FACE[T]S OF FIRST LANGUAGE LOSS

FACE[T]S OF FIRST LANGUAGE LOSS

Sandra G. Kouritzin
University of British Columbia

 LAWRENCE ERLBAUM ASSOCIATES, PUBLISHERS
1999   Mahwah, New Jersey   London

Lawrence Erlbaum Associates, Inc., Publishers
10 Industrial Avenue
Mahwah, NJ 07430

Cover design by Kathryn Houghtaling Lacey

Library of Congress Cataloging-in-Publication Data

Kouritzin, Sandra G.
Face[t]s of first language loss / Sandra G. Kouritzin.
    p. cm.
    Includes bibliographical references and index.
    ISBN 0-8058-3185-1 (cloth : alk. paper) — ISBN 0-8058-3186-X
    (pbk. : alk. paper).
    1. Language attrition 2. Linguistic minorities—Language. 3.
    Sociolinguistics. I. Title. II. Title: Faces of first language loss.
    III. Title: Facets of first language loss.
    P40.5.L28K68 1999
    306.44—dc21   99-17873
                                                    CIP

Printed in the United States of America
10 9 8 7 6 5 4 3 2 1

∞∞∞∞∞∞∞∞∞∞∞∞

For minority language children everywhere;
may they grow up bilingual
∞∞∞∞∞∞∞∞∞∞∞∞

CONTENTS

PREFACE   ix

INTRODUCTION   1

On What Pretext?   3
1. A Pre/text for Language Loss Research   7
    Background   11
    Definition of Terms   12
    Context   13
        Language Loss That Isn't: Language Shift   14
        Minority-Language Families   15
        Individual Language Loss   16
        The Majority-Language Culture   16
    Questioning Findings and Methodologies   18
    Considerations of the Present Study   19
        Life History   19
    Subjects   21

I. FACE-TOUCHING: A STORY BOOK   25

A Musical Interlude   27
2. Ariana: Introduction   31
    The Interview Context   31
    The Life History Context   34
    The Narrative Context   37
3. Ariana's Story: But I'm Canadian-Born   43

4. Richard: Introduction   51
    The Interview Context   51
    The Life History Context   55
    The Narrative Context   59
5. Richard's Story: English Is a Full-Time Job   63

6. Lara: Introduction   75
    The Interview Context   75
    The Life History Context   77
    The Narrative Context   81
7. Lara's Story: An Outsider Looking In   87

8. Brian: Introduction   97
    The Interview Context   97
    The Life History Context   100
    The Narrative Context   106
9. Brian's Story: Nothing Too Deep   111

10. Helena: Introduction   119
    The Interview Context   119
    The Life History Context   123
    The Narrative Context   129
11. Helena's Story: Learning the Rules   135

II. DWELLING IN THE BORDERLANDS   147

Borders   149
12. Introduction   153
    Inhabitants   153
        Nadia   154
        William   155
        Dhiet   156
        Greta   157
        Alexandra   158
        Kuong   159
        Kurt, Cameron, and Julian   160
        Alex   160
        Naomi   161
        Hana Kim   162
        Minette   163
        Nellie   164
        Michael   165
        Charles   165
13. Family Relationships   169
14. Self-Image and Cultural Identity   177
15. School Relationships   187

16. School Performance   **195**
17. The Meaning of Loss   **201**

Discordance   **207**
18. Conclusion   **209**
      . Not a Finale: A Decrescendo   209
              Summary   209
              Implications   211
              Reflections   212

            Appendix A: Life History Selection Criteria   215
            Appendix B: Subject Biographical Information   216

REFERENCES   **217**

AUTHOR INDEX   **225**

SUBJECT INDEX   **227**

PREFACE

The main motivation for this multiple case study is the desire to understand minority first language loss from a descriptive, narrative, retrospective, and personal point of view, a point of view heretofore overlooked in language loss research. The purpose is not to search for causal relationships, nor to assume that first language loss is the consequence, or primary cause of a set of social conditions, but instead to try to understand the meaning of the experience from an insider perspective. This rounds out the picture already painted by linguistic analyses of the language loss process, and by statistical and ethnographic studies. This multiple life history case study accomplishes the following:

1. It describes, from an emic[1] perspective, the intersection between language, identity, culture, and marginalization in some former minority-language speakers.
2. It offers a contextualized, personal, narrative understanding of first language loss during second language acquisition.
3. It describes what it means to lose a language, especially in terms of participation in the social, educational, and economic systems of the community.
4. It offers insight into individuals' perceptions of their communicative adaptation in deficit situations.
5. It opens a window on the lived experiences of people who have lost a first language, as well as on the familial, social, and educational consequences of first language loss.

There are four major sections in this book. Preceding each section are short vignettes, creative commentaries on the text. Having titles in bold italics, these vignettes precede the sections they are meant to comment on; therefore, *On What Pretext?* is meant to be read as a commentary on the literature review that follows it, and can be read either as a straightforward account of how language loss, immigrant experience, and cultural identity have permeated modern literature, or it can be read as a response to the traditional form of the academic literature review that privileges the research genre as truth and penalizes story or poem as fiction. Readers are invited to interpret these vignettes as they see fit, or to ignore them entirely. Some parts of the vignettes are borrowed from literature in poetry and prose, others mobilize artifacts from common culture, others speak to the researcher experience; all have been adapted especially for this document. Their inclusion, and the attempt to give voice to multiple narrators, is intended to address my desire to create a text that is polyphonous, performative, and invitational.[2]

The first section, containing the vignette *On What Pretext?* and the chapter "A Pre/text for Language Loss Research," sets the stage for the rest of the book, introducing theory and research concerned with first language loss. It also briefly describes the research on which this book is based, and the rationale for focusing on life history case studies rather than more traditional forms of second language acquisition (of which first language loss is a part) research.

Part I, "Face-Touching: A Story Book," contains five two-part stories. Following the vignette *A Musical Interlude,* Part I consists of five individual stories of first language loss, told by five different narrators—Ariana, Lara, Richard, Brian, and Helena—in their own voices and words as far as possible. Each story is preceded by an introduction to the story's narrator that describes the interview context, the setting, the atmosphere, the sounds, the social climate, the time of day and year, all of which had an impact on the story that was told. In the introduction, I also give an overview of each person's life so that their language loss stories can be seen in terms of the bigger picture. I also comment on the narrative strategies and language use of each storyteller.

Part II, "Dwelling in the Borderlands," is an emergent theme analysis of the issues concerning, and consequences arising from, first language loss. After the vignette entitled *Borders,* and a separate introduction, it is divided into five chapters—"Family Relationships," "Self-image and Cultural Identity," "School Relationships," "School Performance," and "The Meaning of Loss." It draws on 21 completed life history case studies and 1 pilot study. Extensive use is made of quotations, both to support the claims made in the text, and also to continue to address my concerns with polyphony.

The conclusion, like the introduction, contains one chapter and one vignette. The vignette, *Discordance,* represents the current attitudes toward immigrants and English as a Second Language students in Canada, and is meant as a kind of call to arms. The concluding chapter, purposely entitled "Not a Finale: a Decrescendo" summarizes and raises questions about this and future research, and explains the roles researching, re/searching, and writing have played in my own life.

It is hoped that the understandings arising from this book will not only enable readers individually to validate or change their views of the role of minority languages in public education, but also to critically examine social systems, policy, and educational practice, with a view to:

1. facilitating the best possible language development for minority-language children, indeed, all children;
2. increasing the self-esteem and cultural identity of minority-language students;
3. maintaining the integrity of minority-language families;
4. keeping minority-language students invested in completing and/or continuing their education;
5. engendering equality of educational opportunity;
6. fostering a working antilinguicist multiculturalism.

I know that I have been so influenced.

ACKNOWLEDGMENTS

Any list of all the people who encouraged me, assisted me, or otherwise contributed to this undertaking is bound to be incomplete. I want to thank my doctoral committee, Dr. Marion Crowhurst, Dr. Donald Fisher, Dr. Margaret Early, and Dr. Patricia Duff for all of their time, energy, and caring, and for always allowing me to follow my own lead, while providing me with critique and guidance, without which I could not have written the dissertation on which this book is based. In particular, I extend my thanks to Marion Crowhurst for at all times providing a model not only for the type of academic, but also for the type of person I would like to be. I also thank Donald Fisher for always being a caring, warm, and empathetic "touchstone."

I wish to thank Dr. Jim Cummins, a reviewer of this book, whose support and encouragement have been most appreciated, whose work has given me a vision of ESL academia to follow, and whose suggestions over the years have made me a more careful, more thoughtful scholar. I am also indebted to a second reviewer of this book, Dr. René Galindo, who, above and beyond the call of duty, provided me with detailed and thought-provoking ideas and references, that, I hope, have made this a better book.

A special thank you to Naomi Silverman who, in offering encouragement, support, judicious suggestions, and confidence that I could complete this book while pregnant and then while mothering a new baby and a toddler, became more than an editor, a trusted friend. I appreciate the careful work of Barbara Wieghaus, production editor, at Lawrence Erlbaum Associates.

I am thankful also for the generous financial support I received in the form of doctoral fellowships from the Social Sciences and Humanities Research Council of Canada (752-95-1791) and the University of British

Columbia, and for the British Columbia Ministry of Education Research Grant, and the University of British Columbia, Faculty of Graduate Studies' Mary Simpson Scholarship, all of which gave me the time and resources to engage fully with this research and writing.

I am finally most grateful for the support of my family and friends. My mother and father, Jean and Alex Kouritzin, never said "*if* you go to university," but instead always said "*when* you go to university," and they have stood by me every step of the way. My in-laws, Kozo and Chiemi Nakagawa, have given their love and support, their trust and their name, and have never questioned what kind of unconventional wife their son has married. Thank you to my brother, Michael Kouritzin, and Angie, Trevor, and Vicky; to my sister-in-law, Mutsumi Koshima, and Kazutoshi, Taiyo, and Haruhi; and to Yumiko and Tomoko, who will always feel like family. Thank you to all of the volunteers for this study, to Wendy Pringle-Tanahashi, Katie Sookocheff, and Laura Kaminsky, unparalleled mothers and friends, and to Garold Murray, who listened to this entire manuscript at least twice over the telephone, and did not once miss a word. A special thank you to T. Gilbert Bunch who kindled in me (and countless others) a love of literature, and whose gruff challenge to me to work harder has always inspired me to do just a little bit more.

Thank you most of all to my husband, Satoru Nakagawa, for his love and support, his strength and guidance, his compassion and generosity, his many, many sacrifices...and for Hanika and Tyrone. And thank you to my children for teaching me the most important things of all.

Sandra G. Kouritzin

ENDNOTES

1. This term, commonly used in anthropological research, refers to the practice of working within and against the conceptual frameworks of the subjects of research (Silverman, 1993, p. 24; see also Fielding & Fielding, 1986). I take the term to mean something slightly different from Van Manen's (1992) concept of hermeneutic phenomenology, in that subjects not only reflect on, but also interpret their experiences, and that I too interpret and generalize from the unique and particular circumstances to the seemingly more general and/or characteristic meaning derived from similar or divergent situations.
2. This phrase is borrowed from Patti Lather (personal communication, July 1994) and, in this instance, refers to academic texts that are written with the intent to delight as well as to inform.

INTRODUCTION

On What Pretext?

All good researchers must write a literature review mobilizing the arguments of experts and creating a justification, rationale, and framework for further research—this is one of the basic tenets of social science and educational research. As I have to begin with a literature review, I should explain my crisis in writing it. First, this book, like any other research-based book, is a self-referencing document; the author decides which bodies of knowledge inform the topic, then searches relevant databases, looking under identifiable descriptors. I liken this to peeing in the corners marking the boundaries of intellectual territory. The second approach is to ask "Self, what do you think are the bodies of research that would have a bearing on this phenomenon?" In other words, despite its exploratory nature, this project was no voyage of discovery. To use methodological terminology, like any other author, I began demarcating the academic boundaries of this research project before I began, attending to nonfiction, research, and academic prose, dismissing high-flung rhetoric, letters to the editor, poetry, songs, and fiction, however worthy I felt them to be.

But, just think for a moment—wouldn't it be grand if we could write a review of *lit*'rature (think of Michael Caine pronouncing this word in the film *Educating Rita*), if we could all accept that Carol Shields (1993) was righting/writing acceptable practice when she wrote that

> when we say a thing or an event is real, never mind how suspect it sounds, we honor it. But when a thing is made up—regardless of how true and just it seems—we turn up our noses. That's the age we live in. The documentary age. As if we can never, never get enough facts. (p. 330)

Wouldn't it be liberating to follow these words, as if they constituted academic critique, and to mobilize fiction, poetry, drama, song, art, performance, and all other sensory expressions, in the creation, realization, and proliferation of knowledge?

In that case, I know that I would then ask Garrison Keillor (1985) to speak of one of the parenting dilemmas for immigrant parents who don't speak English, the inability to express themselves fully in a new language:

> America was the land where they were old and sick, Norway where they were young and full of hopes—and much smarter, for you are never so smart again in a language learned in middle age nor so romantic or brave or kind. All the best of you is in the old tongue, but when you speak your best in America you become a yokel, a dumb

Norskie, and when you speak English, an idiot. No wonder the old-timers loved the places where the mother tongue was spoken, the Evangelical Lutheran church, the Sons of Knute lodge, the tavern, where they could talk and cry and sing to their hearts' content.

> *O Norway, land of my childish fancies, thy dark green forest is where my soul goes to seek comfort.*
> *O bird in the sky, tell me—do they remember me in the old home or am I a stranger wherever I roam?* (p. 79)

And while his many-timbered voice read these lines into surround-sound speakers in a dimly lit hall, a spotlight would focus on three old Norwegian bachelors in faded denim overalls, sunburned, shirtless, white chest hair covering their once-brawny, now-sagging, torsos, sitting almost motionless on wooden benches outside a weathered Five-and-Dime, playing gin-rummy, and sucking their dentures, while the grocer, in a dingy, off-white apron, broom in hand, squinted into the sunlight, watching from the door.

And then, to really personalize the torments of immigrant parents, I would print Himani Bannerji's (1990) poignant description of mothers' guilt in introducing what I can best describe as the "Ancient Mariner Syndrome" to their families:

> What did I do, she thought, I took her away from her own people and her own language, and now here she comes walking alone, through an alien street in a country named Canada.
> As she contemplated the solitary, moving figure, her own solitude rushed over her like a tide. She had drifted away from a world that she had lived in and understood, and now she stood here at the same distance from her home as from the homes which she glimpsed while walking past the sparkling clean windows of the sandblasted houses. (p. 141)

The page, a grainy, dark gray photograph of a crowded, unseaworthy, wooden boat, far from land, with Bannerji's words in white, would also contain quotations from Coleridge's (1962) famous poem, including the lines the ancient Mariner speaks—"I pass, like night, from land to land;/I have strange power of speech" (lines 586-587)—and the Wedding Guest's reaction to the ancient Mariner—"I fear thee, ancient Mariner!/I fear thy skinny hand!/And thou art long, and lank, and brown,/As is the ribbed sea sand./I fear thee and thy glittering eye,/And thy skinny hand so brown." (lines 224-229)—which lines, respectively, represent the immigrant and the host experiences.

Next, I would allow Timothy Findley (1986) to speak for my story-tellers about what it means to lose something intangible, something maybe even unrecognized, something connected to one's history, one's identity, one's soul:

> Nothing I can think to say or write reflects my sense of loss. I feel not only dispossessed but impotent. Incompetent. On the one hand cheat-ed of reasonable expectations, I also sense a failure in me to do some duty. Though what that duty might be I cannot tell. Something I wanted to save has been destroyed behind my back. (p. 1)

At the same time, in the background, the music of Joni Mitchell's *Big Yellow Taxi* would play, the end of the first verse coinciding with the end of this passage, and then the volume would increase, allowing Joni's haunting, whispery voice to remind us of things lost. As her voice faded away, the sound of one timpani would begin to reverberate, slowly vibrating until it entered bodily into the audiences' souls, interfering with their heartbeats, and inspiring achingly melancholy nausea.

To illuminate the struggles of the life history storytellers whose painfully summoned words have given birth to this research project, I would, on linen gilt-edged pages, painstakingly copied by an aged monk's hand, have the words of Carol Shields (1993) inscribed:

> All she's trying to do is keep things straight in her head. To keep the weight of her memories evenly distributed. To hold the chapters of her life in order. She feels a new tenderness growing for certain moments; they're like beads on a string, and the string is wearing out. At the same time she knows that what lies ahead of her must be concluded by the efforts of her imagination and not by the straight-faced recital of a throttled and unlit history. Words are more and more required. And the question arises: what is the story of a life? A chronicle of fact or a skillfully wrought impression? (p. 340)

The initial letter, the "A" in "all" would be printed in large, green block font, hand-embossed and decorated in scarlet, with vines encircling its base and rimming the page.

Finally, after I had finished the review of language loss, I would read aloud Denise Chong's (1995) practical words on the difficulty of writing life histories:

> Once my research was done, the challenge was to press it flat onto the pages of a book. Taking on such a responsibility was daunting. There are as many different versions of events as there are members of a family. The truth becomes a landscape of many layers in an ever-changing light; the details depend on whose memories illuminate it. (p. XIII)

as photographs—taken from the same angle at different times of day in color, black and white, infrared, and sepia-toned films of a barefoot child picking daisies on a deserted street in an abandoned gold rush town—

were splashed randomly on the walls of a round room.

But, this is not the accepted norm in academic literature reviews, and so I lay before you a more standard text.

1. A PRE/TEXT FOR LANGUAGE LOSS RESEARCH

So, if you want to really hurt me, talk badly about my language. Ethnic identity is twin skin to linguistic identity—I am my language. Until I can take pride in my language, I cannot take pride in myself. Until I can accept as legitimate Chicano Texas Spanish, Tex-Mex and all the other languages I speak, I cannot accept the legitimacy of myself. Until I am free to write bilingually and to switch codes without having always to translate, while I still have to speak English or Spanish when I would rather speak Spanglish, and as long as I have to accommodate the English speakers rather than having them accomodate [sic] me, my tongue will be illegitimate.

—Anzaldúa (1991, p. 207)

In March 1988, I moved to the island of Kyushu in Japan to take up a job teaching English literature in a small university there. I was one of three "native-speaker" teachers; the other two were Leah, a very experienced 35-ish ESL teacher from London, England, and Emiko, an elderly American woman of Japanese ancestry. Emiko's office was just down the hall from mine, and, perhaps because we were both North American, she often used to invite me to come for a visit over *o-cha* and *o-senbei* (green tea and rice crackers). In my conversations with Emiko, I often found myself unable to understand what she was saying, feeling that our conversation was stilted and somehow disconnected, despite our common "native English speaker" status and our mutual eagerness to be friends.

She often misunderstood my words, or replied in such a way that I knew she had interpreted only the surface meaning. So, for example, when I explained the special wheat-free, gluten-free diet I had to follow to avoid complications from celiac disease, she asked me how much weight I had lost, and offered me a sandwich. Although she was comprehensible, and certainly able to express herself adequately, if not in a native-like manner, I found myself wondering why she had been hired to teach the English language when her grammar, her pronunciation, her lexicon, and her word choice were nonstandard. At the time, I was immersed in my English literature background, and naively assumed that I—and other native speakers whom Phillipson (1992) would describe as being from core-English-speaking countries rather than from periphery-English-speaking countries—"owned" English and had the right to impose our standards of usage on others.[1] When I overheard her speaking Japanese with our department head, I assumed that she was hired for her fluency in that language.

As I became more proficient in the Japanese language, I was able to recognize that Emiko made mistakes in Japanese, that she was often unintelligible to Japanese speakers, and completely unable to read Japanese script. I found that I was able to decipher more of the department meeting agendas, that I could more readily understand current slang, that I was more willing to ask grammatical questions in mid conversation, to make mistakes, to repeat words or phrases when my mouth refused to reproduce the sounds I heard in my head. I now know that, in comparing myself to Emiko in terms of identity development and investment (Peirce, 1995) in both English and Japanese, I was experiencing many aspects of the political and personal dimensions of language learning, associating our language varieties "not just as symbols of group identity, but as emblems of political allegiance or of social, intellectual, or moral worth" (Woolard & Schieffelin, 1994, p. 61; see Crawford, 1992b, for discussions of the dominant discourses and ideologies of English in the United States and Crawford, 1992a, for a historical review of same) and thereby judging us both in terms of our "linguistic capital," which "...like any other form of capital, enables those [of us] who have it to get ahead of those who do not" (Heath, 1989, p. 394).

Over time, Emiko and I shared life stories. She had been born of Japanese immigrant parents in southern California where she grew up speaking English because her parents wanted her to be completely American, and, according to their traditional belief, *"go ni iraba, go ni shitagae"* (when you go to the country, you have to surrender to local customs). In 1942, when Emiko was 16 years old, both of her parents died within months of each other, and, to comply with their wishes, she sailed to Japan to leave their remains at the family gravesite. While she was in Japan, the Japanese bombed Pearl Harbor and the United States declared war on Japan. An American citizen, Emiko's passport was confiscated and she was held in a kind of house arrest. Until the end of the war, she was not allowed to have any English books or to speak in English, though she was told to do some translation for the government. She had one English book that she managed to hide under the *tatami* floor of her house, and which remained her most prized possession. In the final days of the war, she was forced to marry the military son of a wealthy *zaibatsu*[2] family, apparently in the hope that his being married to an American national would save him from arrest and prosecution. During the American occupation, she explained, she lived in the most southern regions of Kyushu, far from Tokyo, and was prevented from leaving the village; therefore, she was unable to reclaim her American passport. She intimated that her life with her husband had been abusive and miserable until his death a few years before I met her, and that she had had little control over her own life. When the American occupation was over, Emiko was the mother of three sons, established, with a family and a career teaching English as a second language in Japan. Without access to the intricacies of the Japanese language, she was unable to advocate for herself, and later, at the time I met her, she said simply "I had nowhere else to go. No one to go to." Having spent their lives experiencing discrimination because their mother was different from other mothers[3], Emiko's sons grew up to have little respect or even tolerance for her Americanness.

Emiko was kind to me. In addition to the friendship and hospitality she offered me, she introduced me to a famous Baptist women's college where I began teaching part-time on my days off from my university. When she "retired" from teaching, on reaching retirement age,[4] and against her will, I learned that her employment and my own had been on different terms. After a 3-year, contractually based period of research, writing, publishing, and teaching, I was guaranteed lifetime employment with generous annual salary and bonus increments. Emiko, it turned out, had, for 30 years, worked on a part-time contractual basis, considered, for the purposes of payment (much less than I earned), to be a native speaker of Japanese, but billed, for the purposes of university advertisement, as a native speaker of English (see Amin, 1997; Nero, 1997; Tang, 1997; Widdowson, 1994; for discussions of a few of the native speaker/nonnative speaker, White/non-White issues in English language teaching). At her retirement, she was not invited to return, leaving a bitter rift in our department.

When I later began doctoral studies in second language acquisition and teaching English as a second language, I found myself thinking about Emiko, and questioning how she might define her cultural identity and the constitution of her cultural community when language "is the means by which members of communities communicate with one another, and how individuals establish that they are, in fact, members of the same cultural community" (Wong Fillmore, 1996, p. 435). I knew that the foreign teachers in our *ken* (like a state or province), did not really consider Emiko to be a member of "our" cultural community, even though it encompassed native and non-native English speakers of all ages and racial backgrounds from Canada, England, Australia, New Zealand, Nigeria, Iceland, Jamaica, India, the United States, and other places. I was also aware that the Japanese cultural community did not consider Emiko to be one of their members, nor did she consider herself to be one of their number. I sensed that Emiko was out-of-sync with both cultural communities, primarily because of her communication and cultural orientation difficulties, but I didn't have the educational background to understand or name her isolation.

Later in the doctoral program at the University of British Columbia, directed to the article "When learning a second language means losing the first" by Lily Wong Fillmore (1991), I began to understand what had happened in Emiko's life, and to piece that together with the way minority language children are generally regarded in public schools— and with my own life. I remembered growing up in an ordinary middle-class suburb with the O'Haras, the Petersons, the Cowies, the Glovers, the Martins, the Carmichaels, the Stanleys, the Carmacks, and the Henrys, and how, because my own last name was Russian, I was always called "Fritzie-bum," or sometimes, "Russian dame". Defiant, I tried to learn Russian words from a book, but, without help, I learned from context only the words for "grandma," "grandpa," "please," "thank-you," "good-bye," and "go to your place" (this last phrase was directed at the dog, but is now the only phrase my husband knows in Russian). From the beautiful items in my grandparents' home, I wove a fantasy tapestry of my Russian history and ancestry that I believed in more than I believed in "the truth"—and was made to feel ashamed when I discovered this made me a liar. With my expanding linguistic knowledge, I became aware that my husband's native dialect is not really a *dialect* at all, but a *language*, which had been forbidden by the con-quering Japanese, and nearly eliminated. I began to feel a commitment to my 105-year-old grandmother-in-law, to my husband's parents and their families, to never forsake the language and culture of their island, and to bring our children up within the glowing embers of the vehement, passionate, and reverent Tokunoshima heart. I became aware that language loss had been a recurring theme in my life, one to avoid if our children were to become not only biracial, but bicultural and bilingual as well.

Keeping in mind words from Shaw's (1977) *Major Barbara* that had foreshamed[5] personal disclosures all my adult life—"Come, come, my daughter! dont [sic] make too much of your little tinpot tragedy" (p. 140)—I decided to tell the stories of people who had once known their first languages, but had lost them when they started school in Canada. I decided to tell my own story only by way of explaining my passion for this topic, and my commitment to the prevention of first language loss during the acquisition of one of Canada's official languages.[6]

In the end, I realized that, for me, a more compelling question than "how do we take English and get it inside kid's heads?" is "should we take English and get it inside kid's heads; what are the consequences?"

As I read about language loss, and then about bilingual education and the education of migrant students in Europe, I became politically motivated to prevent what had happened to Emiko and the other children I read about. Second language acquisition no longer sounded antiseptic or objective to me, but filled with political posturing and hidden motivations. Lily Wong Fillmore's article, and the discovery of a like-minded body of researchers including Jim Cummins, Bonny Norton [Pierce], Tove Skutnabb-Kangas, and Robert Phillipson, led me to feminist research, critical theory, poststructuralist paradigms, alternative ways of knowing, holistic research methodology—and eventually resulted in the research presented here.

BACKGROUND

The theoretical framework informing this book stems from current understandings of what is generally referred to as "first language loss," which usually means restricted minority-language acquisition in a majority-language submersion setting. First language loss may refer to lack of first language development, delayed first language development, or a progressive loss of previously-acquired language ability (Verhoeven & Boeschoten, 1986).

From a wide-scale survey, Wong Fillmore (1991) pointed out the inherent difficulties arising from first language loss. She claimed that while language loss has always occurred in North America, it has never been so widespread, or prevalent, or swift, as at the present. According to Wong Fillmore,

> few American-born children of immigrant parents are fully proficient in the ethnic language, even if it was the only language they spoke when they entered school,...even if it is the only one their parents know. (p. 324)

Wong Fillmore claims that first language loss is more serious than in past generations; that is, she argues that language loss now occurs suddenly between two generations rather than more slowly across several generations. As a result, some individuals are losing the means with which to maintain relationships with their parents, their families, and their cultures.

Given this acceleration and change in circumstance, it seems reasonable that research on first language loss should include a narrower, and more personal, perspective than those that have dominated research to date. To this end, between three and five interviews, each of 2 hours' duration, were conducted with 21 adults who described themselves as having lost a childhood minority first language. Each case study was written in the form of a life story, almost entirely in the words of the narrator. Five representative stories were then chosen for full inclusion in this text (see Appendix A: Life History Selection Criteria), and individual analyses examining the interview context, the life history context, and the narrative context[7] were written for each. In the penultimate section, "Dwelling in the Borderlands," all 21 case studies have been reviewed in an emergent theme analysis, with interview excerpts quoted to enhance our understanding of family relationships, self-image and cultural identity, school relationships, school performance, and the meaning of first language loss.

DEFINITION OF TERMS

According to Van Els (1986, cited in De Bots, Gommans, & Rossing, 1991, p. 87) there are four situations in which language loss may occur:

1. Loss of a first language in a first language environment (e.g., first language loss in elderly people),
2. Loss of a first language in a second language environment (e.g., loss of native languages by immigrants),
3. Loss of a second language in a first language environment (e.g., foreign language loss), and
4. Loss of a second language in a second language environment (e.g., second language loss by elderly migrants).

In this study, we are concerned only with the second scenario as it arises in two distinct situations (immigration and colonization).

A number of terms are either synonymous with language loss or related to it, including, but not limited to, "language attrition," "language shift," "language change," "language death," "language obsolescence," and "subtractive bilingualism". In general, the following definitions apply:

1. **Language loss** occurs "...when [a] minority group member cannot do the things with the minority language that he [sic] used to be able to do....Some of the proficiency he [sic] used to have is no longer accessible" (Fase, Jaspaert, & Kroon, 1992, p. 8). It may also refer to incomplete or imperfect learning of a language spoken in childhood.
2. **Language shift** usually refers to "the change from the habitual use of one language to that of another" (Weinreich, 1952, cited in de

Vries, 1992, p. 213) either by a language community or an individual.

3. **Language attrition, language regression** (De Bots & Weltens, 1991), or **language erosion** (Kravin, 1992; Smolicz, 1992; Taft & Cahill, 1989), "may refer to the loss of any language or any portion of a language by an individual or a speech community" whether because of aphasia, aging, or for any social, catastrophic, or political reason (Freed, 1983, p. 1).

4. **Subtractive bilingualism** usually refers to the loss of the minority language (Landry & Allard, 1991, 1992) during the acquisition of a second language. In some instances, it may at times also refer in a general sense to **semilingualism**, the experience of language loss in minority-language children who are schooled in a majority language "which results in reduced language mastery of both languages" (Carey, 1991, p. 950; Lambert, 1981).[8]

5. **Language death** refers almost exclusively to those languages spoken by indigenous minority-language communities that, when they are no longer used as the languages of schooling, bureaucracy, or government, lose their "primary language" function (**language obsolescence**) and thus lose their viability (e.g., Dorian, 1982; Lanoue, 1991; Pye, 1992; Schmidt, 1991).

6. **Language change** (Anderson, 1982) refers to all of the above, but also includes language acquisition, language learning, and historical linguistic development.

Lacking lexical consensus, I have restricted myself in this book to using the most common and accessible term—*language loss*.

CONTEXT

For the purposes of this book, there are two ways of looking at the extant language loss literature. The first is explanatory, that is, it uses the findings from the existing literature, building hypotheses and theories to work within and against, accepting, within rigorously applied notions of validity and reliability, the truthfulness of the knowledge claims. The second way of looking at the literature is to work in a more critical fashion, seeking to understand how researchers have defined and operationalized language loss in the past, and looking for methodological "gaps," limitations in our knowledge about first language loss that develop not only from missing methodologies, but also from implicit assumptions about the nature of language elements, language use, and knowledge.

Language Loss That Isn't: Language Shift

Much first language loss research has actually been concerned with communal language shift, that is, the gradual substitution of the source country language with the target country language within a language community over an extended period of time (De Bots, Gommans, & Rossing, 1991; Merino, 1983; Pan & Berko-Gleason, 1986). Over several generations, families and language communities become progressively more dominant in the majority language, yet each succeeding generation learns less and less of the minority language spoken by immigrant ancestors (e.g., Extra, 1989; Folmer, 1992; Hakuta & D'Andrea, 1992). Typically conceived, the first generation of immigrants begins as monolingual in the minority language, and may even remain so, provided that they choose to live in a minority-language enclave. The second generation develops bilingually, learning the ethnic language first if the parents use it, meaning that there is a stronger likelihood that children living in enclave communities will learn the minority language as a first language; however, language shift to the majority language begins with the advent of schooling. The third generation usually learns English as the first language, with or without some knowledge of the minority language, while the fourth generation is uniformly monolingual in English (e.g., Appel & Muysken, 1987; Grosjean, 1982, cited in Harres, 1989). As described, this attrition process does not take place within an individual, but between individuals, and therefore it appears smooth and painless, a seamless tapestry of changing colors.

This research tends to be linguistic, often documenting the changes in morphosyntax over succeeding generations without recording the sociopolitical context created by the interaction with the majority-language culture (e.g., Dorian, 1982; see also Markey, 1987, for linguistic definition/analysis of language change, minority language, majority language). When interaction with the majority-language culture is considered in this research, concerns are generally raised about the consequences of language shift, not for the individuals speaking the minority languages, but for the language itself; researchers are interested in assessing the potential for each minority language to survive (e.g., Clyne, 1982, cited in Appel & Muysken, 1987, Giles, Bourhis, & Taylor, 1977; Jamieson, 1980; Pütz, 1991; Wright, 1993/4).

This research is not so much addressed to an individual's *loss* of language, as to imperfect learning of a language by succeeding generations, as that language becomes less relevant to daily activities. Yet, as Wong Fillmore (1991) explains, the language shift process has both accelerated and become more prevalent during recent decades, to the point at which "few American-born children of immigrant parents are fully proficient in the ethnic language, even if it was the only language they spoke when they entered school,...even if it is the only one their parents know" (p. 324). This change in focus from the community to the individual is accompanied by an attendant change in the understanding of consequence. Although the documented consequences of language shift are often communal and linguistically described, familial consequences are personal and social, psychological, and emotional.

Minority-Language Families

Studies of minority-language families have tended to explore the causes of language loss. Taft and Cahill (1989), for example, claim "...parents who are literate and who care about the quality of their children's language are more likely to have children who are competent speakers of the home language..." (p. 142). This implies that language loss will occur in poorly literate homes in which parents are less concerned about their children's language development and education. Indeed, researchers (e.g., Berotte Joseph, 1992/3; De Bots & Clyne, 1989, 1994; Hakuta & D'Andrea, 1992; Harres, 1989; Jamieson, 1980; Merino, 1983; Okamura-Bichard, 1985; Wong Fillmore, 1991) have statistically correlated such things as parental education, attitude, and L1 literacy, elapsed time since immigration, L1 status (both the prevailing language ideology of the source country and that of the target language country), disglossia (which Ammon [1994] has also referred to as a "multiplex social network"), literacy, age, family size, types of daycare or schooling, and other related variables with increased or decreased first language loss. In such studies, more attention is paid to the language than to the individuals who speak the language, and more attention is paid to the causes of language loss than to its effects.

One of the few researchers to consider the effects of first language loss, Wong Fillmore (1991; see also McKay & Weinstein-Shr, 1993) illustrates how language contains more than just its linguistic elements. Language is a "powerful socializing medium" (Schieffelin & Ochs, 1986, p. 172) implicated in identity, relationships, culture, and aspirations, and transmitting information about events, activities, affective domains, tone, mood, the organization of society, the current state of "knowledge," the means to question and evaluate that knowledge, and all other aspects of the social world. When a first language is lost, then, Wong Fillmore (1991) claims,

What is lost is no less than the means by which parents socialize their children: when parents are unable to talk to their children, they cannot easily convey to them their values, beliefs, understandings, or wisdom about how to cope with their experiences. They cannot teach them about the meaning of work, or about personal responsibility, or what it means to be a moral or ethical person in a world with too many choices and too few guideposts to follow....Talk is a crucial link between parents and children: It is how parents impart their cultures to their children and enable them to become the kind of men and women they want them to be. When parents lose the means for socializing and influencing their children, rifts develop and families lose the intimacy that comes from shared beliefs and understandings. (p. 343)

Individual Language Loss

Research that is concerned with individual language loss (as opposed to that within a tightly knit community of speakers) is generally (a) linguistic in nature, and (b) concerned with describing the language loss process. This body of research tends to address the questions: "what parts of speech are most subject to loss?" and "what are the identifying precursors to and features of language loss phonologically, morpho-syntactically, metalinguistically, or affectively?" Studied aspects of language loss include: productive skills, comprehension, circumlocution, retrieval difficulty, visual word recognition, letter writing, hesitation frequency, and length of aspiration. (Jaspaert & Kroon, 1992; Kaufman & Aronoff, 1991; Kenny, 1993; Kravin, 1992; Maher, 1991; Major, 1992; Merino, 1983; Olshtain & Barzilay, 1991; Pan & Berko-Gleason, 1986; Segalowitz, 1991; Turian & Altenberg, 1991; Weltens & Cohen, 1989).

A separate class of studies that could be seen to have an impact on individual first language loss research are those that look at bilingual education. In an extensive review of the literature, Collier (1989) concludes that "...children who reach full cognitive development in two languages enjoy cognitive advantages over monolinguals" (p. 517; see also Harley, Hart, & Lapkin, 1986). In other words, these studies explore, not the consequences of first language loss, but the advantages enjoyed by bilingual children (see Extra, 1989). Loss of the cognitive advantage of bilingualism could be seen as a consequence of first language loss for language minority children if we were to accept Toohey's (1992) argument that we need to regard language minority students in terms of their potential as developing bilinguals, rather than in terms of their deficiencies as "Limited English Proficient."

The Majority-Language Culture

Research on the impact of the majority-language community on minority-language loss also looks more to the causes of loss—particularly in the classrooms of the nation—than to its effects. Ironically, and despite all evidence to the contrary, it appears that many, if not most, teachers continue to believe that maintaining the L1 at home or at school while learning the L2 can hamper cognitive development (McGroarty, 1992, p. 380). Others simply believe that English should be used exclusively at home and at school in order to give students as much exposure to the dominant language as possible, possibly thinking that time on task increases English proficiency (Dolson, 1985; Johnson, 1987; see also Cummins, 1989, for a description of possible rationales for this line of thought).[9] Although teachers who belong to the minority-language community are, in general, more supportive of mother tongue development (Johnson, 1987), they personally have been successful in the type of programs that they represent, and have therefore been "socialized into accepting those values which are connected with that part of the majority society which controls the schools" (Skutnabb-Kangas, 1984, p. 305; see also Wilton, 1994, p. 89).

Looking to language ideology rather than to the beliefs or attitudes of individual teachers may give a more holistic picture. Bourdieu (1982, cited in Ben-Raphael, 1994) establishes an argument for looking at language legitimacy. He argues that during school education, the relative importance of differing linguistic norms (in this case, languages, styles, dialects) are established by the discourse of teachers. Teachers' own use of language models, the linguistic norms that are considered to be prestigious—not only **what** forms are deemed worthy of transmission, but also **who** is worthy of transmitting them (see Toohey, 1998, for an excellent ethnographic example of Bourdieu's theory in practice). Therefore, for children of minority language families, "the gap between the language of the school and that of the family creates a feeling of alienation from the school's world, together with the awareness of being stigmatized as 'inferior,' and excluded (Ben-Raphael, 1994, p. 40). It is little wonder then, that, as Wong Fillmore (1992) has written,

> Let us consider what happens when young children find themselves in the attractive new world of the preschool classroom. What do they do when they discover that the only language spoken there is one they do not know? How do they respond when they realize that the only language they know has no function or value in that new social world and that, in fact, it constitutes a barrier to their participation in the social life of the school? (p. 5)

Wong Fillmore answers that, understandably, children learn English (though perhaps not a standard form of English), but that they also, all too often, lose their first languages as well.

QUESTIONING FINDINGS AND METHODOLOGIES

de Vries (1992) argued that two views of language predominate in second language acquisition (SLA) research; each view of language determines a particular orientation to the operationalization of language loss in research. According to de Vries, when language is viewed in the first way, as a symbolic *system* for the purpose of communication, then researchers define language in terms of properties such as phonology, morphology, and syntax. Researchers begin with a (hypothetical) "norm" and measure loss as deviations from that norm. When language is viewed in the second way, as a social characteristic, resource, or cultural *commodity*, then language loss is measured in terms of the language's vitality and potential for survival—the numbers and age of its speakers, its political status, its use in a variety of situations. Indeed, we have seen that these two approaches to language predominate in the language loss literature.

Understandably, these two different views lead to specific research approaches and specific answers to the second question, "what is loss?" When researchers view language as a system, they are interested in what Lambert (1982) referred to as "criterion variables," linguistic criteria which are seen to identify the loss of specific language skills such as grammatical deterioration (e.g., Jaspaert & Kroon, 1992; Merino, 1983; Turian & Altenberg, 1991), frustration and/or loss of ease with the language, (e.g., Kravin, 1992), code-switching or linguistic interference from the L2 (e.g., Kaufman & Aronoff, 1991; Kravin, 1992), retrieval difficulty, particularly of vocabulary (Kenny, 1993; Olshtain & Barzilay, 1991; Segalowitz, 1991), or phonological change (Major, 1992). Although these studies portray the process of language loss linguistically, they do not document the human factor. When researchers view language as a commodity or social characteristic, they look for what Lambert (1982) has called "predictor variables," those factors capable of anticipating situations in which language loss may occur, which language loss is measured by standardized test (e.g., Hakuta & D'Andrea, 1992; Landry & Allard, 1991; Okamura-Bichard, 1985), or self-report (e.g., MacKinnon, 1990), or both (e.g., De Bots & Clyne, 1989).

Finally, another type of research is based on statistical analysis of census data in which reported first and second language use patterns are taken to represent loss or maintenance of minority languages, which results are correlated with other demographic factors (e.g., Stevens, 1982; Veltman, 1983).

Taken as a whole, studies to date have correlated a number of variables (such as length of residence, age on arrival, gender, attitude toward the L1, birth order, social class, ethnolinguistic vitality, status) with increased or decreased language loss. They have also established a fairly accurate accounting of the linguistic process of language loss. These studies, however, have not adequately considered the social context, nor have they looked at the effects of language loss, nor have they questioned the effects of becoming monolingual in a bilingual environment.

CONSIDERATIONS OF THE PRESENT STUDY

In addition to trying to address these gaps, I wanted to work within a framework that viewed language as a constantly metamorphosing intersection between linguistic elements, identity, culture, history, reality, information and communication. I wanted to acknowledge the interdependence of language, identity, the construction of reality, and the individual, and, because language is a social phenomenon, I did not want to be bound to spoken forms of discourse nor to the first or second language. I wanted to find a methodology that could simultaneously help to define language loss, look at its causes, and track its effects. I wanted to work within a framework that acknowledged that language speakers make choices, and that immigrants often arrive with a strong desire to integrate. I wanted to take into account the understandings and opinions of the people who speak the language under study. Is language not a purveyor of culture? a representation of the real? a vehicle for communication and information? a means for exerting power and control? a means for resisting power and control? a constitution of a social reality? a homeland? something invoked to break silence? a marker of identity and culture? a playful and evocative allegorical force? a linguistic system? Are dialects not languages? Creoles? Pidgins? Patois? Ideolects? Slangs? Interlanguages? Are languages not all of the above?

Because I had not personally lost a language, such accounts as Hoffman (1989) or Rodriguez (1981), haunting personal reflections—autobiographies—about learning to live in a second language while either abandoning or neglecting the first, was not available to me.

Life History

A model for the present research project was found in Cruikshank's (1990) book chronicling the life histories of three women, Yukon native elders. According to Cruikshank, life history is the "collaborative product of an encounter between two people, often from different cultural backgrounds, and incorporates the consciousness of an investigator as well as that of a subject" (Preface, p. x). Life history "tak[es] seriously what people say about their lives rather than treating their words simply as an illustration of some other process" (ibid., p. 1). This latter is the way life history has often been used in ESL research; collected life stories have been analysed for the narrator's use of articles, or length of T-units, or mastery of narrative forms, rather than for what is revealed about a human life.

Through careful study of the theory and practice of life history methodology, particularly in sociology and anthropology where it is most prominent, I came to a better understanding of the potential of life histories when they are viewed as a particular type of case study (see Stake, 1995; Yin, 1994). Where life history seems to differ from case study is in the definition of what constitutes a context, the uses made of multiple sources of "evidence," and in the privileging of individuals' understandings of a phenomenon over the phenomenon itself. Although the case study might be concerned with documenting the immediate physical and emotional context, and may do so over time, life history research focuses on individuals' understanding and recollection of events that have had a substantial impact on their development (the 'lived experiences,' in Van Manen's, 1992 terms). It is not the events themselves that are of greatest importance, but the subjects' understandings of the events, and their later impact on, or resolution in, the subjects' lives.

Rather than take up the narrower definitions of case study found in SLA research (e.g., Larsen-Freeman & Long, 1991; Nunan, 1992), or indeed, than are generally found in education (with some notable exceptions including, but not limited to, Clandinin & Connelly, 1994; Goodson, 1992, Middleton, 1993), I have been influenced by the life history approaches of Bertaux (1981a, 1981b), Bertaux and Kohli (1984), Bertaux and Bertaux-Wiame (1981), Denzin (1986, 1989), Kohli (1981), and Kirby and McKenna (1989), in which the life story serves as testimony allowing the "internal logic" of language loss "to emerge through the practices and representations of its actors" (Elegoët, 1978, cited in Morin, 1982, p. 7), and thus, "researching from the margins" (Kirby & McKenna, 1989). As I have argued elsewhere (Kouritzin, 1995), life history therefore allows the researcher to (a) shift perspective from the extraordinary to the mundane and the collective to the marginal, (b) to describe events or concepts within a historical frame, (c) to work with and write invitational texts, (d) to focus on listening intently and responding in an individual manner rather than on questioning from a format or script, thereby loosening control over the research context, (e) to be reflexive, and (f) to retain a holistic concept of the self and the research subjects.

SUBJECTS[10]

A short note about the subjects in this research seems warranted. Because they were recruited through a newspaper column, the subjects tended to be well-educated, well-informed, articulate, urban, established, and intellectually reflective about their own experiences with first language loss. In order to gain a more rounded sense of first language loss for myself, I therefore also chose to include Kuong, Dhiet, Nadia, and Charles in the cross-case analysis (see Appendix B: Subject Biographical Information), people I had met by chance, or through my work as a teacher who were eager to share their experiences with me. I did not, however, include stories unrelated to Canada, such as that of Teruko, who grew up Korean in Japan, or of Sachiko, who lost the two other languages she spoke after returning to Japan, or of my husband, who never completely learned his islanders' language. I also chose not to include the life stories of my relatives, or of my friends. All of these people, however, remain connected to this research project because, having read bits and pieces of the manuscript, they feel it speaks to their experience.

ENDNOTES

1. This is an ill-founded prejudice of which I have been long disabused.
2. Often defined as the plutocracy, this term has generalized in modern Japan.
3. Neither her sons nor Emiko can be faulted for the rifts in their relationship. Although some laws have been revised, and they continue to be revised, it is still fair to say that children of foreigners, especially foreign mothers, experience stigmatization, and are commonly referred to as "halves." It is very difficult for foreigners, even those married to Japanese nationals, to obtain Japanese citizenship; indeed, during the entire time I lived in Japan, I met only one woman who had become a citizen, and it had taken her nearly 2 decades, fluency and literacy in the Japanese language, an extensive network of government supporters, a thriving business of her own, and marriage to a wealthy and powerful Japanese man. Until a foreign woman is granted citizenship, she does not officially register as a "wife" on the Japanese family register, which is held by the male head of the family. As a result, a wife's name does not appear on her children's school records, and the children are routinely told that they are illegitimate or that they have no mother. I am familiar with one situation in which, when her husband died, an American woman was prevented from returning to the United States with her children because her husband's parents were awarded custody of her children. When I left Japan in 1992, these kinds of stories formed the foundation of common-

sense knowledge and fueled fear amongst foreign wives of Japanese men.

4. It is common practice in Japan, for university teachers, and often for other professionals, to be hired back contractually after official retirement for a period of up to 10 years. Retired rehirees continue to collect their pension for their original employment, and then are paid a reduced salary for their contract work.

5. This word has been made up by the author and means "to feel ashamed of one's words even prior to speaking."

6. The form of this commitment is explained in: Murray, G. & Kouritzin, S. (1997) Rethinking second language instruction, autonomy and technology: A manifesto. *System, 25,* 185-196.

7. Stake (1995) describes three possible paths a researcher might take when developing a case study report: (a) chronological or biographical development, (b) the researcher's view of coming to know the case, or (c) discussion of one or more aspects of the case, which are, he claims, roughly equivalent to Van Maanen's (1988) realist, confessional, and impressionist tales (pp. 127-128). Herein, the interview context section is a confessional tale, focusing on my own collaboration in the research process. The life history context is meant to provide a third person omniscient "rather direct, matter-of-fact portrait...,unclouded by much concern for how the fieldworker produced such a portrait" (Van Maanen, 1988, p. 7), and is, as such, a realist tale. The description of the narrative context sections include "personalized accounts of fleeting moments of fieldwork...carry[ing] elements of both realist and confessional writing" (p. 7) and are therefore impressionist tales of language and narrative usage.

8. One consequence of first language loss is what has come to be known by the loaded term *semilingualism* (see Martin-Jones & Romaine, 1986, p. 26 for European and Canadian references), a form of "subtractive bilingualism" (Lambert, 1975), which has been described as an "...inadequate command of both first (L1) and second (L2) languages..." (Cummins, 1979, p. 222). Those researchers who support(ed) the construct argue(d) that semilingualism "...can be devastating because it usually places youngsters in a psycholinguistic limbo where neither language is useful as a tool of thought and expression" (Lambert, 1981, p. 12). It is, however, Martin-Jones and Romaine (1986) point out, a potentially pejorative and extremely problematic construct that "appears to be defined with reference to some idealized and rather narrow notion of 'full' competence in one language or other" (p. 28). They argue that it is impossible to empirically measure semilingualism, and that "the ways in which children in multilingual settings...learn to draw on the codes in their repertoires have to be understood with reference to community norms of language use and local youth culture, and not with reference to some idealized notion of adult balanced bilingualism" (p. 34). Spolsky (1989) also argues that "if we count as a bilingual only someone with equal and native command of two or more languages, we exclude the vast majority of cases and are left with the least interesting. In practice, then, scholars in the field treat bilingualism as a relative rather than an absolute phenomenon, and consider anyone able to produce [or even understand] sentences in more than one language as the proper object of their study" (p. 100). Although such arguments are important because they challenge traditional notions of bilingualism, which "describes a continuum where those who share a high competence in two or more languages stand at one end and those who are competent in only one language stand at the other" (Baetens Beardsmore, 1986, cited in Ben-Rafael, 1994, p. 38), such criticisms do not, however, in any way change the fact that first language loss occurs, and that there is considerable variation in the language and literacy skills that different children will acquire in both monolingual and

bilingual situations. In one sense, it is an important, though troubled, construct, essential for describing the language ability of two subjects in this research. Unable to articulate themselves in English sufficiently to frame coherent life stories, and yet completely unable to speak or understand Vietnamese, Kuong and Dhiet often expressed frustration with their attempts to discuss ideas or opinions with me. I do not question the intelligence of either subject; Dhiet, in particular, was a talented and imaginative artist. What stymies me is how, without some reference to "some idealized notion of adult balanced bilingualism," I can describe speech that is grammatically nonstandard (in tense, aspect, syntax), limited in terms of vocabulary, heavily accented, aurally based, and restricted in patterns of usage, particularly when the users of such speech recognize themselves that they cannot and do not manipulate the English language as well as even younger speakers who have often been using the English language for a shorter period of time. It would be too easy to assume that English speakers such as Kuong or Dhiet suffer from a learning disability or other innate characteristic that made their failure to learn unique, when, as the increased numbers of such speakers would attest, the difficulty resides not within individuals, but in their social and educational experiences. It seems incumbent upon educators to recognize, describe, and name such a phenomenon, and, as much as I or others may object to the term *semilingual*, which labels the individual rather than the construct (as indeed do such terms as "limited English proficient" [LEP] or "English as a second language" [ESL], which are widely accepted in the field), it is unconscionable to stand idly by debating the relative strengths and weaknesses of terms and operationalizations, while individual children fail to develop their full potential in one or more languages, and while they continue to be frustrated by their own inability to articulate their thoughts.

9. Such beliefs are behind programs like the Head Start program in the United States.

10. Throughout this text, I have used the term *subjects* for lack of a better word. I intend that this word be interpreted to mean "subjects of the stories" rather than "subject to my manipulation"; however, despite this intent, they are indeed subject to my editorial authority.

I. FACE-TOUCHING: A STORY BOOK

A Musical Interlude[1]

When I was in Grade 8, I began to play the French horn in the school band, and soon became proficient enough to play in the New Caledonia Symphony Orchestra. Having chosen to play the French horn because, aside from some vague notion that it was related to Christmas, I didn't know what a French horn was or what it looked like, I was not put off by the band leader's warning that it was the most difficult instrument to play. It is possible to play every note on the musical scale without touching the keys with your left hand, merely by adjusting the shape of your mouth and altering the position of your right hand in the bell. Therefore, a French horn player must develop perfect pitch, and must be able to hear each note, concentrate, and aim for it, before releasing air into the mouthpiece. A French horn player must be able to hear music in her mind that isn't there, but is forthcoming, and then strive for those strains in order to blend herself into the rest of the band, creating harmony rather than discord.

But, what is truly unique about the French horn is its magic. When two French horns are perfectly in tune, and when they play two notes of a chord, you can hear a third horn sounding triumphantly between them. And, between each horn and imaginary horn is the echo of yet another horn, resonating and ethereal. To hear these horns is awe-inspiring; to be a part of it, soul-shattering. Who can be playing these horns but a multitude of angels?

As I see it, an interview is like working toward, and then magically hearing the third horn. In fact, the very word *interview* implies that it is created between two, a negotiated glimpse of the beyond that comes when two people are able, for a moment, to hold themselves in perfect tune. But, you cannot effortlessly hear the third horn; you have to listen carefully, adjust your breathing, strive to be one with the other horn player, taste her[2] spit. You have to try to let go of your ego, to give up your own pace, and dwell within the performance of others.

These stories, then, were not spontaneous outpourings; they represent difficult work. I, the researcher, have not been just a collector of stories, but have also had a major role to play—in determining the kinds of stories to be told, in the story telling, and in the story writing, in always trying to match my pitch to that of (for the most part) novice French horn players. Therefore, no account of this research would be complete without acknowledging the subjects' roles in the process. Although I tried to keep the interviews as open-ended as possible, trying not to unduly influence the resulting music, this was often an unrealistic expectation. Two examples follow.

When I was interviewing Hana Kim, I found that her understanding of an interview and mine were in opposition. A reporter for a major television station, Hana Kim always seemed to give the shortest answer possible, often articulately phrased and extremely "quotable," but intended more to jolt the listener than to create an understanding with her. I assume that Hana Kim's responses were prob-ably typical of her own desires from, and experiences with, interviews. A 20-second encapsulation in dramatic language would be much more appropriate for airing on the evening news than a long-winded narrative filled with digressions and lengthy explanations, even though the narrative is what I was after. I had to work so hard to try to hear her melody, that I would leave each interview with her, my hands and shoulders and jaws aching from the physical strain of willing myself to match her.

Ariana was also a difficult person to interview. Ariana holds a master's degree in the social sciences and she was interested in completing a doctorate. As a result, she also had a strong sense of what a research interview should be like. Whenever I asked a question, or tried to get Ariana to narrate, she would begin with a story, but then delve into opinions about how her experiences were typical or atypical, negative or positive. It would often take several tries before I could get her to tell me stories again; she preferred to speak her mind and to use the similarity in our ages, education, outlook, and professional experience to look for confirmation that I agreed with her opinions. In retrospect, I realize that, while I was trying to blend with Ariana's music, she was trying to blend with mine.

These are not singular examples. Nearly all of the subjects in this research project seemed to have expectations of me as a researcher. They had their own agendas for what constituted a proper interview. They all seemed to have fairly strong opinions about immigration, heritage language education, the rights of minorities, public schooling, acceptable and unacceptable discrimination, and they very much wanted to express those opinions, even in a research format calling for stories. There were times when I felt strongly that, despite researchers' concerns that we are using our subjects, we are sometimes being used by them. If doing research is a political act, so then is participating in the research process.

> But first I praye you of youre curteisye
> That ye n'arette it nought my vilainye
> Though that I plainly speke in this matere
> To telle you hir wordes and hir cheere,
> Ne though I speke hir wordes proprely;
> For this ye knowen also wel as I:

Who so shal telle a tale after a man
He moot reherce, as neigh as evere he can,
Everich a word, if it be in his charge,
Al speke he nevere so rudeliche and large,
Or elles he moot telle his tale untrewe,
Or feine thing, or finde wordes newe
He may nought spare although he were his brother:
He moot as wel saye oo word as another.
(Chaucer, *The Canterbury Tales*, General Prologue, lines 727-740)

ENDNOTES

1. The titles in this book have been carefully chosen. The Japanese word for *interview* is represented by two characters, which individually can mean face-touching. This is, I feel, a perfect metaphor for the type of interviewing in this study, hence the title of this section. The title of this particular vignette introduces a musical metaphor which will be reinforced in Chapter 18.
2. My choice of possessive pronouns is political; I never had the opportunity to practice with another female French horn player. Choosing instruments in high school was a gendered experience. In general, girls chose small wood-winds like the flute or clarinet, while boys chose brass instruments, the drums, or larger woodwinds. I regretted my refusal to stick to gendered norms only for brief moments, like when we traveled; each student was responsible for carrying his/her own music, music stand, chair, and instrument.

2. ARIANA: INTRODUCTION

THE INTERVIEW CONTEXT

Ariana was the second person to call me (prior to 8 a.m.) after the description of my research project was published in Column One of *The Vancouver Sun* on June 19th, 1995; the first person who called was a journalist with the newspaper. Ariana was extremely enthusiastic, eager to begin working with me immediately, and so we set up an appointment for Friday, June 23rd, 1995. Our first meeting together was a difficult one for me personally. I was nearly 14 weeks pregnant, and the evening before had found out that the baby's heart had stopped beating. Consequently, I felt that I had to push forward in my work to keep myself from sitting at home feeling sorry for myself, a decision that I did not regret but which became impossible to follow through with as the initial numbness wore off.

I felt that I owed Ariana an explanation for my haggard and joyless appearance, and so I told her briefly what had happened but insisted that I wanted to continue. This proved to be a good choice for me, if not necessarily for Ariana. Some may think that it may have been a wiser choice to wait until after I had given myself a chance to recover emotionally and physically, but I am glad I made the choice that I did. Perhaps because of my circumstances, I was introduced to a side of Ariana in the first interview that became progressively more unfamiliar in subsequent interviews. She was very kind and very gentle toward me, letting me see some of her pain and frustration without it being too much overshadowed by anger. Coming home from our first meeting, I told my husband, and wrote in my journal, that Ariana and I had a lot in common, and that she was much like me, tough, defensive, and even aggressive to outsiders, but crumbly, soft, and shy with friends and loved ones.

During the second interview, whether because I was more alert, or because Ariana was less cautious, I began to feel that my judgment had been premature, that I was missing something. I remain confused about Ariana's character. On the one hand, I have no doubt that she was painfully honest in her recollections of language loss, racism, schooling, and other life events. On the other hand, I sometimes felt as if she were trying to paint her teaching career as somewhat more coherent than it really was. I often found that she would try to draw me into discussions of ESL theory, pedagogy, and policy, and she expressed an interest in reading several papers that I had written. When I gave her copies of those papers at our second interview, she read them carefully, and then opened our third interview with questions, comments, and even praise for my criticisms of ESL practice in British Columbia. At the time, I wondered what kind of person would choose to read academic policy analyses in her spare time. I believe now that I was still too focused on my research project, and therefore failed to see that she was trying to find many levels on which we could connect. I believe that reading my papers made Ariana feel that she knew me a little bit more, and perhaps let her know that I could be trusted to take a point of view similar to hers. I wish that I had been more astute; we were, after all, the same age and committed to the same field.

At Ariana's suggestion, we met in one of her classrooms, after her classes were finished, at the institute where she was an ESL teacher. I found myself on a squeaky language laboratory stool, behind a narrow desk with Ariana seated two stools away. We both had to turn in our seats to face one another. In the times we met we sometimes changed classrooms, sometimes we had windows and sometimes not, but we never sat across the table from one another, we always had to twist to see one another, and I always sat on her left. This, it seems, made the atmosphere more comfortable for Ariana. When she was speaking, she would look straight ahead, as if concentrating, trying to focus, and searching for the best way to make herself understood. When she was finished narrating a story, voicing an opinion, or answering a question, she would look at me and I would know that it was my turn to speak.

Ariana is responsible for teaching me an important lesson in doing research. After our fourth interview together, Ariana was offered a very prestigious teaching position overseas. In order to verify Ariana's life story with her, I had to write it very quickly. It was the first life story that I pieced together, therefore I found it necessary to make several long-term, grueling, decisions about shape and form in the life stories. After finishing the story, I went to back to her school and dropped it off on August 14th, 1995. I was pleased with the story, except for its excessive length, and was confident that Ariana would also be pleased. On August 15th, Ariana phoned to tell me that she had finished with it. I picked it up the following day, only to find out that she had crossed out half of the story. I was left with very little except her name, the fact that she had lost Cantonese, and a statement that she teaches ESL. All of the things that I had found particularly interesting in her story had been crossed out, and she had marked "Irrelevant, please delete" in the margins. Although I agree that several of the third-party stories she told me had little to do with her life, other than corroborating the current treatment of ESL students, they were also stories that she had told me off-tape, and then explicitly reminded me in the following interview that she wanted to repeat them on tape. I was frustrated, and I prepared a list of reasons that I could discuss with her on the phone, justifying why I wanted to include the directly relevant aspects of her story. In the end, she agreed that if I deleted some of the identifying features of her life and "toned down" her comments, that I could leave it intact.

After our telephone call, I was still frustrated, not because she had wanted to protect herself, but because, as I wrote in my journal, "I am furious that she would say not 'I don't feel this strongly anymore,' but 'this is irrelevant to your study'" (Researcher Journal, August 19th, 1995, p. 18). I felt angry, and I felt guilty for feeling angry, given that intellectually I knew that I did not *own* Ariana's story just because I had listened, taped, questioned, transcribed, and written. I felt that I had not yet had enough experience with language loss life stories to know what was relevant and what was not; I did not relish being told by someone with even less experience. It was not how I imagined research should be. I started to question the value of "member checks," which are so highly touted in feminist studies (the advocacy of which has also become fairly commonplace in research that does not adopt a feminist perspective). Where once I had wholeheartedly endorsed having participants read accounts of themselves, I hadn't really thought about what would happen if they wanted to censor or to change the vast majority of their own words. Despite widespread reading in the field, I couldn't recall the outcome of any such incidents being discussed. I wrote:

> *I'm going to make it absolutely clear that their disapproval does not mean I'm going to edit things out. From now on, I'm not going to mention that I'm going to do this. I can't take the pressure of feeling like I have to write nice things only. That's not right, especially since I'm just taking their own words and editing them together in a coherent manner.* (Researcher Journal, August 19th, 1995, p. 22)

I still think that verifying stories and double-checking for anonymity are extremely important, but I now believe that researchers should make absolutely clear that what they are offering is a chance to comment, to modify, and to have participants' reservations put in print, but not an opportunity for wholesale retraction.

No one reads academic research with the naive belief that the researcher has been objective and impartial any longer, but, unfortunately, that is something that has not been communicated to the general public who, like Ariana, are often the participants in research projects. How could Ariana know that people reading her story would take into consideration that her statements were context-bound, partial truths, the result of our collaboration? Despite claims about bridging the gap between academic and nonacademic prose, current research practices influenced by feminist and postmodern theory have not made many inroads outside the university environment. I have, particularly through my experiences with Ariana, begun to question not only research/ing practices but also writing practices. Who could say, after all, that an "experimental," postmodern academic article, or book, or thesis, or dissertation, which has been littered with poetry, vignettes, and classical allusions, is more approachable, more readable, than one following a known format? It is more personal, yes, less rigid in its truth claims, perhaps, but certainly not more accessible.[1]

THE LIFE HISTORY CONTEXT

Ariana is a third-generation Canadian, both of her grandfathers having immigrated from Canton, China to work on the Canadian Pacific Railway. To place this historically, Ariana explained that when her maternal grandfather brought her grandmother to Canada, he had to pay the Head Tax. She assumes that her paternal grandmother came over after the Head Tax was phased out because she doesn't remember her father saying that his mother had to pay it. Although Ariana mentioned that her family has kept her grandmother's Head Tax document, she seems uncertain even of the decade in which her grandparents immigrated.

Ariana's father and mother were both born in British Columbia, Canada. They both grew up bilingual, speaking only Cantonese inside the home, because their parents never learned to speak English. Ariana's mother speaks, reads, writes and understands Cantonese, while Ariana believes that her father cannot read or write it, perhaps because his mother spoke some limited English, and her maternal grandmother never learned to speak it at all. Therefore, Ariana says that the standing joke in her family is that they are CBCs, meaning Canadian-born Chinese: "we're yellow on the outside, we're bananas, but on the inside we're Canadians" (June 22nd, 1995, p. 3). Like her parents, Ariana was developing bilingually in Cantonese and English, even while playing with the neighborhood children, until she entered school and encountered discrimination.

Ariana, born in 1961, grew up in a rapidly changing community in the Lower Mainland of British Columbia. Although she and her older siblings were the only Chinese-Canadian students in her elementary school, there were increasing numbers of Chinese-heritage students over the course of her public school education. As she points out, in 1995-

1996, children of Chinese descent are now in the majority in the schools that she used to attend, and therefore the kind of cultural insensitivity that she experienced likely wouldn't occur. Putting this in context, she explained that

> *I was a minority so there was no need to address the concerns of a large number of people, foreigners today who are in our country. Back then there was very little, so why shouldn't I be the one who had to adapt to the system and had to become part of the system, instead of other people bending over backwards to accommodate me and my language needs?* (July 20th, 1995, p. 6)

Indeed, in many respects Ariana feels that the current multicultural climate has gone too far the other way in its accommodations for newcomers to Canada. Although she thought it was very important for me to complete this research project and to tell educators, second language learners, and the ESL teaching field that "there's a major concern of losing one's identity" (June 22nd, 1995, p. 6) when first languages are neglected and lost, she also expressed shock at how much more newcomers to Canada are entitled to today than when her grandparents immigrated:

> *It astounds me that oftentimes I see students with very low levels of English, but yet they know how to extract a number of benefits from the government. I'm like "How did you know that?" I didn't even know that such an agency or Ministry was around until they started showing me letters, and I'm like "what is this?" So, it really is mind-boggling.* (July 13th, 1995, p. 14)

She, at first glance, appears very divided on the issue of services for newcomers to Canada. In fact, it seems that while Ariana strongly endorses first language maintenance and cultural support programs and also fully supports the teaching of ESL, she is more skeptical of other settlement and immigrant family programs that do not have a direct bearing on language.

Of course, Ariana's opinions are likely shaped by her own occupation as well as experiences. Ariana is an ESL teacher who has taught an enormous range of ages and English abilities. Trained in elementary education, she began working with adults while working on a graduate degree, and continued after she completed her degree. She has taught in a number of different types of educational institutions, educating visa students, Language Instruction for Newcomers to Canada (LINC) students, university transfer students, and regular high-school students. She is a very dedicated teacher, considering herself a master teacher, and often taking an advocacy role for the ESL students that she comes in contact with.

Indeed, Ariana related a number of third-party stories during our interviews that attested both to the past and to the current situation for ESL students in the Lower Mainland. For example, she told of an immigrant Cantonese acquaintance, two years older than she, who had entered school without speaking English. As there were no ESL classes at that time, Victor was sent home with a note that said "Don't bring your child back to school until he can speak English." The parents, having no other resources, made Victor watch TV for 12 hours a day until he was allowed to enter school. According to Ariana, Victor then lacked confidence throughout his school career. As she said, even if the teacher had no training in ESL, she should never have been so callous toward a small child: "That's unforgivable, and that's really—that's uncalled for. You don't do that to anybody...." (July 13th, 1995, p. 15).

Ariana also told several more recent stories. One teacher was baking cookies with her adult ESL students in their classroom at a local elementary school. When they were finished and had cleaned up, the school principal came in and accused the ESL students of washing their dishes in the toilet. When the teacher expressed disbelief, he summoned her into the hallway, and told her to go into the toilet cubicles in the girls' bathroom and check out the mess. She looked into the bathroom, and told the principal that all she saw was blue and green paint. Apparently another teacher had told her students to empty their leftover watercolors into the toilets. Ariana commented,

> *And what that seems to say to me is that there was so much ignorance out there about ESL students and about the people from different countries and different cultures, that they seem to think that newcomers to Canada are somewhat barbarian, and that they don't know how to clean dishes, and that they are very crude in their personal hygiene, and that they would wash a cookie tray in the toilet! It's so absurd, and so very insulting, that I think really attitudes have to change towards ESL students, and toward newcomers....* (July 13th, 1995, p. 1)

Ariana also told me about ESL classes being housed in basement rooms, storage areas, and cafeterias, both in public schools and in private educational institutions. She was enraged by teachers who she saw as exploiting their students, teaching for the first 15 minutes of a class and then giving out worksheets for the class to work on silently at their desks. She said that she received numerous complaints from her adult students who were parents, and from children in school who needed additional tutoring, that ESL teachers were untrained, old, sick, and incompetent. Ariana remarked that,

> *...things like that really make me sick. That they're getting a wonderful salary,*

and they're supposed to be there to help the students, and they're not. And how come these very students who are in the ESL classes...have to go and hire a tutor later on in the evening to help them with their English? Why is that happening? To me, if the ESL teacher is doing his or her job, there's no need to have a tutor on a regular basis. (July 20th, 1995, p. 1)

Every time that Ariana told one of these stories, she became an advocate for all ESL students, pushing for greater understanding, more institutional resources, and better trained, more caring teachers. Perhaps because of her background, Ariana's choice of career is a personal mission, something that she does not forget when she leaves the classroom after school.

THE NARRATIVE CONTEXT

One of the most striking things about Ariana is the tension she exhibits between, on the one hand, not wanting to be Chinese, not intending to learn Cantonese, and feeling a complex, tangled, and bemused abhorrence of the "old ways" and the "hocus pocus traditions" (July 13th, 1995, p. 18) of her cultural heritage, while, on the other hand, wishing that she had maintained her Cantonese language and culture, and regretting that she had internalized what she referred to as "being racist against her own race" (July 20th, 1995, p. 6), feelings which characterized her childhood recollections. During our interviews together, she often revealed her disdain for the cultural practices of some of her relatives and her disgust that they not only would not abandon traditional rituals even 20 years after immigration, but also expected her to participate in them. Although I encountered racism against one's own race many times, and in many degrees, in no one was it more pronounced than in Ariana:

...I find it very annoying when we get together for family reunions and they're insisting we do this, this, this, and I'm going "why are we doing this? That's how you people do it, but you're in Canada, why not try the Canadian approach?" (June 22nd, 1995, p. 4)

...but they had a very different perspective and when it comes to very, very traditional Chinese things, after somebody dies, and even after the birth of a baby, it's supposed to be a cleansing process, they cook this, what I find absolutely offensive soup, that just smells up the whole house, but they believe in that. But then, as a cousin, they want to give it to me, and they tell me "drink it" and I tell them "I can't drink that. I respect what you do, but I just can't bring myself to drink your exotic concoctions.... (June 22nd, 1995, p. 4)

I think Chinese is b-b-b-b, and so nasal and whiny sounding.... (June 22nd, 1995, p. 7)

Based on what I've heard, and based on what I've seen of their standard of living, if you could call it that, I'm sorry, I cannot go to a country where there is no real running water, and they have no real sense of cleanliness or of hygiene, and from what I've—[heard]—I'm not impressed. And I could not go where to me it seems backward. I couldn't. (July 13th, 1995, p. 8)

I mean, that's fine for their mother to hang on, but I can't really understand why they would want to hold on to hocus pocus traditions. And I'm going "My God, you guys, get with the program. This is Canada." (July 13th, 1995, p. 18)

During our third interview, I questioned Ariana about these and other strong statements she had made, and Ariana thought about it for a long time. Because she was so concerned about how she had managed to adopt those attitudes, in our last two interviews together, Ariana expressed dismay about her opinions. She did not say that her feelings had changed, but she was concerned about, and disturbed by, her own racism. What saddened me is that Ariana did not forge her attitudes in a vacuum; they are a reflection of the cultural prejudices that surround her. Although I would hesitate to make too much of it, I wondered at Ariana's choice of pseudonym. "Ariana", I mused, "Aryan-a."

At the same time, Ariana stressed her envy of present-day immigrants who are, in what she feels is a more culturally sensitive climate, encouraged to maintain their languages, their cultures, and their religious/political beliefs. When queried, Ariana said that "impatience comes from being denied—I guess the right or the privilege to maintain my language when I was growing up" (July 13th, 1995, p. 14).

Throughout her story, Ariana speaks of "losing out" because of not being Canadian enough as a child, not having blond hair and blue eyes, not speaking the English language, not having her cultural heritage respected. As a result, she worked hard to become part of the majority culture, and even became proud to have "assimilated very nicely, thank you, and...forgotten all my Chinese" (June 22nd, 1995, p. 3). Today, Ariana is still losing out, not because she isn't Canadian enough, but because she isn't Chinese enough to fit in with the current climate of multiculturalism. As an ESL teacher, she is expected to participate in multicultural days, but she doesn't know anything about the Chinese New Year, festivals, traditions, or ideals. She doesn't speak the language, and doesn't feel a part of the community:

...and even in our own country where people are encouraged to have French, Japanese, Mandarin, whatever, we can't even do that. And we can't even participate in our Chinese community because I feel like I'm an outsider. And sure other people have the luxury of speaking English and Chinese, but I really

envy that, and if I were to participate—I know I'd be ostracized because, well, "you're Chinese, but how come you don't speak the language?" And my sense is that I turned my back on them in the earlier days, so why should I be allowed back into the Chinese community? (June 22nd, 1995, p. 10)

Ariana says that she will never feel fully a part of "mainstream WASP culture," and is still not interested in learning about her Chinese heritage. Having lost out twice, that is, being first too Chinese, and then not Chinese enough,[2] Ariana is "angry that when I was growing up, there was just so much lacking in terms of educational resources and services" (June 22nd, 1995, p. 10). She believes that, even if multiculturalism had come about as late as when she was 10 years old, she would have been able to maintain her language and take pride in her culture. For Ariana, multiculturalism has been a mixed blessing.

I was struck, too, by Ariana's choice of words when she commented on multiculturalism today:

I'm really glad that I chose ESL because, even though I was deprived of my cultural background, I'm glad now that I can make amends in some way and make sure that my students maintain theirs, and that they are not to be ashamed of speaking Chinese or Japanese and that they are not ashamed to be wearing their traditional outfit to school when we have a multicultural day. (June 22nd, 1995, p. 5)

When I initially questioned her about why she used the term "make amends," as if she had done something wrong, Ariana explained that she meant trying to compensate in some way for her loss, and vicariously experiencing heritage and cultural knowledge through her students. When I stated, "It really struck me because you often talk about the guilt that you feel, and you're trying to apologize for having your language *stolen* basically" (July 13th, 1995, p. 18), Ariana tentatively agreed that there may be a deeper meaning to her words, and that she wanted to give it some more thought.

This was not the only occasion on which I was attracted by Ariana's choice of words. At various times during our interviews, Ariana referred to having been "given a raw deal" (June 22nd, 1995, p. 5), or being "gypped" (June 22nd, 1995, p. 5) by cultural attitudes that forbade the use of Cantonese. The loss of her language, having it "stripped from [her] when [she] was younger" (July 20th, 1995, p. 6), Ariana feels, has "really robbed [her] of [her] cultural heritage" (July 20th, 1995, p. 4). Ariana views her language not so much as lost, but stolen, indicated by her attribution of agency. Language loss was something that was done to her, not something that she willingly participated in. Moreover, when I asked her about the strong language and violent images she used to describe the loss, or rather, theft, of her language, she did not express surprise at her words, reiterating instead that "I really feel it's been a personal assault. I've been denied certain things; it was taken away..." (July 20th, 1995, p. 6).

A second thing that struck me about Ariana's word choice was her frequent description of herself as "Canadianized" (e.g., June 22nd, 1995, p. 4; p. 5) rather than Canadian. This was not unusual, particularly among the visible minority subjects (see Chapter 14 below), but I did find it especially interesting because Ariana is not an immigrant, but a third-generation Canadian. When I later spoke to Ariana about her identity attitudes, asking her to clarify whether she was Canadian, or Chinese, or Chinese-Canadian, or whether she felt more comfortable with some other label, she replied

> Oh, now I feel that I'm definitely a part of the Canadian society, the part of—well—the WASP establishment. I feel that I am a part of it now because of having gone through all my schooling here, my education here, working here, I feel that I certainly am Canadian and identify very strongly with being Canadian and not Chinese, because of all the newcomers, and not one of them. (July 13th, 1995, p. 19)

Of particular note, Ariana does not equate being Canadian with being born in this country, rather, being Canadian comes from schooling, education, and the mastery of English. Moreover, Ariana's strong identification with being Canadian stems from the influx of new Chinese immigrants whom she views as different from herself. Recent immigration patterns have pushed her into representing the WASP establishment, a very odd circumstance because Ariana's constant descriptors for WASP society are "blond hair, blue eyes" (June 22nd, 1995, p. 5 (twice), p. 7, p. 8 (twice); July 13th, 1995, p. 2). This, it seems, is the other side of Ariana's ambiguous attitudes towards her Chinese heritage—an equally ambiguous "Canadian" identity. When I asked her if she could perhaps clarify her identity for me, she paused, and then finally answered, "That's tough....I don't know. I don't know" (July 13th, 1995, p. 19). Given that Ariana clearly identifies knowing the Cantonese language with being Chinese, saying "Well, I just feel that I'm not really Chinese, because if I were Chinese, how come I can't speak it?" (July 13th, 1995, p. 12), her confused racial identity is inextricably linked to her language loss. Rather than viewing this as a strength, as being able to draw from two different cultural traditions and two different language systems, she views it as a negative characteristic, in that she fits comfortably with neither culture.

I was also struck by Ariana's distinctive vocal patterns. I found myself wondering whether I was listening to her "real voice", or her "teacher voice", if she naturally spoke in this manner, or if, like myself, she spent so much time around non-native speakers of English that some of her expressions and her intonation became non-standard. I wrote in my journal after meeting with her:

> *I wouldn't really call [her accent] a native speaker accent. Many forms of the language that she uses are very unusual and her key phrases are things like "but I'm Canadian-born." To me, this is quite strange. I would also describe her intonation as nonstandard. It's not that it's really so much nonstandard as that her voice always seems to be out of place, like a lecture to a million people without a microphone.* (Researcher journal, August 17th, 1995, p. 17)

I noticed, while transcribing the tapes, that her intonation is exaggerated, and that her sentences tend to rise in intonation at the end. Yet, rather than making her seem tentative and questioning, it seems to me that she is asking for collusion, seeking my understanding. Despite the complexity of her sentence structure and the comprehensiveness of her vocabulary, her grammatical/linguistic choices are often nonstandard; for example, the phrases "I am enviable of," "to enroll for Japanese lessons," "say derogatory names about my racial background," and "I admire that there have been" all appear on page one of the transcript of our first interview.[3] In addition to these nonstandard utterances, Ariana displays a lot of hypercorrect speech; for example, she uses the noncontracted form, saying "whose first language is not English" and "oh this is not good" without stressing the negative. Because Ariana is a highly intelligent, highly educated, young woman, I found myself wondering whether her nonstandard language was a result of her linguistic development, of being exposed to nonstandard English on a daily basis at work, or of a certain difficulty with oral performance. Although I would tend to discount oral performance difficulties as a factor because Ariana was able to employ extremely complex sentence patterns without grammatical error, it is possible that she could not attend to sentence-level and phrase-level performance simultaneously.

Finally, a look at Ariana's story would not be complete without noting her parents' participation in her education. Many language loss studies cite parental illiteracy, lack of educational commitment, and an attitude of "benign neglect" as contributors to first language loss (see, for example, Merino, 1983). Ariana's story clearly shows an enormous parental commitment to Ariana and her siblings' education, and considerable effort invested in helping the children to develop bilingually, and yet their best efforts were thwarted by the educational system. I think there are three things worth noting. First, in order to combat the racism they had encountered, and which led them to tell their children they'd have to be twice as good as blond-haired, blue-eyed Canadians, Ariana's parents felt they had to drill their children on proper English usage before and during their school years. Second, this practice led to a situation in which both English and Cantonese became permissible home languages. Therefore, third, as long as the educational system demands that parents assist their children in their acquisition of English language and culture, instead of encouraging them, and even assisting them, in having their children maintain their first languages, language loss will continue to occur, even in the most highly educated and linguistically aware families.

We will now turn to Ariana's story, the story of being a Canadian-born Chinese woman.

ENDNOTES

1. This is similar to a point made recently by Tierney (1995) who claims that much of this inaccessibility is due to bad writing rather than difficulty of concept (p. 386).
2. This sentiment is also documented in a different context in Wilton's (1994) examination of Chinese-Australians.
3. When she enrolled in a doctoral program and sought my editorial advice, I later had the opportunity to read some of Ariana's academic prose that exhibited the same features.

3. ARIANA'S STORY: BUT I'M CANADIAN BORN

Hi, my name is Ariana and I was born in Vancouver many, many years ago, in 1961. My parents are Canadian-born. Dad was born in Victoria and Mom was born in Vancouver. It's interesting, I think, that even though my parents are Canadian, I was encouraged to speak Chinese, particularly Cantonese, at home with my parents. I think this was due, in part, to the fact that occasionally my grandmothers would visit, and of course they never spoke English, and so we had to converse in Cantonese. Although I can't say that I remember vividly my early childhood years, I know that later all my little story books, my little "Golden Books," were in English. There weren't any Chinese books in our house.

I spoke Cantonese up until I was about 4 years old, and then I began playing with the kids in the neighborhood. When my older sister entered the public school system, she lost Cantonese very quickly and so then there was really no need to speak it. We all spoke English thereafter. As I was growing up, all the children in our neighborhood spoke English; we were the only Chinese kids on the block so to speak, so after I played with them, I lost my language very, very quickly. I recall being at school and being teased. There were a number of racial remarks made about the fact that I was Chinese, and, even though I never spoke Chinese at school, the other kids in my class would taunt me and say derogatory names about my racial background. In my days, there was no such thing as multiculturalism; what we had instead was cultural insensitivity. Some students tried to mimic the Chinese language, and of course, being a very sensitive person, I felt "Oh this is not good," and so, in order to have friends, I felt I had to speak their language, so quickly my Cantonese was dropped. When I was going to school, it was never overtly said, but there was the innuendo that "you're in a Canadian school, everyone speaks English so you had better speak English—and don't ever utter a word of Chinese." I grew up feeling that I was to be ashamed to be Chinese, and, of course, to speak Cantonese was forbidden.

My Chinese cultural heritage was really shunned after I started school, because kids would make racial jokes and remarks about "you chinks." When I heard that, I was so hurt. I remember a classmate saying, "Ariana, just ignore him. Just ignore him." I'm really quite surprised looking back on it because even the teachers knew that the kids were going "Chinky, Chinky Chinamen," but they wouldn't say anything. And the boys—I guess boys will be boys—would pretend to be Chinese, going "Chinese, Japanese, dirty knees, look at me." And then the other students would start mimicking the Chinese sounds; even though it wasn't even Chinese, they'd start trying to sound like Chinese, and that was so hurtful. I was ashamed to be Chinese. The teachers would see it but they'd prefer just to turn away, and not stop and say, "Look that's not nice. That's not a nice thing to do picking on other kids. It doesn't matter that Ariana's Chinese," and so nothing was done to stop that. We had to become very Canadianized, and act like our fellow classmates who had blond hair and blue eyes, and dress like they did, and match all our nuances and speech attitudes to theirs. If we hadn't done so, we would have been ostracized and then who would we have had for classmates and for friends? And, at that time, my sister and I were the only Chinese students. So, we made a pact: "Let's not say that we're Chinese. Mom and Dad said that we were born in Vancouver; that's what we'll tell them."

And even later with the advent of multiculturalism when teachers would ask, "So what do you do for Chinese New Year's," I'd smile and say "Oh no, I don't observe Chinese New Year's; I observe January 1st." And this is what's so sad about having lost it. Part of my identity has gone down the tube. Yes, technically I'm Chinese, I was born Chinese, but because I was born in Canada, and my parents are Canadian-born, and I've lost the language, I don't feel that a real part of me belongs to the Chinese culture.

So what I grew up with was a tenet of "Lose it quickly and learn English as quickly as you can" and to this very day, it's all been English for me. I even asked my parents, "Did I actually speak Chinese?" and they said, "Of course you did when you were little," but I have forgotten it for so long, I don't even remember. I apparently repressed it because I was just so ashamed to speak it, that there are times when I asked, "I don't really think I spoke that language, did I?" My mom and dad would say "yeah, you did. When you were little, you spoke it very beautifully and now you've lost it." And now when people ask my mom, "Mrs. Chan, how come Ariana doesn't speak Chinese?" my mother replies, "Well I feel that if Ariana is Canadian-born, she's going to be working in Canada and Ariana will probably be dying in Canada, so why shouldn't she know English perfectly?" Moreover, my parents experienced a lot of racism and my mother always told me that if you want to get ahead and get a good job, you've got to be twice as good as a person who is Canadian-born and fits the typical Canadian ideal of blond hair and blue eyes. I was brought up very firmly that you've really got to give it that extra something to make sure that you're successful. The basic message from my parents was "Learn the English language, and learn it well and if you happen to remember Chinese fine, and if you don't well...."

In a way, I had an advantage when I started school, even though I had spoken Cantonese as a child. My dad and my mother are both teachers. Both my parents and my older sister wanted to make sure— and I guess this is consistent with our Chinese culture; they're high achievers—that I understood sight words, and so even before I went to school they sat me down with little readers, and my sister pretended she was a school teacher, and she would drill me on sight words just to make sure I was up to scratch with the other, Caucasian, kids. So, going to school itself was not a problem because I had a head start from my own family, being nurtured, and they made sure that I was a part of it, or even above the other kids, when we started Grade 1. They encouraged me to read and ask questions and they always made sure that I answered in full sentences, orally and written, because they wanted to make sure that I had good form before I was sent off to school. Therefore, thank God, language wasn't a problem for me. I saw what people who didn't have English-speaking parents had to go through, and it was really disheartening.

I didn't really have any problems at school, not academic problems. In Grade 11, however, when I was taking a composition course, I was really offended by the woman who was teaching the course. She was hard on everyone and very obnoxious, but she said to me—she looked at one of my writings and she said to me—"Why don't I send you to ESL?" I was so offended. I told my mom, who told another teacher at the school that my writing teacher wanted me to take ESL. The teacher went, "What? Ariana's Canadian-born!!!" I was so insulted. I didn't have any verb tense, or subject-verb problems at all, but for some reason...! That woman was going through a very, very tough time herself and she was picking on even kids with blond hair and blue eyes and saying, "Do you call this English?" and she'd throw it down and insult their writing. For me, it got so bad that the principal intervened on my behalf and said "About one of your students, Ariana Chan....she's Canadian-born you know, and her parents are teachers...why did you tell her to go to ESL?" and she said, "Oh, well, you know, she's Chinese and I just think she needs ESL." But, she was so quick to judge. She just assumed that because I had black hair and I was the only Chinese student in that classroom that I was misplaced and that I should have been in an ESL class, not in a regular writing and composition course. You know, I asked my dad to read my essay because he loves writing as well, and I asked my sister and they said, "This is good. All you have to do is just expand on your ideas." I gave what I thought was enough, but I didn't develop the ideas adequately and it was misinterpreted as "She needs ESL."

I was actually really careful when it came to writing. My dad sat me down during the summer months and he said, "well nothing against you personally, but I just want to make sure that when you graduate from high school, you're a good writer." He said that he had many students who can't write, and I said, "But dad they're Canadian-born" and he said, "It doesn't matter. Nobody taught them how to write." So, over the summer, my dad sat me down parsing, doing all the subject, verb, predicates, and he made sure that we had a very good handle on grammar. Even going through Grade 4, one teacher commented to my mom "Oh, your daughter seems to know her subject and verb stuff really well." So, the grammatical aspect was not a problem, but just because I didn't expand on ideas, this high school teacher of mine wanted to send me to ESL. I had a problem with form and content rather than the run-of-the-mill mechanics, and it was misinterpreted. If you didn't put a name on it, it would be the same as all the other kids with the blue eyes and blond hair, but because this little girl with black hair handed it in it was "why don't we send her to ESL?"

I guess that's another factor that sort of contributed to my losing the language, the fact that both my parents speak English very well, and they were teaching in English and using the language with their students, and that's why it was never impressed upon me to speak Chinese at home, because everybody, mom and dad, spoke English. The rare times that my grandmothers did come over, mom and dad were the translators. And so, over time, there was no need, I guess, to maintain the Chinese language.

In fact, I'm really ashamed to say I was very intolerant with my maternal grandmother because she never spoke English and I felt she wasn't making an effort to learn *my* language. I remember being very intolerant with her, and even to the point of going, "Oh, if she's coming up, I don't want to talk to her." I'm really ashamed that that's how I felt because I kept thinking, "Doesn't this woman know English? She should make an effort." My dad's mom had a little bit of English so I could talk to her, but anything complicated, my parents would have to translate. I also remember being annoyed with other relatives who were coming to visit. My parents would say, "This is auntie so-and-so and uncle...." and I'd be like, "They can't speak English. Why are you dragging me along to this boring dinner when I have to listen to Chinese?" And, I didn't want to even be associated with relatives who couldn't speak my language. In retrospect, that was very bad because I lost out on a very important relationship, but it just goes to show you what I was inundated with and what was going through my thought processes: "If I was made to feel bad speaking Chinese, for being Chinese at school, well why shouldn't these people who are visiting me know a little bit of English?"[1]

I admire that there have been a number of efforts to change our whole approach toward children whose first language is not English, and also for the government to have this whole business of multiculturalism. It's really sad that I don't have a word of Cantonese and I'm totally lost when people are speaking Cantonese. What's even sadder, I understand more of what my Japanese students are saying to me than I do of what my Cantonese students are speaking to me. On the down side, I really regret losing my Cantonese language, because I find even if I wanted to relearn the Cantonese, it would be difficult. I've taken a little bit of Japanese, and I can say right now that Chinese is very tonal and so it's going to be an uphill struggle for me to learn Chinese again. In fact, I guess in some ways it's been instilled in me so much as a kid to lose it, that I'm even ashamed to even try to learn Cantonese, and in fact I've even gone so far as to enroll for Japanese lessons, not Chinese lessons. That's the sad part of it.

And, as an ESL teacher, I admit I am enviable of the young people coming over today, be it from the former Yugoslavia, Hong Kong, or Japan. They are encouraged to speak their languages, and they are able to attend weekend schools to maintain the languages. I envy that because in my day it was "Lose it quickly," and so I had to lose the Cantonese language, and now it's lost, and I feel a part of me has been lost with it. I don't know if I'll ever be able to get the Cantonese back. It's going to be a struggle. It's a very sad state when you lose your language and you learn another language and when you see people being encouraged to maintain their languages today, but in my day it was "hurry up and lose it," and there was no support for multiculturalism or the fact that I came from an ethnic background. I just feel that I'm not really Chinese because if I were Chinese, how come I can't speak it? I've always believed that language and culture are intertwined, and if my language was stripped from me when I was younger, what the heck can I say about the Chinese culture? I can't relate to it. I can't communicate with them.

Oftentimes my students even tease me and say, "Hey Ariana, you say you're Chinese but how come you don't understand?" And that's why I feel that I lost a part of my identity. I use the analogy of being a banana—yellow on the outside but white on the inside. I look at it as an assault on my identity. I guess now as First Nations are wanting to preserve their languages—they have a voice and they're doing something about it—but nothing was done in my era, and I really feel that it's been a personal assault. I've been denied certain things; it was taken away and that's why the strong feelings, the very intense emotional feelings that I have toward losing my first language. And that's how I feel. And I don't know. I guess if I made a concerted effort I could try to learn the language, but because of what's happened in the past and because I feel so ashamed to be Chinese, I don't have this desire to learn Chinese. In fact, I want to learn Japanese, and it's going to take a lot of...it's going to be a major project and a major uphill battle for me to sit down and want to learn Cantonese.

I have to admit that when I see people down at the store, speaking very loudly, some Caucasians give me this disgusted look. I just smile and say, "That's not me. I'm Canadian-born." I say, "I know these guys have no respect for our land and no respect for our space and all that" and the Caucasians sort of look at me. And I say, "Well that's typical Hong Kong behavior and I would have to say that's typical Taiwanese aggressive behavior." And I tell them quite bluntly, "Sure I'm Chinese on the outside, but I'm Canadian-born and I agree with you, it's very annoying when you go to McDonald's or some public place, and you can't really enjoy your meal, or you can't really talk to friends because those people are speaking so loudly." Because of what I've...what's been ingrained in me, I really don't like that at all. I get very annoyed when people assume that I'm going to respond in Chinese to them.

I'm afraid I don't have a lot of patience for Chinese people or for China. Based on what I've heard, and based on what I've seen of their standard of living, I don't want to go there. I'm sorry, I cannot go to a country where there is no real running water and they have no real sense of cleanliness or of hygiene. I could not go to a place where it seems backward. I couldn't. I've been to east Malaysia where it is somewhat backwards, but for some reason China seems to be a lot more backwards than east Malaysia, so I wouldn't be ready for that, not at this point in my life. If I were a bit older, I guess I should go there just to see where my roots are and all that, but I'm not ready for that yet. I have no qualms about going to other third-world countries. I'll go to a third-world country, but I don't want China.[2]

I'm really glad that I chose ESL because even though I was deprived of my cultural background, I'm glad now that I can make amends, compensate in some way, and make sure that my students maintain their languages, and that they are not to be ashamed of speaking Chinese or Japanese, and that they are not to be ashamed to be wearing their traditional outfits to school when we have a multicultural day. I'm glad that I'm able to step back and say, "Okay even though I was given a raw deal, I don't have to be like that. I can change and help make sure that people foster better understandings between Canadian-born people and immigrants and even if you are Canadian-born and are from a different ethnic extraction, be proud of who you are and maintain that culture and that language," because so much is lost if you don't.

There's a major concern of losing one's identity when immigrants come to a new country, and they're afraid. They don't know: "Are they really Canadian or are they Chinese?" Just the other day, we had our multicultural day here, all the little kids came in and danced from Bosnia, and I thought that was so wonderful because already they're maintaining their roots, yet they're still getting used to the Canadian culture, but there was that almost like an option, they had a choice to keep it if they wanted to, but in my days there wasn't that choice and...it was never said overtly but through innuendo and covertly it was "hurry up and become a Canadian." And that's why I chose ESL, because I wanted to give the students a second language which is ESL, but also to impress on students the importance of maintaining their own cultural heritage.

I was made to feel guilty for being Chinese, and now there is a certain amount of guilt or shame that I don't speak Chinese. It's embarrassing. It's embarrassing when you see high school kids with blond hair and blue eyes speaking Japanese or Chinese. I feel that I've been gypped, and I feel guilty that I turned my back on my own culture, not by choice, but because of circumstances. And I can't even participate in my Chinese community because I feel like I'm an outsider. Most of the other people have the luxury of speaking English and Chinese, but I really envy that and if I were to participate...I know I'd be ostracized because I don't speak the language. And my sense is that I turned my back on them in the earlier days, so why should I be allowed back into the Chinese community? This is one thing that, in some ways I can't help; I am angry that when I was growing up there was just so much lacking in terms of educational resources and services, and there wasn't that training to be sensitive to people who spoke other languages—and even their culture.

ENDNOTES

1. Ariana adopted a different tone of voice whenever she was trying to represent her thought processes or what she or other people were saying. On the audio tapes, it is very clear that she shifts from story or opinion narration to performance, a shift that was accompanied by different gestures and facial expressions.
2. It is interesting to note that Ariana does not say "I don't want to go to China," but rather, the more emphatic "I don't want China", as if she is rejecting it in herself as well.

4. RICHARD: INTRODUCTION

Language spoke through him, and not—as is the usual case—the other way around.

—Shields (1994, p. 85)

THE INTERVIEW CONTEXT

At about 11 a.m. on the sunny morning of September 5th, 1995, I approached a townhouse cooperative that had always captured my imagination. I had lived in the neighborhood while it was being built, and I remembered thinking how beautiful it was, one of the first complexes built with high ceilings, recessed balconies, and enormous windows. It was slightly less beautiful on the morning I first went to meet Richard. In many places, the siding had been torn off the buildings, exposing rotted two-by-fours.[1] Men worked throughout the complex on new roofs, new balconies, and new framing, so the noises of hammering, sawing, falling lumber, and shouting drowned out the more familiar sounds of seabirds, children, and traffic.

I was filled with apprehension about meeting Richard. Although I had grown up in an area with a large First Nations' population, I had had virtually no contact with First Nations people before. We had gone to different schools, lived in different neighborhoods, shopped in different stores, had different interests. Later, while in university, I was occasionally enrolled in graduate courses with one or two First Nations' students, but my experiences with them were limited to academic discussions about classmates, profs, required readings, and postcolonial theory. I greatly admired those students whom I had met, and was therefore consumed by the desire for Richard to also admire me. I felt that this was *the most* important life history, the one that would finally confront the us/them dichotomy that I had known all my life. Having heard the word at a peer's dissertation defense, I realize now that I was ready to be "bewitched" by my assumptions about First Nations' culture. I was predisposed to becoming enchanted by Richard, a man who, I already knew, was not only a Cree, but also a writer, an actor, and a poet—other spiritual manifestations that had already worked their magic on me.

Richard, long greying hair, bare feet, pitted complexion, dressed in an Oka T-shirt and jeans,[2] answered the door and welcomed me. The dining room we passed through was filled by a large desk and books, with pages of foolscap covering every surface. The living room contained a sofa, dining table, and chairs, small television, bookshelves, and a low table arranged so that, as Richard explained to me, the room became circular. Decorating the room were beaver skins, black and white portraits of First Nations' people, sweetgrass, driftwood, and a large Ukrainian wedding bread belonging to Richard's wife.

I set up my tape recorder, accepted a cup of coffee, and was immediately caught off guard when Richard asked me how much the honorarium was that I had offered to all participants. I replied that it was $50. He countered by saying that he could give me the best interviews of all the participants, but that he would do it for $100. I said that was fine with me—and it was. Richard then congratulated me for offering an honorarium, explaining that too many academics had studied First Nations' people extensively and never thought to give gifts. He felt that my gesture, and willing acquiescence to his request, were a sign of respect and honor. Taken aback, uncomfortable, I thanked him.

Of course, his comments ensured that I would never return to his home without bringing something with me. To the next interview, I brought croissants, muffins, and cinnamon buns for breakfast, and was permitted a little closer relationship, symbolized by my being given a tour of the townhouse. To the next interview, I brought some Japanese beer and cigarettes that I had been given, explaining that he was the only smoker I knew. Richard, pleased, told me that tobacco was the most honored gift in Cree culture. At the end of that interview he walked me to my car, called me a friend, and hugged me. This continued throughout our varied contacts. I think sometimes, perhaps to my discredit, that I have been trying to apologize for hundreds of years of discrimination. Yet, I also feel that it is a reflection of how much I love to give gifts to people—especially to people who are as appreciative as Richard. And then too, I feel reluctant to be seen as an exploiter; I want to give something back, even if I can only afford tokens.

It was at a particularly interesting time in British Columbia's history that Richard and I negotiated his life history. In the fall of 1995, a little-known spot in the province's interior, Gustafson Lake,[3] was featured daily on the front pages of the newspaper. A group of First Nations'[4] peoples from Canada and the United States had gathered for an annual Sundance ceremony on land owned by an American rancher. At the completion of the ceremony, several of the Sundancers refused to leave the land, arming themselves, and setting up camp. The Royal Canadian Mounted Police (RCMP) set up barricades to try to force them out. The situation grew steadily worse as sides were taken throughout the province, and shots were exchanged. My reaction was intense and indicative of my own cultural biases: "Just leave them alone, you American bully.[5] You're not using the land right now; they're not hurting anybody. Besides, what arrogance leads you to believe that vast tracts of land can be privately owned, especially vast tracts of land in a country that has not adopted you as a citizen?" My reaction was not the dominant one.

Each time I arrived at Richard's home, it was to find him watching the news for information about the standoff. He mentioned that I should phone him prior to each scheduled interview because he might go to join his brothers at Gustafson. While Richard and I were meeting, the situation was settled "peacefully," meaning that the First Nations' peoples were arrested and charged without loss of life.[6] Although most of our discussions about Gustafson Lake and other land claims took place off tape, I am certain that the emotional intensity/rancor of some of Richard's statements was intensified by the situation, particularly as it grew more acute, around the time of our September 19th interview:

I don't know who said this,—Byron I think he said "Oh, the English,[7] the British, they think the rules of their tribe should be the laws of the universe", right? and there's a lot stated in that, right? Because I, as a Cree—although I would laugh about it, what he is saying—there's a lot of truth in that humor, and that's the difference in how we look at worlds right? In our world, the native man, the Cree man, looks at his world in terms of the totality without breaking it up into fragments...whereas the English man would look at even his language as providing a tool for ulterior motives perhaps, like law, British law...if you make it complicated enough you can absolve yourself of a lot of what you do. (September 19th, 1995, p. 7)

English is a very wily language, you know, and I think treaties bear that out—any kind of agreement with the Englishmen, bears that out, with the British. Wily, you know, like a coyote, like a trickster language I would call it....And I think that the English man is like that a lot. You can't trust—you know, he's breaking every treaty he's ever made, you know, and I'm not just talking about the English man, I'm talking about the Canadian legal system, which is implicated by its adoption of the English common law. You could sign an agreement knowing full well that you're entitled to break it—and it's like that....And we know very well what we're doing is not worth the paper it's written on, right? And they know very well that what they're doing is not worth the paper it's written on, so—who's the more honorable man? (September 19th, 1995, pp. 7-8)

Gustafson Lake, you know, the rules the Canadian law makers, the rules they've set up don't apply to us. Because you can't take a nation and make it into a city state, and treat it in the context of subjectivity. You can't do that, and that's what's happening, right? (September 19th, 1995, p. 11)

And we have to define the boundaries and parameters of jurisdiction of each of the communities that live in Canada before—you know, you don't go selling land you steal, you know. I mean, how absurd a notion that is right? Or you don't tell me that what you're going to give me of my land....The whole legal system was premised on the needs of only the conquerors right? In a democracy, the system is also premised on the needs of the conquered, you know? Quote, unquote. We've never been conquered. We've never been slaves. Why do we have to act conquered? (September 19th, 1995, p. 21)

Richard's rancor made me feel ashamed. I wanted to object to his use of *you* and have him substitute *they*. My people, who were not really my people because they did not represent my heritage nor my views, had basically entered into local war with his people, who were not really his people either, but another sympathetic nation. Ironically, in one interview, Richard explained that it was the English language that "brought native people together," because the English language gave the First Nations' people in North America "a common tongue," while, "in the old days," Richard would not have been able to communicate with the members of other nations (September 12th, 1995, pp. 5-6), a phenomenon that Lanoue (1991) referred to as "Pan Indianism" (p. 93).

During each of our interviews, Richard sat back on the sofa, coffee cup between his feet on the floor, sometimes leaning back, sometimes forward, always running his right hand through his hair. I sat facing him at the dining room table on a slippery wooden chair, which necessitated my changing positions frequently as different parts of my anatomy became numb. Our interviews were never less than 3 hours long, during which time I probably spoke fewer than 10 minutes. Although I tried to limit the amount of speaking I did in all of the life history interviews, concentrating instead on attentive listening, I spoke least of all with Richard. Some may accuse me of "losing control" of the interview context; however, as I wrote in my journal:

> *[Richard] is what I would call a great interview. One question...twenty minutes of "rambling". He seems to enter a trance-like state that I have no desire to interrupt. I don't think that allowing people to ramble is in any way dangerous. They are answering my questions in their own way, in their own time, and they are answering their own questions as well. I think that if I feel they are rambling, it's because I'm not understanding. I think that this view comes from a really limited position. If I feel they are off-topic, then I have an agenda that I'm imposing, and a view of their lives and loss that may not be compatible with theirs. My husband has told me in the past that I have a very strong "my pace", a characteristic which is antithetical to the notion of interview as I see it.* (Researcher Journal, September 23rd, 1995)

During interviews, I work hard to suspend "my pace" and adapt to another's. In Richard's case, I needed to learn to "flow in Indian time" (September 5th, 1995, p. 17) and wait.

During our first interview together, Richard specifically requested that I not use a pseudonym for him because it was very important that First Nations' peoples' experiences be recorded and claimed. During our second interview however, I began by asking for a "rounder sense" of his family and his life, to which he replied that he would need "to revert back to being anonymous" (September 12th, 1995, p. 1). He alternated between the two positions so that I was never sure whether to use a pseudonym or not. In the end, I chose to use a pseudonym in order to protect Richard, his family, and his community, from any mistakes that I might make.

THE LIFE HISTORY CONTEXT

Now 48 years old, an age of which he seems sometimes unsure, Richard was born the son of a Rock Cree trapper and a highly respected midwife in Van River, a town of about 1,500 in northern Manitoba. He was the second youngest in the family. Richard explained that he came from a family of

> ...originally eleven children, five boys—seven boys actually—and four girls, and we are now seven of us, and three of my brothers have died through a very common disease at that time—but they were so helpless, you know, like smallpox, or not smallpox, measles I believe, or maybe smallpox, who knows? (September 12th, 1995, pp. 1-2)

Three of his brothers died before he was born, he thinks, because he can't remember them at all. That left his family with seven children, three boys and four girls. He didn't say what happened to the other missing brother. I was particularly intrigued by Richard's inclusion of deceased siblings in his family, especially given that he neither remembered them, nor recalled what exactly caused their deaths. This seemed very important to me, and made me feel connected to his mother, who must have kept alive the memory of her dead children.

There was a wide range in ages among the children in Richard's family, therefore they all "grew up in separate eras" (ibid., p. 2). Most of the children, particularly the elder children, had a "very minimal education," about 2 years of formal schooling. His eldest brother, for example, who, Richard claims, is the most intelligent person in the family, went to school for 2 years and then turned to trapping like his father. Three of his sisters and one brother went to a sanitarium for tuberculosis where "they got into the educational thing" (ibid., p. 2), his brother becoming a master carpenter, his sisters all entering "the helping fields" (ibid., p. 3) as medicine women, healers, and midwives. Richard insists that all of the family except himself, his younger brother, and the youngest of the sisters, were self-educated. I believe, given the professions he describes, that he means they apprenticed themselves to their elders in Van River instead of leaving to enter formal educational institutions off the reserve.

The three youngest children left Van River and entered the residential school system. Richard explained that his father had "a lot of foresight in terms of society and where it was headed" (ibid., p. 3), and he knew that trapping, fishing, and hunting weren't going to be viable options in the younger children's lives. His father foresaw the day when they would be living in cities, in apartments, and townhouses, and insisted that they go to school. Richard first started school on the reserve, a school which went up to Grade 6. He attended Grades 1 and 2 in the Catholic school system on the reserve, and then went on to residential school. The Van River Catholic school system had been run for 40 years by one teacher who had built up a reputation and trust with the people, despite being "set in his own ways of elitism from his French background" (ibid., p. 6). The teacher chose the best and the brightest students—including Richard—to send out to different residential schools, "almost like to compete or to show" (ibid., p. 6), as if the students were championship horse stock. Of course, Richard explained, all the students were curious to leave the community to see what was outside and so they all wanted to go to residential school. They could see that the returning children were different somehow, and they all wondered "when is it going to be my turn to go out, and how will it affect me?" (ibid., p. 7) Richard later commented, however, that

> *the luckiest ones were the ones that didn't go anywhere to this day....And they're the ones that prospered, and gained from the whole situation, and thrived in our culture, because culturally, spiritually, as men and women, as parents, as providers, and so on,—they had it the best. They had the right upbringing. Their parents were there. They had role models. They had the training for their livelihood. They had love, support systems, and so on, everything the guys that went with us didn't have, or the guys that went out lost out on. Right? And—but that's the way it was. That was the reality, and that's still the reality of it today, and I have no complaints about that. I survived that. I worked around it. I'm going to outlive a lot of it, a lot of the degradation and humiliation a lot of those people...put us through, that I'm going to outlive them by sheer force of stubbornness and will.* (September 12th, 1995, p. 7)

> *I still maintain that those guys that stayed home are the lucky ones because they never had anything taken away first of all, and then they never had to question the value of it, because they lived its value everyday....How undignified one lives without the values of one's culture, one's upbringing— or—that's why I consider those guys lucky—and girls, women, men and women, that didn't leave the community to go to school, because they were shown how to be good human beings, and I had to search how to be a good human being. I wasted a lot—not wasted—but, I suffered a lot in that search....* (September 12th, 1995, pp. 17-18)

4. RICHARD: INTRODUCTION   57

Richard continued in residential school and made a life for himself outside the reserve. He claims not to have finished high school until he was about 23 years old, dropping out at least three times, and then dropping out of "some of the best universities in the country," by getting "sidetracked...by the situation as far as native people were concerned in the early [19]70s" (September 5th, 1995, p. 13). He became politicized, and, while in college, worked summers for the Union of British Columbian Chiefs in public relations. He later became an activist, worked for the Manitoba government as a policy analyst, and became involved as government liaison in Ottawa, "always in relation to the Indian Movement" (ibid., p. 14). At the age of 23, he began thinking that he was old, and that he needed to settle down and get married. He married an urban-raised Sauteaux Metis woman. For 7 years, he lived thinking

> *"I might as well stay where I am now. Here I am, so I might as well stay there because this is all I know"; that's all of life I knew. That's the only way I knew how to survive, was to go to work 8 to 5, or 9 to 4, the case at that time, and live for the weekend, I guess, and live for the holidays, and live for the spaces among the business, and then one day I just decided "well this is bullshit man," you know? "This is really bullshit; there isn't fuck-all here," you know?* (September 12th, 1995, p. 11)

Feeling unfulfilled, knowing nothing about his spiritual practices, or his stories or his history, or his language, and married to a woman whose priorities were a house in the suburbs, picket fences, children, and security, Richard became tormented and decided to go home to Van River. Breaking up their marriage was, he said, "one of the wisest things we ever did as two people in love, and perhaps the only wise thing we ever did in our marriage" (September 5th, 1995, p. 19). It is unclear whether or not Richard and his first wife have remained friends, but he retains both love and respect for her.

After returning to the reserve, Richard intended to go to law school, but, when a cousin decided to run for chief and offered him a job, he stayed. He assumed that it was going to be easy to relearn his language and reacquaint himself with his culture, but he found that it took more than 5 years, even though he claims that all Cree children know their entire language by the age of 8,[8] the age at which he left the reserve. Interestingly, Richard commented to me that, had he not relearned his language, he would never have been able to participate in my research project. He only understood what losing a language meant because he had relearned it, and thus realized what he had lost.

Richard eventually became involved in formulating reserve

education policy at the time when they implemented schooling in Cree from kindergarten to Grade 12, because "studies have found that a person learns faster in their own language" (September 5th, 1995, p. 8). Yet, it didn't seem to me that research studies would have had too much bearing on the decision, given that he alluded to a controversy over the policy, saying "how could it be right or beneficial if we thought of it, right?—now if an English man found it, how could it not be right or beneficial?" (September 5th, 1995, p. 8). I felt that the decision had come first, the justification second, a feeling that was backed up when Richard explained to me that his people believe that all decisions will affect the next seven generations, and bad decisions, such as treaties, become crises in the seventh generation. When he stated that, "I'm sure six generations ago, someone must have thought 'Oh well, you know, it's going to be a global society, so people have to learn English, the English way....'" (September 5th, 1995, p. 5), I came to understand that the policy that Richard worked on was changed in order to avert a potential impending crisis. In fact, Richard later commented that a proper education would have been to learn to be a trapper, and to learn the ways of his ancestors, but also:

> *I should never have been taken away to be educated. I should have stayed home to be educated. Now, my—the real practical aspect of that same idea is to have been educated right in the community, speaking my language, but also learning, having traditional education, traditional as meant by the school system, public school education. But in my language. A public school education in my language, in my home, with my people. With my own teachers, native teachers. Like the way it is now, right?* (September 19th, 1995, p. 20)

This belief extends to Richard's own children. During my first interview with Richard, he received a telephone call from Van River about his eldest son who wanted to live with him and go to a school in Vancouver. In that way, I became aware that he was a parent. Although he didn't mention his children to me while the tape was rolling, I was curious to know whether he had ensured his own children were developing in the Cree language, so I asked him. His two daughters are developing in their mothers' native tongues—Ojibway, and the Dene language, Chippewan—while his sons are all Cree and being brought up in Cree. Telling me that, having had no role models while away in residential school, he was "not the greatest parent in the world" (September 12th, 1995, p. 3), Richard explained that, therefore, all his children were being raised, at least in part, by their grandparents, because grandparents have the time and the language to share with them. It is very important to him that all his children know their languages: "They have to have a solid base first in that language in order to have a solid base in life...." (September 19th, 1995, p. 5).

Richard remained on the reserve for 16 years, relearning his language, learning the spiritual aspect of being Cree, and working for the community. Two years before I met him, he chose to leave Van River again. The simple reason, he said, was that he left for love, to be with his girlfriend in British Columbia. The more complex reason was that he had come to a "watershed" in his career, having finished making a contribution to his community as a leader and a council member. He had talked for years of becoming an actor and writing a book, and so he decided it was time to "be a writer, and starve—or prosper" (September 12th, 1995, p. 12).

THE NARRATIVE CONTEXT

Richard was one of three people I worked with who came from oral cultures; the other two were Lara (Finnish) and William (Welsh). Interviewing Richard, Lara, and William was completely different from working with other storytellers. Their initial undirected life stories were longer and more detailed than average, while each question I asked would act as a catalyst for more stories, ideas, or opinions. They each seemed to have an understanding of "life history interview" as opposed to "interview," and although their definitions differed one from another and from mine, they worked at their narratives as craft. Despite their dominance or monolingualism in English, they all appeared to use speech or story traditions from the L1.

In Richard's case, the most striking linguistic feature was his extensive use of metaphoric and poetic language, a property that is evident in his life story, and one that he associated with the Cree language. In this quotation, which I find moving, Richard was struggling with what he saw as the confines of the English language, to explain to me the richness and descriptive power of Cree:

> Our language, the Cree language, my language, is a living, breathing entity as far as I'm concerned. It's another entity. It's—the language is my landscape; that's where I live. It's not only a physical environment...,it's an expression of the spiritual. It's an expression of the higher man, of the higher being within us as a community. It's an expression of a totality of Cree, of one aspect of humanity. It strives to live and to prosper like we all do. It changes you when you know the language; it's a poetic experience, and sometimes it's an overwhelming experience....The Cree goes way back into the bush, in our case, and it comes from the river. It comes from the fire, the earth, I think the rocks...started talking. I think it was given to us from the Creator through nature, how to speak their language. You know? It's descriptive, you know? It's unique. It's like a rock. It's in how it's shaped and what it does and how it

looks, and it's in the texture and it's in the coldness of it, and the roundness
and the smoothness of it. (September 5th, 1996, pp. 25-26)

Another key characteristic of Richard's language was his playfulness
with the language. Several times during our interviews, Richard used
foreign phrases that weren't quite correct (e.g., "my modus operate"),
nonstandard pronunciation of English words (e.g., "mollibility"), or he
made up words (e.g., "empackaged"). I have chosen not to correct any of
them in light of one of his comments:

For instance, in the process of a conversation, in English, I'll throw in
absurdities into it right? I'll use it backwards, or different. I'll use a word; I'll
invent words....I like doing that because I get a joy of doing that. It's like a
game, right? It's like bouncing a ball. I like the English language. I like any
language I use that I can be flexible and mollible [malleable] and I can bend it
and bounce it the way I want it, off of whatever I want, whatever wall or ceiling
or whatever right? Because I try to make it alive, right? I try to make the
English language as alive as the Cree language and that's hard. But, by
inventing words and by inverting them, as long as I get close to the meaning,
people will know what you're talking about....I like throwing curves when I
speak right? And especially English, it's easy to throw curves because you can
find two words that have similar meanings or words that sound the same but
are different...and it gives it more of a—more color. (September 19th, 1996,
p. 23)

Of course, the down side to Richard's nonstandard English, which is
magnified by nonstandard intonation,[9] is that the English Richard
speaks in order to become "a good, little, brown-white man" itself marks
him as an outsider. This was something noted by Pye (1992) in his
research into language loss among the Chilcotin in British Columbia.
Pointing out that Chilcotin is the language of those families who "have
not made it" (p. 79), but that Chilcotin children are not learning a
standard dialect of English, he asks "Why...would the Chilcotin switch to
a language that is no more acceptable to the dominant culture than
Chilcotin?" (p. 84). Yet, Richard's case is even more complex. He never
spoke English with his parents and only for a short period of time with
his siblings. His only contacts with English came from reserve school,
residential school, and government work where, presumably, standard
English was modeled. Not wanting to point out to him that his English
pronunciation and intonation were nonstandard, I did not ask him
whether it was conscious, like a form of rebellion, or unconscious.

A particularly interesting narrative feature in this story is that
Richard is a natural storyteller; he was one of a minority of participants
who did not speak directly to me, or even look at me, but instead seemed
to enter into a kind of trance and soliloquize. Oddly enough, the only
other person who did this was William, the only other speaker of an

endangered indigenous language. The result is that this story is the least-edited of all of the life stories. Although in other stories, I found it necessary to change the narrative construction used by participants in order to establish/maintain coherence, it was unnecessary in this story.

Another interesting aspect of Richard's narrative is his uncertainty about his own family structure. At various times, he seemed uncertain of his age, the number of siblings he had, and his relationships to people. The impression that he gave me was that his bonds with other people appear tenuous. He displayed a strong allegiance to "his people," meaning the Rock Cree, but showed little emotional attachment to his family, his children, his wives, or his friends. Despite numerous promptings, Richard told few stories about his life on the reserve, his time in residential school, his life as an activist, his work as an actor, his relationships. Instead, he tended to relate expository narrative and opinion, always in relation to himself. I found myself wondering what role language had to play in this. Had the loss of his language and culture in residential school broken the primary bonds with his family, as he hints at various times? Had the fact that most of his relationships until the age of 30 necessitated second language communication inhibited close relationships with them? Was he unable to tell me about the relationships with his family because the relationships were in his first language and he was speaking to me in his second language? Again, not wanting to ask him an awkward question, I did not follow this line of questioning.

As a final comment about Richard's narrative, one of the most prominent recurring themes is the battle between good and evil. In Richard's narrative, the reserve and Van River are good, while urban landscapes are evil. Speaking Cree is good; speaking English is evil. Education in Cree is good; education in English is evil. First Nations' customs are good; English-speakers' customs are evil. And yet, Richard is conflicted. By his own admission, he still wanted something that the reserve couldn't offer him, and so he left. He still has "White-world" aspirations, in that he often spoke of material goods that he wanted to possess, despite his frequent assertions that such things had no meaning in his life. I feel that this is very much tied to his language loss. With the English language came a host of ambitions and expectations. He writes in English; he acts in English; he conducts his business life in English. Having now been successful in English as an activist, and having achieved success in Cree in Van River, he has now returned to the world outside the reserve in order to try to achieve success in another capacity—as an actor, a poet, and a writer of English.

ENDNOTES

1. This housing cooperative was built in the late 1980s, one of the first buildings constructed to resemble California styling. Such buildings have spawned what has come to be known as Vancouver's "leaky condo" crisis.
2. Richard later told me that he was often successful in landing acting jobs because he looked and sounded so much like an "Indian."
3. Richard pronounced this Goo-*staf*-son, and usually he did not say lake.
4. First Nations is the chosen form of third-person address for Canada's native population.
5. Although I knew that it was a false assumption, I somehow felt that the Sundancers would be treated with more respect if the land was owned by a Canadian.
6. In May 1997, it was determined that the Royal Canadian Mounted Police had acted with unnecessary force in the Gustafson Lake incident. The Sundancers were convicted and jailed.
7. Richard usually referred to dominant Canadian society as "the British," and to all English speakers as "the English man." He does not recognize Canada, or the Canadian national anthem, though he does acknowledge "God Save the Queen" and the monarchy with whom treaties were signed.
8. Compare Richard's own beliefs that, it must be noted, can be attributed to his considerable experience in working on the Van River School Board, with the conclusions Collier (1989) reaches after lengthy consideration of existing research:

   From birth through age 5, children acquire enormous amounts of L1 phonology, vocabulary, grammar, semantics, and pragmatics, but the process is not at all complete by the time children reach school age. From ages 6 to 12, children still have to develop in the first language the complex skills of reading and writing, in addition to continuing acquisition of more complex rules of morphology and syntax, elaboration of speech acts, expansion of vocabulary (which continues throughout a person's lifetime), semantic development, and even some aspects of phonological development (p. 510).

   Cree, though it has been assigned a written form, is primarily an oral language, prompting us to question whether these kinds of conclusions can be applied to the Cree language.
9. One of the most prominent intonation differences is that in two-word phrasal verbs, Richard always stresses the first rather than the second word. He would say "*got* strapped" rather than "got *strapped*".

5. RICHARD'S STORY: ENGLISH IS A FULL-TIME JOB

I'm a full-blooded Cree Indian, raised in Van River in northern Manitoba. I went to residential school at an early age. First of all, where I went to school, my first experience with languages other than Cree was from my sisters, who were a bit older, had already been to school for a couple of years, and they said it was really important that we were prepared before we went to school to know the English language, plus some of the things to expect in school, such as the alphabet, numbers. So, they took it upon themselves—one sister in particular—to teach us English, numbers. So, she taught me this unusual strange language, and so by the time I got to school, I was already ahead of other students, because they were all other Cree students, but, having a basis of the language, I was able to articulate my thoughts; I was able to tell the colors, could count to a hundred and so on and so forth.

My family is a really intelligent people, and being as I was always considered a bright person, it was expected of me more or less [that I would do well]. The school I went to...was conducted by a French gentleman from southern Ontario who believed...in total immersion. [He believed] that a person, in order to learn a language, had to speak and only hear that language, so that was my case in his school. We were encouraged to speak only English, in the schoolyard, in the classroom, all over, so we did that, and so I learned the English language quite easily and quite fast because everybody else was speaking it, and we were reading it—as soon as I learned how to read—and what I found was I enjoyed it. I enjoyed English. It was an adventure in a new language. Everybody had impressed on me, my folks included, my brothers, my sisters, everybody, how important it was going to be for me to know the English language because it was going to be the universal language of my life and also the language of nonnative people and the outside world.

My older sister Shaney, she was the boss, so whatever Shaney said, that's what happened. Shaney said, "Now we speak English." She was the one that taught me as a baby to learn English. She insisted, "If you're going to do something, you do it well. If you're going to learn the English language, you're going to learn the English language well. Because that what's gonna determine your success or lack of it." So, she took it upon herself to give us the English world. For a while, us kids, we would talk to our sister in Cree, but it was not encouraged. It was not discouraged either but it became almost an appendage, useless.[1] We communicated in our language until the point where the English

63

language overcomes the Cree; it's like being buried by an avalanche. All of a sudden, the avalanche happens. All of the English words fall on you and you die. The Cree dies for a while. The Cree is never dead, the Cree will never be dead, but the language becomes less important.

So, I learned the language and I became fluent. I liked school. I liked reading. I liked stories. I liked storytelling; I liked writing. As soon as I learned how to write, I loved it. And it seemed that English was a magical transformation; it was like entering a new world for me. And it was an adventure. And I had no qualms about it. You know, I had no prejudicial thoughts about race or nationalism, so it was no problem.

And then I went to a residential school, where Cree was a minority. My language, my Cree people there, were a minority. Aside from the Cree, there was Ojibway, Sauteaux people, Sioux people, and so they outnumbered us by quite a bit. And the fact that everybody talked a different language there, it was more convenient for everybody to speak English, to communicate. We had to speak English in order to make friends and it got to a point there I started speaking only English at a very early age, 8 or 9 years old, and English became my life, my modus operate. When we were only Cree together, we talked our language to hear it, right? We made each other happy by talking our own tongue, but then if somebody else would join the group, maybe a Sauteaux or Sioux, and we'd start the whole thing of speaking English again for our friends. It was a matter of integrity. There's a lot of honor to be maintained and part of the honor of our society is to make people feel comfortable, and so that's why we'd all speak the common language. We all eventually adopted English as a full-time job.[2]

It never occurred to me then, and things didn't occur to me like "Well, should I save my language?," "I should not lose my language," because when you're at that age, when you're a kid, it's secondary to play for instance, or making friends, or having adventures. It's secondary to a lot of things. One thing I remember was my favorite teacher, she told me "don't ever forget the language, because that other language of yours makes you like two men." And, how true that is. That's how I feel now. But, we weren't so prejudiced and conditioned to have adult thoughts, so, we just went about. I just went about and reveled in the English language. I became quite articulate at an early age because of reading. Because I loved reading, and I was a writer already at that age. I liked stories; I liked making up stories, doing literature.

For the next, well I don't know how long, 'til I was about 30, I was speaking English, because, after that, I kept going back to school every year. When you're in residential school, you have very minimal contact with your family till summer. You don't go home for 10 months. You get letters from your family but they're in English, because you don't know how to read Cree. When I was a kid, I didn't know how to read the Cree syllabics,[3] so my mom and dad would get someone, one of my brothers, one of my sisters, a friend, a nephew, or whatever, and say "Okay, well, sit down, we're going to write a letter to Richard, and this is what I want to say and you write it down." So, I took my letters and I answer back in English and ask someone to interpret them for my folks back home. There was no contact; there was no phone calls, you know....your family became not your family anymore. They became the people "back home." No matter how much you love them, or care about your family, you are literally taken from your parents and put in this strange environment and that becomes your world. It's being totally removed, being totally isolated from anything resembling culture or language. You become, for all intents and purposes, of the system, a brown-white man. A brown-white man. That's what they want to make you. The dominant belief at that time was "Well for the Indians to succeed they've got to learn the language; they've got to assimilate; they've got to become White."[4] And that's what the residential school system was. It was the politics of destruction essentially, as far as I'm concerned. One day everything is there, the next day everything is gone, and then there's no communication with the parents until the next summer and then you have summer holidays and then you're back home, but you don't speak the language anymore because all your peers, yourself, you're speaking English, you're communicating in English, but you do understand Cree. I shouldn't say you don't speak the language, I mean, you don't forget your language in 1 year. You don't forget your language for several years. At school you communicate with your Sioux friends, your Ojibway friends, and so on in English, and you begin to accept that as a fact of life. You don't question it. You're a kid, a teenager; you have too many other things you're questioning to worry about language.

At home, in the summer, everybody knew English so we didn't have any problems speaking or communicating. Did have problems with attitude. We were told that we'd become arrogant; we'd become nonlisteners. In native society, you learn through example and through listening, but we lost that in the process of education, I think. And, when we went home, our parents—not just mine, my friends' too—they'd say "There's something wrong with you. You don't listen to us anymore. You don't listen to the good things around us, right? You're stubborn." Stubbornness is what became a problem. We became stubborn toward our own parents, our own language, our own tradition. We became whiplashed; we succumbed. We had a lousy attitude; we became rotten kids. We were beautiful kids before that, and then we became rotten because we had other models now. We had outside ways, and they were not necessarily good for traditional models. But, in some ways, you know, we retained our communication in Cree. I mean, I'm not saying that everybody on the reserve all of a sudden spoke English, at a certain age, or a certain period, but I'm saying that English was an easy form of communication, it was almost a lazy form of communication as far as we were concerned; we didn't have to think anymore, us kids. We communicated in English because it was easy; it was like play as opposed to the seriousness of Cree. When you spoke, when you worked, when you had to communicate in Cree, it was a serious matter. You had to be serious because this is your culture; this is your tradition. Everything was empackaged in the Cree, but English was a frivolous thing. It was frivolous, and you didn't have to worry about offending the saints and the heroes of the Cree world by speaking English, because there were no saints or heroes in the English language.

So, when you had gone to school, Cree would have been natural, but after you began school, you lost that ease. I don't know if it's sociological; it's symptomatic of something 'cause when we got back, the kids you grew up with, the ones that hadn't gone to school yet—everybody was always wanting to go to school—those kids became almost distant, like you had formed new kinship, new relationships with other kids. It's like getting up, going out the door, and 10 months later you appear at the door again and the people inside the house are like "Where'd he go? Why has he changed? What happened to the poor kid?" They couldn't understand us, not just in language, but they couldn't understand the transformation of what happened to us, why all of a sudden we had many different priorities and different outlooks; I don't know. I've never been on the other side [that is, someone who never left the Cree homeland] so I couldn't say. Someday I'll write about it and figure it out, but it was not easy anymore to be Cree. I think we hid behind the English language too. Because it was not easy to admit that you had become an uncultured, uncivilized, person. It was not easy to admit that you had lost the most precious thing you ever had, which is your Cree tongue, your Cree soul, your Cree language, your culture. It was not an easy thing, even as a kid, to realize that something happened: "What the hell happened? How do I deal with that?" So, you deal with it by speaking English, and that way you don't have to face the hurt of the loss. You know, that's just my own personal opinion, but thinking about it, in retrospect, you hide behind the language of the dominant society for a while. The ease with which we could offer our heart by way of language wasn't there anymore, so we choose to use an unfeeling language.[5]

I don't know where their heads were, but their priority was to educate these Indian kids, these children, to educate them, to make them forget their language and their culture, to make them forget everything...forget everything that they ever learned that was beautiful so they can become something else. You know, you can all of a sudden become contributing members of society as...as our society wasn't considered a contribution. It was, I think, for me, the residential school system, and the whole question was: it was the politics of destruction pure and simple, but it failed. It was something that failed, that didn't happen, we're still here, we're stronger than ever and we'll never be destroyed, you know; I know that. And language, the question of language was just one of the things used to do that. But that didn't work either. We're still here and I still know my language, my own mother tongue just as well as I know English right?

You shame people away from their language, you shame them into speaking yours, you know? You become ashamed to know an ancient dying language, Cree. It's like being ashamed of how you're dressed, you know? You want to dress like everybody else, except for sure your shirt will have a patch and your knees will be poking through. So, you try to take off these garments and put them away or burn them, or out of sight out of mind, and put on new garments. I put on a tie, a white shirt, and *your* skin, sheepskin, and so on, but you're very susceptible, because you haven't really made up your mind about this—other people are in the process of making up your mind about it. So, you just go on lies, thinking you're cool because you speak English, you're cool because you don't speak Cree anymore. It's better because now you're white, right? We're apples, which means red on the outside and white on the inside, right? And, it's still happening. People want to live in big suburban houses with white picket fences and two incomes, two cars and all the latest gadgets; it still happens. My people still want to be White, but we didn't identify it as being *White*; we identified it as being different. At a young age, it's a gas to be different. It's cool. The thing to be is to be different. Adopting another language was just something about being different. People looked at you in a different way, admired you because you knew English, because you dressed a certain way, because you went to an exotic place to school far away. It was an innocent acceptance with a very major consequence with the Cree language, because you were just armed with the awareness of innocent children, put into a system that tried destroying us, and you either "go with the flow" and get destroyed there, or you get lost in the flow.

When I left school, I entered the business world for a career. I lived in cities. I married a non-Cree woman, a non-Cree speaker, and so I didn't hear...[pause]...well, I heard, my friends would visit and they'd talk a bit of Cree, but usually even the friends from home, everybody, spoke English. You know, we spoke English as a means of communication, because it was the handiest thing; you didn't have to think "what's the word for such-and-such in Cree?". And we didn't realize what we were losing, or the hazard we were getting into by not speaking our language because it was impressed upon us that you had to speak English in order to succeed, in order to know what was going on in the world. English was it. English was the world, my world, my friend's world. So, none of these things [that] have transpired between the age of 8 to the age of 30 was any help as far as the retaining of my own language, because you know for everybody it seemed to be the going thing. You know, get an education, go out and work, live in an English world with nonnative people, and your own language, your own culture and so on, your own people were far-removed; [they] lived on the reserve and were up in northern Manitoba, in a different world from the immediate experience.

Not only that, but I also became a writer, a poet and a writer, and I reveled in the English language. I fell in love with the English language because of its complexity, its mollibility [malleability], its preciseness. One of the first things I remember as a kid [is] thinking "well this is a neat language; you learn x number of words, you put them together in a certain way, insert them into a paragraph, and then you can play with them, juggle them around, and have different thoughts and assert them"—there was so much you could do with the English language because it was a written language as opposed to an oral language: "Now I will also have the means of transmitting my thoughts to a written page." It was exciting and I could make up things. I could make up a fantasy through the English language, and that's exactly what I did, so it became a second skin; it was so natural.

I had no thought of I was getting rid of anything else in relation to the implications of forgetting my own language, or [what] I like to think as a *leaving* of the language for a while. See, I didn't think I'd forget my language; that's what happened. I didn't forget it; I figured "Okay, I have this Cree language, I'll always think in Cree,...I'll never forget the language". I mean, it was my body, my soul, my spirit, how can I forget a language that's so beautiful, that I was born with? So, it never occurred to me that I could forget it. I always thought later "Okay, it's in *abeyance*, and once I go home and am back with my people, it will come back naturally." And that was not to be the case I found. Later on, when I went home at the age of 30, I formed a thought in my mind of something

I want to say in Cree, and I would try saying it and draw a blank, or, at the least, form the language in my mind, say it, but it would come out different. And I was frustrated, but now I'm fluent again, in my language, and so my language died for a while; between the ages of 8 and 30, for all intents and purposes, it died. It was gone; it was in the ether. I came back and I readopted my language; it was not so much a relearning because in your mind you never forget the language, but in the speaking....it doesn't work out. You do forget you know, like you do forget what words mean; you come to pronounce them and something else comes out.

So, at 30 years of age, I went home, 'cause by that time I had gained a lot of experience in the field I was going to enter. I had worked in a lot of places, so it was time to go home and contribute some of my own education, my own knowledge, my expertise, on behalf of my people. When I went back, it was not as simple as I thought it would be. I mean I thought, "I'm a Cree man, born of a Cree soul, and that's never lost and nobody can kill that, and I'll just stretch away from the English. Now the English language dies, and then the Cree language lives and I'll continue from there," but that was not to be the case, unfortunately.

I remember, when I went back, the first few times as a leader, when I had to speak in front of a group of people in Cree because they were my people. And the words came out really funny. People laughed and joked about it because I was not a Cree speaker; I was an educated man. I represented education to them, so I'm trying to speak, I'm trying to bring up my ideas across to my people, regarding the Northern Flood committee for instance—a referendum was to be held and I was in charge. I had to speak in front of a gymnasium of my people to bring this idea across. There's no word for referendum, first of all, in Cree. There's a lot of thoughts in Cree that have no equivalent in English, and vice versa, and, not only that, but even in the simplest basic Cree, I'm mumbling, and I figure, "Okay this is how you say it," then I'd come to say it and it comes out wrong. People laughed and I laughed because...but they're not laughing at me, they're laughing at the words that come out. They're laughing 'cause it sounds so funny, but they're not laughing at me as a person or me as a Cree; they're laughing at me because "Poor guy right? He doesn't know how to speak. He's illiterate right?" That's what's going on. I stumbled and I bluffed through. My people, the elders, took it upon themselves: "Okay, well this kid wants to get involved; he's half-ways bright, so let's give him a hand." And they took it upon themselves to become my mentors politically, as well as socially, as well as language, which is the culture, you know? They taught me, not in the sense of "Well, this is how you say that word" but teaching me... For example, the first thing I learned when I went home was that I was too aggressive and I was too much in a hurry. I learned to be less in a hurry; I learned to flow in "Indian time" meaning "the right time is when it happens." In teaching me these things, they're always teaching me in Cree, right? Because it's the only language they speak. A lot of elders, my parents included, they can understand the English language but they never speak it. There was no way they were going to succumb to another nation by speaking English to them. I imagine it would be like a defeat and they were not a defeated people. They were not a conquered people, so there was no way they were going to speak as a conquered people, like I do. Then, over time, I learned in my soul the Cree thoughts and the Cree spirituality, Cree philosophies by how they spoke to me, by kindness, and with love and with understanding and with patience, or forgiveness right? They forgave me the fact that I lived until the age of 30 and forgot about my people. I never came back. I never contributed anything till I was 30.

It took me about 2 seconds to be comfortable with the Cree, but about 5 years to become comfortable with speaking in public. I didn't say a word until I was sure—unless I was standing in front and a hundred people were looking at me because I'm public speaking—then I have no choice. I stumbled through though, and, by the time I left, I was one of the most articulate leaders in the community. In the Cree language. In those years that I was back home, I became very articulate, not because I made a point of it, but because people took the time, the patience, the understanding, the love to give me back my language. They loved me enough to give me back my language, and for me it was an act of love, but also an act of war. I went back because there was a war between my people and the rest of Canadian society, and this war had to be fought with words, right? I became a warrior of ideology through language. I was picked to do that somehow. I don't think I was picked to be a great leader or a great problem solver, but I was picked to deal in language. I'm only a messenger; I bridge ideologies and races. I'm a go-between; I offer ideas back and forth. And I needed to do that, to fulfill myself, to become whole again, to become a whole man. I had to do that, so I went and did it.[6]

So, I was immersed again for the next 16 years back into my community and I became a Cree speaker again because everybody around me was a Cree person; everybody spoke Cree; we thought in Cree, we laughed in Cree, we cried in Cree, we loved in Cree, we died in Cree; everything was in Cree and it was fantastic. It was great. It was like falling in love again with an old lover, but a true love. And English, what's English? English is nothing anymore. English is something that you use at work to communicate in the form of the written page again. English was something we all paraded around with when I got back home again for 8 hours a day, and then we were back to Cree. English was a business thing. English was how you spoke to bureaucrats and business people, how you communicated, throughout the day at the office with those people who meant anything to your function, and then when you left at 5:00 o'clock, you were Cree. Different mind-set. Totally different way of looking at things in Cree as opposed to English. English became inadequate when I started speaking Cree again back home, because, you know, coming from an oral tradition, being an oral people, Cree was where it was at. Cree could accommodate the Cree wants and needs more than English could. English became lacking; it was not as colorful; it was not as useful—it was dry. Cree became a more colorful world, became a more precise world. You could describe things in Cree you couldn't describe in English.

The language, my tongue, my Cree tongue is like another person; it does things that another person would do. If you're not using it, it will sleep; it'll get bored so it'll move away from you. It will sit down elsewhere and contemplate things, try to figure out what's happened, and this is what the Cree language did, in my case. Because I wasn't using it, what was the sense in it hanging around right? So, it was in abeyance; it went away and became still, and went to sleep, until one day, when I was about 30 years old, I went back home. It was so happy to wake up. You know there was a new day, a beautiful day, so he jumped up and said, "Well, here I am you know; enjoy me again. Let's live life over," and we did that. And we did that, living life over at 30 years old.

Now that I have learned Cree again, my language will always be there waiting for me, because my language is me. It's my culture, it's everything that I am, it's my landscape in life; it's the one constant in life, right? Someone will always light a fire, someone else will always be keeping the fires burning, so I have an option of always slipping back and being warmed by that fire. Whatever age I am—I may be 90 years old—I'll be able to go back and warm myself at that fire and have that fire burning inside me. If I had not readopted Cree, I think I would be an Englishman. I would be living in the larger world, in English, but I wouldn't be very happy. I'd be a misplaced person. I'd be a little, brown-white man I guess; there'd be still something missing. Losing the language is like losing half the man you are. Not to lose the language makes me twice the man, so the loss of the language is the loss of the soul, I think, for an Indian person. It's the loss of the essence of the soul, not to know the language, because you never know how beautiful you are until you know your language...because you can only be described in a foreign tongue, right? If I hadn't reawakened Cree, I wouldn't be able to talk to you now, because I wouldn't know...I would have nothing comparative to speak to you about right? So that, essentially, in a few words, is the history of my language loss.

ENDNOTES

1. Reflecting on what I had read about residential schools (e.g., "'we'd get a lot of strapping'...already hungry children were denied meals, forced to remain with their arms outstretched in a 'push-up' position until they collapsed, and encouraged to inform on other students" [Grescoe, 1996, p. 19]), I asked Richard if he had ever been encouraged to give up Cree. The only active discouragement he recalled happened in Van River:

    Nobody has ever suggested that. But I think it was done indirectly through a lot of people have done it indirectly, a lot of educators, teachers,—Canadians. You know, like, my—by penalizing my Cree, or my Cree over the English, right? By ridicule when I was younger, when I was child, 'cause I spoke Cree. It's a good way to make us all forget the language pretty fast and minimizing it is—well, that I'm used to because always my culture has been minimized by the so-called— dominant society—. And, the one teacher when I first started back home in grade school—we had to speak [English] in the classroom and in the yard, in the immediate vicinity of the school, but not once you left that boundary. And the rationale for that guy was that when we left that community it was going to be an English world sure enough, right? And, I heard that you got strapped if you spoke your language at that time. I never—I never got strapped because I didn't speak my language in the classroom. I was very careful about that, right? Because I had never been strapped so I didn't know what it was about, right? And, I certainly didn't want to find out. (September 19th, 1995, p. 22)

2. This particular expression is one that Richard used repeatedly, and seemingly without thinking about it. English is associated with work and a joyless existence, while the Cree language is the language of love, life, and happiness.
3. Apparently, Richard still does not read the Cree syllabics, nor can he understand High Cree.
4. Richard adopted a clipped British accent to express this idea, acting in a paternal fashion by looking down his nose and raising his chin.
5. Richard explained what he meant by an unfeeling language:

    For me anything that does not depend on its oral history or oral communication is pretty well dead; English happens to be one of those languages because you can write English down and a page is dead, you know and the writing, computer board, is a dead language, it's a visual, it's visual as opposed to heart, as opposed to oral is not an exchange anymore; it's a one-way communication. Whereas in oral there has to be an exchange; your language is alive as you're speaking it, in the same sense as you're alive as you're using it and the communication is instantaneous. You're living the language and, in English, you're not living the language. In English you're putting the language down in history books for posterity for instance, or to put up on the bookshelf, and English has its beauty, but it has its limitations, and that's one of them. (September 5th, 1995, p. 11)

6. I think it is very important that Richard here describes a balance between the Cree and the English-speaking culture that is missing from the other stories, but resonates with Bhabha's (1994) description of the "third space," which is "somehow *in between*,...occupying an interstitial space that was not fully governed by the recognizable traditions from which you came" (p. 190). Richard's balance perhaps results from his linguistic renaissance, which allows him to communicate with both the Cree and the Canadian cultural traditions. He has therefore not been confined to an either/or position, but has been able to adopt a both/and orientation.

6. LARA: INTRODUCTION

THE INTERVIEW CONTEXT

When I lived in Point-middle-of-no-where, Japan, I wrote in a letter to my Mom that one of the great things about living in a city with fewer than 20 other native English-speakers was that I learned to be friends with people whom I would not normally choose to spend time with— just because we spoke a common language, and we were thrown together a lot. My "White" social circle was diverse in terms of age, background, education, racial attitudes, country of origin, lifestyle, and just about every other conceivable social category. In doing this research project, I was blessed with the same kind of phenomenon. When I think back about the time I spent interviewing people and visiting their homes, a quartet of women aged 45 to 52, whom I would not normally have crossed paths with, from Belgium, Holland, Japan, and Finland, represent to me the pinnacle of what working with life stories should be about. Minette, Greta, Naomi, and the subject of this story, Lara, all shared with me tea, food, companionship, curiosity, and each of them was able to bestow and receive often distressing details, which sometimes led to tears.

I reflected often about why these four women had such an impact on me, and finally concluded that it was partly the circumstances of their lives, and partly the circumstances of mine. Each of them had been profoundly influenced by World War II, Minette, Greta, and Lara immigrating because of European devastation, and Naomi being born and then held in an internment camp for its duration. Each of them had faced the deterioration and mortality of parents, which had made them aware that their closest links to their first languages were stretched to breaking. Each of them felt that they were at a particularly reflective point in their lives, and mentioned that reading about this study in the newspaper had triggered a flash of recognition, an "aha" response. Each of them was herself the parent of at least one daughter who was still struggling with "becoming" rather than "being" in terms of career, family, and education. And, I think, because of my own circumstances, I naturally fell into a surrogate daughter role, especially when I was pregnant, then not, then pregnant again. I don't know how else to explain it except that each of these four women palpably loved me, and let me love them in return. It is unfortunate that, within the limits of this particular work, I cannot detail all of their stories.

I spent two evenings and two mornings in August and September,

1995, at Lara's architect-designed house by the sea. We sat on big red leather wing-back chairs facing floor-to-ceiling windows, while outside on the balcony, her fierce little dog complained to anyone in his field of vision. The windows were always open so we could smell the salt air, and hear the passing traffic. Every time I was at Lara's house, we were repeatedly interrupted—by her daughter, by another daughter and her boyfriend, by a neighbor, by the police looking for a former resident, by the telephone, by her dog begging for attention, by her homestay student—and each time I was amazed by Lara's ability to adapt from her role as storyteller, to mother/neighbor/house owner/friend, and back to storyteller, seamlessly, without losing a single thread of her story.

And, it was such a fascinating story. Lara seemed to really enjoy the uninterrupted oral narration aspect of the interviews, at ease with relating a life story. She spoke directly to the tape recorder rather than to me,[1] and I found myself listening to her as if I were a child listening to a legend or a fairy tale, rather than listening with a mind to research, writing questions, and making quick notes. I wrote that,

> *I love to listen to her. I find that I too enter almost a dream-like state, and have trouble bringing myself around to really concentrate in a researcherly way because I'm so busy listening to the story.* (Researcher Journal, August 20th, 1995, p. 23)

As a result, I found that I was constantly "making discoveries" while transcribing Lara's interviews. Many of her comments that were directly relevant to the research project had completely passed me by.

Lara is very soft-spoken, and has a musical quality to her voice. I remembered reading F. Scott Fitzgerald's (1953) *The Great Gatsby* when I was younger, and being struck by the description of Daisy as having a voice so low that people would automatically lean towards her when she spoke (p. 6), one that, for some reason, I remember being described as "full of money." Lara, too, had a low-pitched, yet "thrilling," voice that sounded more like an echo of itself than itself. Moreover, its musicality and timbre made me think that she was speaking very slowly, almost meditatively, yet, when I began to transcribe the interview tapes, I discovered that she actually spoke quickly, so quickly that I had trouble hearing every word, and had to turn the transcriber speed down. Yet, I recalled no trouble hearing and understanding every word while I was in her presence.

I think that the music in Lara's voice is particularly interesting, given that loss of the lyricism of Finnish is what she claimed to most regret losing. During our third interview together, I asked Lara to try to tell me exactly what it meant to her to have lost the language, and she replied that,

> *Well, I think the Finnish language is an extremely lyrical language. It's almost like half-singing almost, and there's some real character in it, and you don't see that in the English language, or you don't hear it in the English language very often, except perhaps if one makes a concerted effort to put some lyricism in, when they're talking in poetic verse or whatever. But, in Finnish it's just part and parcel of the language, and it really really provides a character definition that we're lacking, and I don't know how to describe it....It feels like there's a real void there. It feels like there's something missing and I'd really like to tap into that and I can't tap into it in the English language, and I can't tap into it in the Finnish language either right now.* (August 30th, 1995, p. 3)

Lara then asked me to stop the tape because she had a video on which some people were speaking Finnish that she wanted to play for me. I listened carefully to their words, and while I admit that Lara did not sound particularly *like* them, I feel that she spoke English with a kind of musical fervor that the Finnish speakers also showed in their language. The difference, if I were to put it into metaphoric terms, is that while the people on the tape were "singing" a lusty folk tale, Lara was "singing" the melancholy song of a heavily pregnant fisher's wife on her Widow's Walk, pacing beneath a gray-purple sky.

THE LIFE HISTORY CONTEXT

One of the first things I noticed about Lara is that her back was absolutely vertical, and she held her head perfectly erect, even when lowering herself into a chair or raising to a standing position. One of the first things Lara told me about herself is that she had been in a very serious car accident several years previously, which had broken her back, leaving her unable to return to work, and living on limited means. As a result, Lara said, she had been going through a very reflective time in her life, with considerable emotional turmoil, considering her first language loss, and the various losses in her life. As Lara described it,

> *It was really finding out who I am and what my purpose and place in the world is, which I still haven't determined at this point. But I feel much more comfortable in that I suppose that I've come to the conclusion that I will always be an outsider from whatever perspective I look at my life. As a Finn I'm an outsider. As an Anglophone I'm an outsider. As a Canadian I'm somewhat of an outsider because I fit nowhere really, but then, perhaps all Canadians are outsiders as well, so maybe there's a common thread there. And the best that I can see for myself is that hopefully my children are going to be well-adjusted and will not have the same crisis, so to speak, that I've had.* (August 30th, 1995, pp. 3-4)

But, as Lara did, I should begin at the beginning, rather than somewhere in the middle.

Lara was born in a small seaport city in Finland, that she believes was very beautiful, though she doesn't have any visual recollection of it. She was born into a family that could trace its roots back over 400 years on her father's side, while from her mother's family she inherited the oldest recorded Finnish family history. Her mother's family history is recorded in four volumes, beginning in the year 932, and attests to their upper-class social position and attendance at some of the first Finnish universities that were established in the 1700s. Although her family was of the elite, the bulk of the Finnish population were peasants who were uneducated and illiterate, and who relied on oral history and the telling of stories. According to Lara, when Finland broke away from Russia and Sweden at the turn of the century, the new government decided that the Finns had to be educated quickly, so a law was passed stating that anyone who wanted to get married had to become literate. Within one generation, everybody in the country had learned to read and write, and the churches took over the teaching of language. The oral traditions were written down. The Kalavalas (sagas) were recorded, and Finland became an extremely literate society. Lara wanted me to know that the story of language in Finland was complex, and very rich.

Lara's mother and father both were educated to speak five languages. They knew Swedish, Finnish, Russian, German, and a fifth language that Lara can't remember, but that wasn't English. If their family had stayed in Finland, Lara too would have spoken five languages; her parents were appalled at the miserable second-language education students received in Canada. Of course, if their family had stayed in Finland, many other aspects of Lara's life would also have been different. Of all her cousins living in Finland, only one owns a home; the others all own apartments or condominiums. On the other hand, all of them have summer retreats on a lake with a sauna and a cabin because it's more important for a Finnish family to have a cabin with a sauna in which to spend the summer months, than it is to have a house.

Lara was the middle child of five, the last sibling born in Finland. She has a sister 10 years older who Lara feels is both brilliant and a fine artist, but who is institutionalized with schizophrenia. Lara believes that the stresses of moving to Canada, having to learn the language, and never being accepted into the community, coupled with living through the bombing and the horrors of the war triggered her sister's schizophrenia. Lara's brother, 5 years older, is now an environmentalist; however, he was also very troubled at school, dropping out in Grade 9 to work in unskilled labour. At the age of 21, he finally realized that he was too intelligent to continue working where he was, and finished high school in 1 year, followed by an honors degree and Master's in zoology. Lara feels that he dropped out of school because he felt like an outsider in the system. As an example, she told me that he brought home a report card with the name Adam Johnson on it—he had changed his name to a more Anglophile name because "that was just more acceptable" (August 30th, 1995, p. 4). Lara herself did not complete a degree, though she attended four universities, taking a wide variety of arts and science courses, and completed a diploma in computer data base design.[2]

The two younger children, both boys, were born in Canada, the youngest one 14 years after Lara's own birth, yet neither of them had a particularly easy time fitting into society either. Lara's immediate younger brother, the only family member she felt close to, was not interested in school, and she remembers him having particularly poor grammar. He died in a car accident at the age of 18, before he realized his potential as a professional hockey player. The youngest brother went to university, got a degree in English, and works for a social service agency; however, Lara claims that he still has difficulty with English. Because her parents never spoke English well, and because they were busy people with little time for family, Lara believes that all of her siblings are poor English communicators.

At the end of 1952, when Lara was 2 years old, the family boarded a New Brunswick-bound ship, part of the third wave of Finnish immigrants to Canada.[3] After landing in Halifax,[4] the family was sent to Winnipeg, Manitoba, where her father found a job and moved the family a short distance to Lakeland. Lakeland was a Francophone town, which had a large settlement of Finnish immigrants living on the east side of the river who had come to work on a hydroelectric project. A single-lane bridge connected the east side of the river to the west side, and the train also shared the bridge. Lara remembers their house very clearly, an old farmhouse that must have been built around the turn of the century. There was no heat except for a wood-burning stove, and no insulation. A hot water tank that had to be filled by hand was attached to the stove—but their family was lucky. Most of the recent immigrants lived in two-room cottages without foundations and the pipes would freeze all winter long. Although Lara said that even the most poverty-stricken family would not consider living under those conditions anymore, Lakeland remains the scene of her fondest memories, the place that she refers to in her story as "home."[5] Even though she moved away from Lakeland at the age of 6, after living there for only 4 years, Lara still maintains contact with other Finns who had lived there. She is therefore able to say that there was little interaction between the Francophones and Finns, and no intermarriage. While her fellow Finns married

Ukrainians, who lived to the south, and English speakers who dwelt in the north in Lakeland, they did not have anything to do with the French Canadians. The bridge, it seems, was a physical metaphor for the emotional isolation, creating "outsiders looking in" to town.

When Lara and her family moved into a large city 2 hours away, her life changed dramatically. Her father, having been transferred to "head office," then spent most of his time on the road. Her mother, bored and frustrated without a career, took over a lunch bar in an industrial area, and eventually opened a number of restaurants in the area. Lara and her siblings were largely left on their own, an isolation that was intensified by their frequent residential moves while the family climbed the socioeconomic ladder.

Lara doesn't speak much about her time at school, except to say that she was not permitted to enter school until she was 7 years old, and then she was only allowed to begin kindergarten. Her older brother and sister were also put back a grade, but they were quickly moved ahead to their normal peer groups. Despite her family's attempts to have her moved ahead, and in spite of the fact that she was by far the brightest student in her class, Lara was kept behind. She feels that there was some kind of resentment against her that worked to her disadvantage.   Lara remembers her kindergarten teacher really disliking her, and not allowing her any leeway, even to go to the bathroom:

> I wanted to go to the bathroom, and when you're a kindergarten student you've never been in a social group like this before. You don't think that you have to go to the bathroom at certain times, you think "Well geez, you know, I've got to go to the bathroom"; the urge is there. You've got to be forgiving, you've got to let them know that "well try to think about...go[ing] to the bathroom, even though you may not have to go," that type of thing. And there was no grace there for me, but there was grace there for other people. And I recognized that early. (August 21, 1995, p. 20)

I questioned Lara about why she thought she had been singled out for such deep dislike, asking too if she remembered other teachers. Although she changed schools many times as the family lived in nine different homes during her school years, Lara remembers virtually always having the same principal, the principal who refused to promote her to her proper grade when her father tried to intervene.   Lara remembers feeling persecuted, thinking that she didn't want to have to deal with her anymore, that she had had enough. Lara told me the reason that she was held back:

> I think that [language] had a lot to do with it; I think the fact that I was a year older, I think the fact that I was much bigger than the rest of them... very tall

for my age. And I think the fact that I was much smarter than the rest of them. And I don't know if I was intellectually smarter, but I was just smarter because I was older. I think there were a lot of things going against me, definitely. I think the language issue was one of them. I think that...we were perceived to be lower-middle class, illiterate people. I don't think they thought of us as educated people who came from an educated home, and I can understand it....It was difficult to communicate with our parents; it was difficult for [our parents] to communicate with us, communicate with teachers, so there was a barrier there.... (August 21, 1995, p. 20)

In high school also, Lara had difficulty with her own placement within the education system. Her parents were very concerned when she was in Grade 10 because the school wanted to put her into the general program rather than the matriculation program. At her parents' insistence, she endured aptitude tests and IQ tests, which placed her in the 99th percentile, so the school finally relented and put her into the matriculation stream. Lara feels that there must have been "something on the school records right from Day 1...that followed [her] all the way through" (August 30th, 1995, p. 10), but her parents were unable to obtain access to her school records and so her placement difficulties remain a mystery even today.

But, for the most part, Lara avoided talking about her education and postsecondary education, glossing over, too, her early marriage to an Icelander, another "Arctic person" and her move to British Columbia. She had two daughters, and was later divorced. She does not speak much about her ex-husband, except to say that he also came from a very old family, able to trace their roots back over 1,000 years. Lara feels this gives her children a sense of "groundedness" that her daughter's friends envy. They have 121 first cousins, and know a little bit about them all. They have roots on both sides of their family, and this, Lara feels, will help them in times of personal crisis.

THE NARRATIVE CONTEXT

The first thing that I noticed about Lara's interviews was the complete ease she seemed to feel with oral narration. The second thing that I noticed was that her stories seemed to be constructed like legends, or, perhaps, Nordic sagas. She always tried to give me a complete picture, detailing not only what she felt was important in her life to the topic of language loss, but the relevant stories of her parents' lives and the entire Finnish national history as she knew it as well. When I told her that she was the only participant at that point who had told her story in that way, she expressed surprise, and asked me how others had managed to tell their stories at all; she could conceive of no other way.

This was very interesting to me for several reasons. First, Lara had not formally studied or deliberately read about Finnish history. Rather, what she knew about Finland came from childhood stories told to her in the community sauna in Lakeland. Later, when she heard mention of parts of Finnish history or culture, it was like a flash of recognition to her. She knew that she had heard that information before, and she knew that she had learned it in Finnish, so hearing it again in English was an important validation for her. This confirmed what I had started to believe in this research project: Memories are memories and are not necessarily stored in any language. Several participants had mentioned to me that, while they could not hear the soundtrack for their memories in their heads, they could remember the essence of what was said. I am starting to believe that, although it is common for ESL teachers to encourage their students to try to think in the target language, we do not have sufficient understanding of what that means. If memories are stored without regard to language, then perhaps we can reason that people do not think in any language. Perhaps we think in the abstract and through conscious processes transform that into language.[6]

The second reason I found her stories about Finnish history interesting is that they were new to me. Not only were they new and intriguing, but they were also relevant to language, immigration, and cultural issues, often containing some kind of moral precedent. For example, Lara told the story mentioned previously about the need for Finland to become literate in a very short period of time, and the country's literacy requirement for marriage. I sensed profound admiration on Lara's part for such an ingenious solution.

Another of her stories dealt with the problem of refugees. To repay part of her war debt, Finland had to cede a section of her territory to Russia. The inhabitants left and moved into the remainder of Finland because they didn't want to live in Russia. The Finnish government decided that they would not build refugee camps because such camps "have a habit of staying where they are and lasting generations and generations" (August 21, 1995, p. 17). What the Finnish government did instead was to force everybody who had any space to take the refugees into their homes, because the incentive to get them employed and settled would be very strong. All Finns were taxed 10% of their wealth, which monies were given to the refugees to reestablish them in their own homes. In 3 years, the entire population was housed. Lara commented, by comparison, "I mean, how many people are still, 25 years later, living in refugee camps for the Vietnamese problem?" (August 21, 1995, p. 18). And I have to admit, there was part of me that admired the Finnish solutions, however harsh they may first appear. Of course, such policies, and our reaction to such policies, cause us to question who policies are designed for. Are policies designed in the best interests of the refugee, or in the best interests of the voting public?

The third reason I found her method of narration so fascinating was that I was reminded that Finnish was originally an oral culture. I found myself wondering if Lara, like Richard, had internalized part of the Finnish language tradition without realizing it, and translated narrative structure into English. This again set me to musing about what language loss is, and what it means, and whether speaking English while using Finnish language traditions qualifies as a kind of language hybrid.

And I wondered as well, whether it was familiarity with the patterns and metalanguage of Finnish, or the ability to understand some elementary Finnish, that led to Lara's feeling that, with 6 months' immersion, she could be fluent in Finnish to at least the level she had reached when she started to learn English. Lara estimates that she had once been fluent to about 75% of a standard adult norm. I was struck by Lara's claim because it was so common among the participants in this research project. So many seemed to feel that the language was buried deep within themselves somewhere, if only they knew how to find it (see Chapter 15).

Oddly enough, Lara, one of the most articulate interviewees in this study, expressed a lot of concern about her English language ability. In our first interview together, Lara expressed her opinion that her English language ability today is still influenced by having lost her first language because she is not able to call on the words she needs when she needs them. Although she has no trouble writing, because she has the opportunity to be thoughtful and to edit her word choices carefully, she just doesn't seem to be able to monitor her oral performance, a problem she attributes to her interrupted language development and to the communication problems in her home. Lara also said that very articulate people intimidate her because she is always aware of the grammatical errors that she makes in her speech, and she would like to be able to speak more perfectly. In fact, Lara is so uncertain of her English language ability, that she is cautious about correcting her children's grammar. On those occasions when she has tried to get her daughters to speak with more precision, they have told her that no one speaks that way anymore. Lara is inclined to believe them, especially when it comes to new slang, because she feels that she is completely unable to understand it. Lara finds that she cannot judge the gist of new expressions from the context.

In this uncertainty, Lara is very much like a second-language speaker. My first- and second-hand experience has been that a second-language speaker will not correct, or even question, a native speaker of that language, no matter how flagrant the error. Second-language speakers always feel that slang, idioms, and humor are the hardest things to understand in the target language because so much is culled from often unfamiliar cultural norms. Second-language speakers are often very critical of their own oral performance, not believing that they can express themselves well because they could do better in their first languages.

Yet, Lara is not really a second-language speaker. She has little recollection of Finnish and therefore, if we were to take the 1996 Canadian census definition, she is a native speaker of English. Her uncertainty likely comes from the poor English language skills she heard modeled at home, and the feeling she mentions often throughout her interviews, of being an outsider looking in at Canadian culture. She feels like an outsider looking in at language use as well. Moreover, I believe that her lack of confidence can partly be attributed to being what she calls the "transition" person in her family. Lara's two older siblings began attending school at Lakeland, where they learned to read and write both English and Finnish. By the time the family moved to the city and began using English in the home, her older sister and brother were 16 and 11 years old, respectively. They remain fluent bilinguals. Lara's two younger siblings were born in the city and never learned to speak Finnish at all. They were completely monolingual in English. Lara is the only person in the family who began developing in Finnish and then suddenly switched to English, rather than developing bilingually. She feels the shame of being the only person in her family to have lost a language, and she seems to feel insufficiently grounded in language. Using Cummins' (1979) "iceberg" metaphor, Lara suddenly switched from one language to the other and was never able to transfer concepts from one language into the other. Instead, she had to redevelop concepts in a second language, learning everything again "from scratch." This could, understandably, lead to lifelong uncertainty about the language.

A final comment I wanted to make about Lara's story was that she was the first person to articulate the source, not just of the linguistic difficulties she had with her parents, but of the cultural difficulties as well. In her life story, Lara points out that her parents remained 1950s-style Finns. Because they could not speak English well, they did not change with the times in Canada, but because they were separated from the Finnish experience, they did not become Finns of the 1990s either. Instead, they remained mired in a kind of time warp, which they shared with other Finns who had immigrated at the same time. This was something that I had never even considered, and yet, as soon as Lara said it, I thought "Of course!" Ironically, considering Lara's feelings of language inferiority, I was always grateful for Lara's amazingly articulate ability to explain this to me. When I later heard others struggling to understand and verbalize the cultural disparities in their homes, I was able to listen and hear echoes of Lara's explanation. When the tape was turned off, and we were talking off the record, I would paraphrase Lara's words to other participants, and they would exclaim "that's it." I was told to thank her for being "one smart lady" who had managed to precisely explain a common experience. Fortunately, I was able to pass several messages of thanks on to Lara for her wonderful descriptive ability.

ENDNOTES

1. Though she did not seem to enter a trance-like state in the same sense that Richard or William had. While Richard and William spoke as if I wasn't in the room, Lara seemed to be speaking to a large, unseen audience.
2. Although she had not completed a degree program, Lara was later admitted to a Master's program on the basis of her accumulated credits.
3. Apparently the first wave, at the turn of the century, consisted primarily of loggers and fishermen, while the second wave, in the 1930s, was fearful of the unrest in Europe and wished to avoid another World War.
4. I am not sure if Lara mistakenly thought Halifax was in New Brunswick, or if they disembarked enroute.
5. I think this is a testament to the strength of memories and knowledge of early childhood. It is unfortunate that, having lost Finnish, Lara would be unable to ever go home again.
6. Indeed, I became even more convinced of this recently when I was asked to participate in a "think aloud" research protocol. As I was trying to articulate my thoughts, I kept feeling "this is not what I am thinking except in the very narrowest, most linear part of my mind." I did not feel that I had access to what I was really thinking.

7. LARA'S STORY: AN OUTSIDER LOOKING IN

I guess I'll start with my name. My name is Lara Johanneson and I was born in Finland, in 1950, during a period in Finland's history that was very difficult. When I was born in Finland, it was a very tumultuous time and very difficult for many of the people. After the war ended in 1945, the Finnish government decided that, in order to repay the war debt,[1] everybody would have to work an extra day each week for the government, and the sixth day's wages would go to repaying reparations. No emigration was allowed from Finland because it was felt that the strict reparations would cause a mass exodus from Finland. So, when 1951 came along, the war debt had been repaid—I should say that Finland's the only country that repaid its war debt—and at that point the Finnish government opened the doors to emigration.

The times in Finland had been very, very hard. There was mass starvation. Finland was completely razed during World War II. No money was given to Finland to rebuild and they had to do it all from within. In 1951, Russia realized that Finland had become a very industrious, wealthy nation, and they were making overtures to take over Finland again. A lot of the people who had been through the war decided that they weren't going to stick around for another war because they didn't think that Finland could handle it. Russia had militarized their population and Finland wouldn't have the advantages that they had had during World War II. So, my parents were part of the mass exodus leaving Finland.

We moved to Canada; we took the *S. S. Europa* to Halifax. We landed in Halifax and we were sent to Winnipeg, which was part of the Canadian policy to distribute immigrants, instead of ghettoizing them in specific areas. My father was an engineer in Finland; he didn't have engineering papers here. My mother was a nurse in Finland but she couldn't work as a nurse here. My father found a job working in steel construction in Lakeland, about an hour-and-a-half-drive northeast of a major city. They quickly found out that he was a brilliant man and mathematically inclined, that he could proof an engineer's mathematical formulas right on the spot and tell immediately if there were any mistakes in it. So, he quickly worked his way through and became an engineer.

Now I think I need to go back a little bit into their history. My father was orphaned at a very young age, but not orphaned in the sense that you would expect. My paternal grandmother was institutionalized and my paternal grandfather, for some reason, didn't raise my father. He was sent into an orphanage. My paternal grandfather divorced his wife and remarried and had another child, but never took my father home. I think that life in an orphanage was very harsh and very strict and my father became a very quiet, very thoughtful person; the result was that I didn't get much conversation from my father.[2] And then my mother's mother died when she was 5 or 6 years old. Her father was a sea captain and he was on the ocean a lot, but the oldest brother said that he would raise them. He finished school and he raised them. My mother also has been a very quiet person who hasn't really communicated very well with any of us. I think this had a major impact on the rest of us.

My mother and my father both learned five different languages in Finland, but anyway, they couldn't speak English. My father and my mother never really learned the English language very well. My father was very good with the English language in engineering, but when it came to speaking to us, I would say that both my parents were at an elementary-school language level in English. Perhaps that affected their ability to communicate with other people in the English language community, and maybe they were looked down upon in spite of their education. Maybe others assumed we were uneducated and illiterate, but, at any rate, we were kind of outcasts. I always sensed that there was something really different about our family and I'm not sure quite what it was. I think that language played a major role when it comes to that. I think that we were perceived to be lower-middle class, illiterate people. I don't think we were thought of as educated people who came from an educated home. I can understand that. It was difficult to communicate with our parents. It was difficult for them to communicate with us, communicate with teachers, so there was a barrier there, but that doesn't mean we weren't an upper-middle class family.

Getting on to my life, I lived in Lakeland from about the age of 2 until I moved to Winnipeg at the age of about 6. In Lakeland, the west side of the river, the town, was French-Canadian, while the east side of the river was a huge Finnish community and everybody spoke Finnish. We had a very tight Finnish community because we all lived on this one side of the river, and the east side was only connected to the town by a single-lane bridge, which the train also used. I'm not sure if I was articulate in Finnish; I expect I wasn't articulate. I don't think I could have been, given that my mother and father were very quiet people. And, I never started school in Lakeland, though my brother and sister did. Because of the large Finnish population there, the school even made provision for the students to learn to read and write in Finnish.

I remember many of the people in Lakeland, and I remember many things of them. The interesting thing is that I don't remember events in Finnish anymore, and I don't remember them in English, but I remember the essence of what was important to me. I try to think back to when people were talking to me and I just can't remember the words; I can't remember them at all. I think one of my earliest memories is when I was about 2 years old. My brother and sister had a towel and we were scooping up minnows by the side of the river. I remember laughing and giggling and watching these minnows jumping up on the towel, and I remember pointing at them and I remember I said, "Look, look" but not in English, and I don't remember saying it in Finnish, but I know I had to have said, "Gato, Gato." The whole experience is still so vivid. I remember saying things and I know what I said but I don't remember actually what I said. And I'm not sure if that's the experience of losing your language or if it's just that that's the way children remember.

There's so many things that various women in the community imparted about my history, in an oral history. I remember many of the things that were told to me but I honestly can't remember the words that were said; I know that I was told, for instance, that the Finnish people would bake that hardtack bread with the hole in the center twice a year and hang it on birch poles across the kitchen ceiling, and whenever they would need it, they would break off a piece. I was told all about Finnish history after World War II, and I know all of these stories, but I can't remember when I was told them. I remember the sauna was where this really transpired, where the children would sit on the lower rungs and the older women would talk to us as they were sitting up higher, and they would tell us stories, and they would pour water on us to cool us off, and gently brush our skin with birch leaves to release the oils and just feel the meditation a little bit more. I remember many stories that were told to me and I know what those stories were, but I can't remember a word, which is just amazing to me.

Anyway, my language experience ended when I left Lakeland, and I very rarely went back to visit these people. When I did, I couldn't communicate with them. And most of them had very poor English language skills. I learned all of the history that I know of Finland prior to when I left Lakeland, and it was reinforced by my own reading afterwards, and then I recollected all of these things being told to me in Finnish. And it was really important to me to get that validation as well, to realize that it wasn't my imagination, this really was the truth; these were stories that were told to me. When I read the histories I remembered being told that, and I identified with it, but I remembered just like snapshots; you remember little bits here and there, but you can't tie it together until the common thread is drawn for you.

And I always felt like I was an outsider looking in. I never really felt like I was part of the community. And it's funny how at an early age I was feeling that. I never felt that prior to moving into the city, but moving to the city I always felt like I was an outsider looking in. And I'm not sure what effect the language had on it.

As I said, my Finnish language experience ended when I was 6 years old and I moved into the city. When we moved there was a transformation into English. I think what took precedence for my parents was that we integrate into society; they thought that was more important than our maintaining our culture and learning our mother tongue. Once we left the environment of Lakeland, it just became much more difficult to maintain it, and I don't think an effort was really made by them to make sure we maintained our culture and our language. So, we never really had the language experience in English or in Finnish after that from my parents, and we all came out of our home with various degrees of English-language skill.

And, I realized that I had stopped learning my language when I left Lakeland. I remember feeling kind of bad, sad, but it wasn't a really embarrassed or disgusted anger with myself; I just felt like I'd let myself down. But, I still feel somewhat that I belong to my culture, though I feel removed. I don't think that it would take me long to integrate back into it because of my early experience. I have no doubt in my mind that if I immersed myself in Finland, within 6 months I would probably be fluent in the language up to the level I was at when I started to speak English.

Interestingly enough, I'm sure that I must have been able to speak a few words of English when we moved into the city, but my mother ended up taking me to four or five different elementary schools, trying to get me in. Now you have to remember that I was older than most children, and they wouldn't even take me. They said, "No, just leave her for another year playing on the street and she'll learn to speak English and then we'll take her into kindergarten"; I guess that was their way of dealing with ESL for a child who had never been to school. I remember being dragged from school to school, and I knew my mother was stressed. I couldn't understand what was going on because I just thought, "Well, I'll just start school and I'll be okay," and I remember wanting to say something to the people at the schools, but I don't remember what it was specifically I wanted to say. I suppose I just wanted to let them know that it would be okay if I started school, but I think after that I recognized that my English was very important, and you had to be understood.

I remember it very clearly, and that's one of my few memories, of being dragged—I remember going to the school closest to me, Portwood, and I remember going to Timms School, I went to Fellows School, I remember going to another school, but I can't remember the name of that one. I remember going to the three key schools that were closest to my home, and they turned me away. They turned me away from kindergarten. The next year, they had to take me at Portwood because I was 6 years old, but they didn't have to put me in Grade 1. They could put me where they wanted because schools were all-powerful then. They put me in kindergarten. The irony here is that the principal of the school when I started was Nancy Sherman, and though we moved nine or ten times climbing up the social ladder, she followed me to all the major schools that I attended. I remember thinking "My God, why do I have to have her again?" I just had this instant dislike. I guess it was because of my experience. I just didn't want her in my life.

I never really learned any English and no one would play with me. I imagine if someone had been in school previously then they'd have to take them, because my brother and sister went to school immediately. They were brought down a grade—because they were country hicks, I suppose—but they were quickly moved up. So, when I went to school I was almost 7 years old. I was twice as big as any child. I couldn't speak English very well I'm sure, if I spoke any at all. And my teacher disliked me.

I knew that I was proficient in English to the same level as everybody else by the time Grade 1 came along, and I was far ahead in ability. And I think at this point language discrimination did come in because I really should have been moved ahead. My father went to school and said, "She should be moved ahead a year" and they said, "No, no, no, no," that my English was not good enough. And my father couldn't argue. His language wasn't good enough to assess the situation. So, I was always a year behind and I was always way ahead of everybody else after that. They were just sticking to their guns, I guess. I know academically I was far ahead of anyone else in my classroom. At first they said, "Well, she can't speak English"; within 6 months I was as fluent as the rest of them. My parents were concerned—my father even said that he recognized that the language at home wasn't as good as it could be—but I guess when my father went in to fight, he still couldn't speak very well. I know that my aptitude tests were excellent, because my parents got them in Grade 10. The school wanted to put me into a general program, and my parents said "No," to put me into the matriculation program. So, anyway, they got my aptitude tests done and finally they relented and put me into matriculation, but I don't know what the reason to hold me back was. I don't know why it was—but this followed me all the way through school.

I don't remember ever really being ostracized for my language as such, and I don't remember ever having an accent, but I'm sure that I did. I'm sure that I made major mistakes in the English language and I think that had a major effect on why I now find it very important to speak English well. I know that when I first moved into the city, kids used to make fun of me and they would repeat things that I would say when I didn't think that there was anything unusual in the way that I had said them. They'd laugh and giggle or whatever, so I know that they were making fun of me, but I don't remember it clicking that I was saying it wrong. I don't remember that kind of problem, so obviously I must have corrected myself pretty quickly. I still make a lot of mistakes grammatically, but I'm at the point where I don't care anymore, and I don't try to figure out which is which because I just find it too hard.

I think that English was important to me, because I recognized this poor communication that we had in our family. I think that, in my family, we have problems where we can't talk to each other openly because we think too much when we're talking. We're trying too hard to understand rather than taking things at face value. I often attributed that to the fact that we had this other language. I think it's something that becomes habitual because you have to do it at some point in your life in order to understand what is going on. Because, when we listened to much of what our parents said when they were speaking to us in English, we had to deduce what they were trying to say, to try and understand because they weren't getting it across in the way that a normal parent who had good language skills would.

Although I was very good at school, I found Social Studies hard, and it came down to the English language. We were asked to do analysis of writings with regards to social studies, and we had to make inferences from those writings and I couldn't make the connection. I couldn't see how people could pull that information out. When the answers came, I remember thinking "They're so simple. Why couldn't I understand them?", but then another twist would come up in the problem and I just couldn't make that connection. And, I remember English grammar being exceedingly difficult for me. I really did try in English, but I found it hard. I applied myself more than I did with anything else, but my marks didn't reflect that application. My marks were from 85 to 90, but most of my marks were over 90. To this day, I'll look at a sentence and I'll say "I've done something wrong here; I don't know what it is." But, literature and writing I was very good at. My English teacher in Grade 11 actually told me that I should be an English teacher, and a writer, a poet. I think poetry suited me because I didn't feel bound by any grammatical rules necessarily.

I do remember being in about Grade 1 or 2 or 3—I'm not too sure—my mother trying to speak to me in Finnish and I was so frustrated and I said "speak English because I don't understand what you're saying to me." And, I think that she was trying perhaps to push my level of Finnish, or bring it back, because she realized that I was losing it, and I was exasperated. And I suppose the frustration isn't really with my mom; it's more with myself but it's focused on my mother. Trying to discuss this with my mother is very difficult; she doesn't want to speak about it and I think she has a lot of painful memories and I think it's painful to her to see that we've mostly lost the language and the culture. But, we do things that are part of the Finnish culture. That I've tried to maintain because I think it's important for my children to know their heritage and I think too much heritage is lost as it is.

There were many things that I couldn't discuss with my mother because I couldn't communicate with her. I felt she couldn't understand what I was trying to say. Maybe she did and she was just so set in her ways that she wasn't open to any conversation and maybe she wanted to dictate to me; I don't know. When I spoke to my parents, we spoke in English and that was it. They communicated what they could, but I'm sure that they never really understood what we were trying to say. And you have to remember that when we left Finland, it was the 1950s and my parents culturally were 1950s-Finnish; they never never developed beyond that. They were 1950s Finnish, and when we moved into Lakeland I think that they maintained that era in their way of thinking about society as a whole. You have to realize that people in Finland moved beyond that and were now 1990s people, and my parents never really integrated and adopted the North American culture either.

I have to let you know that the last 5 years, I've spent a lot of time thinking and reflecting because I was in a serious car accident in 1989 and my back was broken. I guess you go through a period when you get really depressed and you really start to examine your reason for being. I think that as a result of that, all of these types of issues start to come up and you start to think of things that perhaps you wouldn't have thought of previously. But, this is the first time I've ever really had a discussion about my language with anyone. I've had a lot of thoughts about it, and a lot of these thoughts I've had to myself, but not through reading or discussing it with anyone, just reflection more than anything else. Definitely, I was aware of having lost my language and I was aware that my language to this day is affected by it, in that I'm not able to call on the words I need when I need them. I know the words that I need; I understand them; I can read them; I can write; I can really write exceptionally well, but to verbally speak the English language is very difficult for me, especially trying to find the exact word that I want to use. I know that I have it in my vocabulary, but it's not on the tip of my tongue. I'm trying to search for the words that would be most appropriate for what I'm trying to describe. Perhaps I get too caught up in trying to be accurate in my descriptions, looking for a specific word to use so that I'm more precise in my definition of something. I know I have the word in my vocabulary, but I just can't get at it for whatever reason. I don't understand why I have these problems. If I scroll through the language in my head, I recognize it but I just have such a heck of a time getting that word out.

I suppose I look with envy at people who are able to access words so quickly and have such command of the language where I have to be so much more thoughtful. When I was in college I was getting A+s on my essays, and when I went to university, it was the same thing, but I wasn't able to articulate what I wanted to impart. I guess I need a slower pace to be able to do that, and I just can't seem to talk at the same time. And also people who are very articulate can intimidate me to a degree as well, because I'm really conscious about the grammatical errors that I know I'm making. Sometimes I'm so intimidated—maybe intimidated isn't the word for it—but I just sit back in awe and I just want to listen to articulate people and see if I can learn anything from them. It's their vocabulary, their structure, content, and the ability to describe precisely what they're trying to say, and in such an elegant way that it appears easy, so you know how difficult it really is. I've often wondered "What did they do to get to that?" and "I would give anything to be like that," but that's not the truth of the matter because if I really would give anything to be like that, I would be like that, wouldn't I?

As a matter of fact, I haven't totally lost the Finnish language. There are still words that I don't need to translate. The last few times I spoke to my mother I made a concerted effort to try and figure out if I remember the words she spoke in Finnish. There are things that I remember in Finnish, but I don't identify them as Finnish. I know instinctively what it is, but I don't translate it. I mean, they're equal. I think the words I remember were so fundamental, so elementary, that they were the first words out of a child's mouth perhaps. I had 4 or 5 years, or 3 years, whatever it is you need to get them so embedded in your mind that you can't lose them. But, as far as the language, perhaps as I was getting closer to 5 and 6 years of age, that language when you're learning the words, perhaps I used them more and then, perhaps, retained them.

As far as speaking goes, I could say something in Finnish if I needed to, but it would be very elementary, very rudimentary. I don't think I could say anything higher than perhaps what a preschool student or child would say. I can understand some things, not a lot. I can get by and introduce myself. I can say some things that I might want, like "I want a glass of water." I could ask for a glass of milk—the things that a child would want to be able to do, but as far as explaining myself, and where I want to go, and explaining what I'm trying to do, there's just no possible way of doing that because that's not something that a child would try to explain. And, I no longer have the capability of understanding the stories I grew up with. I tried to listen to the sagas on the Finnish channel and I didn't understand a thing. It's something that I would have to read in English, I think, and then maybe it would bring back the memories of the stories I was told, but there's nothing that I really remember regarding the sagas.

Yet, my daughters claim that I can speak Finnish because my mother comes over quite frequently and stays, and she'll speak to me in Finnish and I'll say "no" or "yes," and respond, and then they'll say, "You can speak Finnish!" I try to explain to them that, "Well, no, no, I can't speak it; I couldn't repeat what she just said to me." When my mother is here, I am not at all speaking. I'm listening to Finnish and responding to it in English. In fact, the last time that I ever tried to speak Finnish, I must have been about 18 years old, in Grade 12, and my uncle came from Finland. He was dying, and he wanted to see my mother and her siblings. And I wanted to speak to him very much because he couldn't speak English. I tried, but it was a total failure, and after that, I never tried again.

Still, I feel a certain affinity with other Finns and try to stay in touch with the culture. Where I live now is an old Finnish community. It's not a young one, so it has been assimilated. I think that's probably why I fell in love with this place, because it's just like home. This is what the area around Lakeland was like, and this is what Finland was like, and I know right away when I hear a Finnish accent. I can even pick out the accent of the person who did speak Finnish up until they were about 10 or 12 and then moved into English; there's a distinct sense of the rhythm of the language. The Finnish language is an extremely lyrical language, half-singing almost, and there's some real character in it. You don't see that in the English language, or you don't hear it in the English language very often, except perhaps if one makes a concerted effort to put some lyricism in. In Finnish, it's just part-and-parcel of the language. It really provides a character definition that we English speakers are lacking. I don't know how to describe it. I don't know how to describe having lost it; it feels like there's a real void there, like there's something missing. I'd really like to tap into that lyricism, and I can't tap into it in the English language and I can't tap into it in the Finnish language either.

When it first dawned on me that I'd lost my language, there was a sadness, a disappointment, and a sense of tragedy. I think the tragedy is still there, but over time my attitude toward it has changed. I suppose that it was inevitable in the way that our family handled the language issue. There's still a sadness and a tragedy, but it's not as deep now as it once was. And if I could do it over again, I would certainly love to change things. But I can't, obviously, and I think I'm more accepting of it.

As far as consequences from losing my language, I would stress that I couldn't communicate with my family members from Finland when they came here to visit. That was hurtful to me—and for them, too. And I think, having lost my language, I, in essence, lost a lot of my culture. No matter how much I try, I don't think I'll ever really understand it. If I'd kept it, I think I would have kept a sense of myself, my own identity, much more; I think that when I'd gone through the turmoil that I've gone through in the last few years since the accident, perhaps I wouldn't have had to go through much of the soul-searching task that I had to go through. I was really finding out who I am and what my purpose and place in the world is. I still haven't determined that at this point, but I feel much more comfortable because I've come to the conclusion that I will always be an outsider looking in from whatever perspective I look at my life. As a Finn, I'm an outsider; as an Anglophone, I'm an outsider; as a Canadian, I'm somewhat of an outsider because I fit nowhere really— but then perhaps all Canadians are outsiders as well, so maybe there's a common thread there. I suppose there's a certain death of self when you lose your mother tongue as well, that perhaps you don't ever get back, don't ever find...don't ever resurrect.

ENDNOTES

1. Lara explained to me that Finland was allied with the Axis Powers during World War II. Having been invaded by Russia, Finland bought arms from Germany, which forced the country into an Axis alliance.
2. As a young man, Lara's father then served in the Finnish military during the war. She believed that her father had served as a kind of Guerrilla, cross-country skiing in to Russian camps and slitting the throats of soldiers while they slept, but she made clear that this wasn't something he spoke about. Instead, she felt that his war experiences had likely contributed to his adult silence.

8. BRIAN: INTRODUCTION

THE INTERVIEW CONTEXT

I chose to include Brian's story for different reasons than I chose the other stories. Brian is one of only two people who volunteered for this research project claiming that losing his first language really hadn't had that much of an impact on his life, that it really hadn't mattered to him at all. Therefore, because he fit into my definition of "outliers" (see Appendix A), I should not have included his story as one of the five major narratives. I reconsidered in light of the stories that emerged.

In the beginning, I miscast Brian and therefore nearly excluded his story. When I first reread his transcripts, I agreed with Brian's self-assessment that he had not been terribly much affected by the loss of Korean. He was polite, popular, possessed of a fine ironic wit, and very cavalier in his descriptions of his struggles to learn English and the loss of Korean. Even when I asked him why he had chosen to participate in this research project, and why he had telephoned me to volunteer, he replied that,

> I didn't want to really. I mean, it wasn't something where I had to get something off my chest. It was more probably just because you were a UBC student, just to help a UBC student out, just because I'm a UBC student. It wasn't really, you know, "get out of this cloud", it was just to help out another UBC student. (July 6th, 1995, p. 14)

Brian explained that, because he didn't even remember speaking Korean, he didn't have "any feelings" for the loss of his language. At first, I took him at his word.

But then, I began to question his motivation a little bit more deeply. The first meeting that I had with Brian took place at the University of British Columbia's Main Library, in the basement. I had allowed Brian to choose the place because I wanted him to suggest somewhere convenient for him. When he chose the campus, I assumed that he was enrolled in courses, or had work to complete there. When I found out that he had taken the bus from his job downtown to meet me at the university, I told him that I would be happy to meet him anywhere, that he didn't need to worry about making things convenient for me, and I also offered to drive him home—about 90 minutes away by bus—an offer he refused because a friend was coming to pick him up.

The second time we met, Brian again suggested that we meet at the university, this time in the Student Union Building (SUB). I asked him if he was sure that the SUB was a convenient location, and he said that he had some things to do out by the campus that day, therefore it was a good place for him. I told him before we met that I would drive him home after we had finished. During our interview, and the discussion which followed it, I found out that Brian's family was very private. He mentioned that he didn't know how old his parents were,[1] that he didn't know anything about their childhoods, that he would never have discussed anything of a personal nature with either of them, preferring to have those kinds of discussions with friends or school contacts. Brian wasn't sure why his parents had come to Canada, though he assumed it was to pursue "opportunity," nor did he know how old they were when they immigrated, nor did he have much knowledge about their lives prior to coming to Canada. When I asked Brian if it might be possible for me to interview his parents, he said he didn't think they would consent to being interviewed, but he would ask them. He thought they'd be embarrassed by their poor English, and unwilling to answer questions. I asked him, if that were indeed the case, if he would mind speaking to his parents about his language loss; I wanted to check whether his parents might be able to fill in a few details that Brian was missing. He thought that would be fine. Yet, I realized his parents were more than a little bit private when I drove Brian home. After pointing out his house, he asked me to drop him off a few doors away. He didn't offer an explanation. I didn't ask.

Our third interview was also scheduled out at the university, very soon after our second interview. We met in the basement of the Student Union Building, and one of the first things that Brian mentioned was that his parents refused to talk to him about language loss when they found out that he was participating in this research study. They were very upset that he had volunteered. I offered to give back his transcripts and tapes, but he wanted to complete the interviews. I began to suspect that talking about losing Korean, and about the times when it had affected his life, was something that Brian found himself benefiting from. Even though he knew his parents were directly opposed to his participation in the research project, he still continued with it. Even though participating necessitated inconvenience for him because he obviously couldn't meet me at his home, he still expressed a keen interest in working with me. I therefore reformulated my opinion of how much impact losing Korean had had on Brian's life. I thought that it had had a greater influence than he recognized—or was willing to admit.

Perhaps to my discredit, I also wanted to include Brian's story *because* he participated in the face of his parents' opposition. Although I suspected that it would limit what he might say, I wanted to explore their negative feelings about his participation. Unfortunately for my purposes, I was left mostly with speculation. Brian did not know why his parents were so private, though he did feel that it was unusual. Brian and I discussed several possibilities (see Chapter 13). We came up with many possibilities, but no conclusions, except that first language loss was something that his parents did not want to discuss, with me or with Brian.

Another reason I wanted to include Brian's story is that I completed my interviews with him before I completed my interviews with anyone else. Although I started interviewing several other people before I began working with Brian, we scheduled our interviews tightly into the space of about 3 weeks, because of Brian's work commitments. Because Brian's story came first, I felt that I had not developed the knack of actively listening to stories, nor had I really begun to synthesize the stories into any coherent patterns, nor had I made any concrete decisions about how the life stories would take shape after the interviews were complete.[2] I wasn't particularly adept at asking questions that would lead into stories rather than opinions or short replies. I wasn't confident about what kinds of questions to ask the subjects, whether I would give them a direction and prompts, or whether I would be able to access the kind of stories that I wanted without leading. Finally, apart from some vague notion that Chaucer's *The Canterbury Tales* was a fitting model for the stories and their introductions, I didn't know what kind of narratives would be written. I thought it was important to see what kind of story would be produced between a "raw" life history interviewer and an equally "raw" interviewee. I thought that together we might produce the closest thing to a story that was uninfluenced by a priori theory that I was going to be able to write. I also wondered what a more experienced (or perhaps jaded) eye might bring to the analysis later, whether I would see only missed opportunities, or whether I might also see some merit. In the end, analysing Brian's story, I saw more missed opportunities— but then, that was the case with all of the life stories.

One other fact about Brian's life made me eager to include his story. Brian describes his life as "pretty static" (July 6th, 1995, p. 15) by which he means that he lived in the same house all the way through school. He attended one elementary school, one high school, and in general led a pretty constant life. He didn't need to make new friends during his school years, nor did his family become disrupted in any way. There are therefore few other losses in Brian's life other than the loss of his first language. And there are few outside influences that would have been considered traumatic, therefore it is more difficult to speculate about possible disruptive influences that may have predisposed him to first language loss.

THE LIFE HISTORY CONTEXT

Brian's parents immigrated just 2 or 3 years prior to his birth. His father, who had completed a college diploma in electronics, was able to find a good job in his field, after completing an English course and spending some time engaged in employment that Brian knows nothing about. His mother, on the other hand, who was an artist with a university degree in art in Korea, was never able to return to her talents in Canada, perhaps because she never did take English language courses and never became very familiar with the language. She would sometimes take on a part-time position designing and painting greeting cards or working in a flower shop to augment the family income when they had a specific goal in mind, but she never worked as an artist after immigrating.

Brian was born in November 1973 somewhere in the Lower Mainland of British Columbia, but he isn't sure where. In the first years of his life, before Brian started school, he and his parents moved many times, to many different municipalities in Greater Vancouver. Brian doesn't recall much of his life at that time, nor has he talked to his parents about it. He knows that his father recently celebrated 15 years with a major B. C. utility company, but he doesn't know what his father did during the years when they moved from place to place. The family eventually settled and bought a house just prior to Brian's entry into school. They chose to live in a predominantly Italian neighborhood in which they were the only Koreans, practically the only Asians, and they isolated themselves from the Korean community. Especially considering that Brian's mother never learned to speak more than a few words of English, I find it surprising that they isolated themselves so completely. Brian claims that his parents didn't stress the importance of integration into Canadian society—in fact, they avoided outside social contact—so it is doubtful that could have been their motivation.

Although at first I dismissed Brian's family as very strange, I slowly came to believe that Brian just didn't sufficiently understand his parents to discuss too much with them. Brian told me that, even in day-to-day conversations with his parents, particularly his mother, frustration and misunderstanding was the result. His mother and father would often exclaim "oh, you should start learning Korean again" (June 21, 1995, p. 2) because they were unable to communicate what they wanted to say in English. Brian also gave examples of the kinds of things he still understands in Korean,—"commands mostly. Just 'hurry up,' 'get this,' 'go there,' things like that" (July 6th, 1995, p. 6)—which he claims represent the type of conversations he has with his parents. He also mentioned that his mother cannot use time or monetary expressions in

English, and he doesn't understand Korean numbers at all. Not only did this lead me to believe that Brian and his parents just don't share the language skills to be able to talk about the past or anything deep or personal, but he also claimed that,

> *To begin with, I don't really think I really talk to them about things like this, so that's where I mean I still talk to my friends mostly about things like that. And so, when we do talk, it's mostly about the weather's nice, and I mean it's not that shallow, but in terms of social things, it's mostly with my friends that I discussed that stuff.* (July 6th, 1995, p. 8)

Although Brian claims he "doesn't" talk to his parents about social things, I suspect, given several of his other comments, *that doesn't* is a direct result of an original *couldn't*.

At the age of 3 or 4, Brian was enrolled in an English-speaking preschool with a Caucasian teacher, which "...was okay then because it wasn't—it didn't revolve completely around languages; there was a lot of arts and things..." (June 21, 1995, p. 1). Brian was therefore in Grade 1 or 2, he isn't sure which, when he was first sent to an ESL teacher. He remembers his ESL classes as being very helpful and very comforting to him. He was the only Asian in ESL, and even the Italian students who were in ESL classes with him were better off in English than he was because they had had some exposure to English prior to beginning school. Brian had been exposed to English only at preschool where, presumably, he didn't interact socially very much because he didn't learn very much English. He knows that his English skills were poor because he remembers clearly being in his regular classroom, and whenever he was called on to do something, he would start crying because he didn't understand what was going on.

Brian's first- and second-grade teacher was Japanese-Canadian, while his ESL teacher was Indo-Canadian. He feels that having visible minority teachers made his adjustment easier, partly because they recognized the need to help him "not only with my language, but with—with just the customs and traditions of the western—you know, western, or Canadian—or Canadian, life" (June 21, 1995, p. 1). But, one thing about his ESL teacher's practice was disturbing to me. When Brian didn't seem to be making fast enough progress in learning English, she suggested to his parents that they begin speaking English at home to help him, a very common theme among participants who lost their first languages. Brian credits her with being "the person I have to thank for my language abilities today" (June 21, 1995, p. 1). Yet, at the same time, he recognizes that the language shift in their home signaled the beginning of the loss of Korean. Moreover, several other statements that

Brian made, indicate that he is somewhat aware that losing Korean wasn't entirely necessary to learning English well.

First, Brian mentions that the Italian students who formed the bulk of the ESL class have remained his friends throughout the years. He therefore knows that the majority of them still speak Italian at home, and have remained entirely fluent in their first language. He speculated that,

> *I don't know, maybe they're—possibly it was because they had some English already, like most of the Italians, and so, you know, the ESL teacher didn't have to say "don't speak Italian at home" because their English was a bit better, so I probably think that was the main reason.* (July 6th, 1995, p. 2)

Brian is obviously aware that home-language shift caused his language loss, but, what is more interesting are the reasons he attributes to his teacher's recommendation. Although the language loss literature frequently cites parental language shift as one of the causes of first language loss (see, for example, Pan & Berko-Gleason, 1986), and although other researchers have claimed that teacher attitudes ranging from outright disapproval to benign neglect of the first language are often contributors to parental language shift, to my knowledge, no one has ever looked at whether this advice is more often given to students who begin school completely L1 monolingual. If this is the case, there may be reason to further stream ESL students, separating those who have less language ability from those who have more in order to prevent this kind of advice from being dispensed. There is also a need to inform teachers about the possible consequences of their advice.

The second hint Brian gave that giving up Korean at home wasn't entirely necessary is found in his description of his parents. He said of them,

> *I think that when I started out especially, my parents were pretty protective of me, and they didn't let me hang out with other friends quite a bit, and because of that I think I really only talked to my parents—for a while anyway. And I think maybe that was one of the reasons—if I could talk to my parents just in Korean, that wouldn't have helped. I would have just learned English at school, and then come back and speak Korean.* (July 6th, 1995, p. 4)

Here, Brian seems to be pointing out that his parents' choice to isolate themselves from the community also contributed to his first language loss. The problem, it appears, wasn't so much that Brian was speaking Korean at home, but that he wasn't speaking English anywhere but in school in formal circumstances. Had he been able to spend more time interacting with his peers, would his English language development have been hastened without reducing the Korean input he received at home? When I asked Brian what he thought, he replied only "probably" (July 6th, 1995, p. 4).

Brian also displayed a tendency to blame himself for developing monolingually rather than bilingually. Rather than connecting the different strands in his life to recognize a pattern that robbed him of his first language, Brian pointed out that many Asians have been able to keep their first languages while learning to speak English. He therefore concluded that "I guess it was just me" (July 6th, 1995, p. 2), implying that he was somehow innately linguistically inferior to other people and that is the reason he had lost his first language. He implies that he just wasn't smart enough, or perhaps not hard-working enough, to be able to learn and keep two languages. This was something I came across often in my research project, finding myself offering reassurance that participants were not of below-average intelligence and should certainly not blame themselves for what we both regarded as an unfortunate linguistic situation.

Brian did well throughout school, even making it into the top reading group by the time he was in Grade 3. He does admit, however, that he probably didn't belong in the top reading group, that his teacher liked him and wanted him to rise to a challenge and so she placed him in the group. But, his Grade 3 teacher also engaged in classroom practice that I find questionable, particularly when there are ESL students in the class. According to Brian, they often wrote standardized school tests and the teacher would

> read out the names of people who failed, ones who didn't do well, so they'd have to write it again. But I remember one time when I didn't pass and everyone else—in my group anyway—did pass, and she read out everyone else's name, but I guess spared me the disgrace. I would have been pretty upset if I heard just my name. She did that a couple of other times too, and I think that was pretty good of her. Just to be singled out for failure—I don't think that's—. (July 6th, 1995, p. 4)

Brian was really grateful to the teacher, a teacher he remembers as being Caucasian, for trying to spare him embarrassment, but I'm afraid that my own reaction to his story is less generous. First, the teacher wasn't doing Brian any favors by placing him in the top reading group where, as he said, "I knew I didn't belong" (June 21, 1995, p. 2). When he received not only the lowest mark in the top reading group on the standardized tests, but the lowest mark in the entire class, I am left to wonder what her rationale for setting him up for constant failure could possibly have been. Second, reading out the names of students who fail a test seems rather cruel. I think the fact that Brian remembers that class so clearly, and that he pointedly remembers the teacher's racial background, both speak volumes about how much he feared public humiliation. I, for example, do not remember anything at all about my primary grades except for a substitute teacher who handed back tests once from the highest to the lowest grade, and I got the highest grade so I was very proud. I remember making a mental note of who got the lowest marks and, to this day, I remember the names and/or faces of the classmates who did. I don't think these are the kinds of memories we should be carrying forward into adulthood.

Third, and finally, the teacher was, however unintentionally, setting Brian up for failure. When he passed into Grade 4 and he had a different teacher, he was demoted to the intermediate reading group. Brian subtly criticized his Grade 3 teacher, saying that demotion to the intermediate group, though embarrassing, "...helped because...I was with people who were at my level, and I worked hard at it" (June 21, 1995, p. 2). It is characteristic of Brian, in these interviews, to cast a positive light on all of his experiences, even ones that were polar opposites.

Brian continued through school without difficulty. His marks improved as he became more and more familiar with English, though, like Helena (see chapter 11), he always got good grades for his writing content and poor grades for his grammar. He also feels that his pronunciation is rather poor, giving as an example, not knowing whether he should say "taciturn" or "takiturn." Given that most people wouldn't even try to use this word in normal conversation, I feel that Brian perhaps is using a very elite comparison group, some of his peers at university, in order to judge his own English abilities. He agreed that is a possibility.

Intriguingly, although Brian can still understand several basic Korean commands, he, like Lara, would be unable to repeat what he just heard his parents say. Even more intriguingly, despite being unable to speak Korean at all, Brian often finds that other Korean people talking to him on the telephone will recognize his ethnicity. As an example, he explained that he worked in a telemarketing job recently and he had to telephone a lot of Korean people at home. He said,

> I didn't know they were Korean, but, for some reason they could understand that I was Korean even though I was speaking English. Because, because of my hesitations and the way I talk, it's still—they could tell I'm Korean, and I found that a couple times. A couple times they just asked me straight out "are you Korean?" and I'd go "yes." (June 21st, 1995, p. 3)

Brian has also found that his Korean ethnicity has been recognized by Korean students at his part-time job. Working as a conversationalist, testing the oral proficiency of immigrant students in an international school, he has found that the Korean students feel a special affinity for him, and he for them.

In all honesty, when I spoke to Brian during our interviews, I could not understand why other Korean people would recognize his speech patterns as Korean. The only differences I detected were word choice mistakes—like saying "he took me under his arms" (July 6th, 1995, p. 10) instead of saying "he took me under his wing," or nonspecific grammatical errors. Even when I spoke to him on the telephone, I didn't notice anything that would have marked him as Korean. He used common slang and a number of the features of casual speech markers, making him sound like any other young adult I had been acquainted with. I began to wonder what the markers for having once spoken Korean are, and whether there are markers in every language that would help to identify people who had once previously spoken that language. This idea was reinforced by Lara's claim that she was able to detect the accents of people who had spoken Finnish up until the time they were 10 to 12 years old, and that she was able to distinguish the level of fluency people had attained in Finnish by their accents.

After finishing high school, Brian began studying genetics at UBC, following a course of study his parents hope will lead to medicine, but which Brian wants to end in graduate school and genetics research. He lived in residence every year, at first preferring to travel home every weekend, and later preferring not to go home at all. In his first year of university, Brian's roommate was also of Korean descent, but Brian found him fairly difficult. Having never spent time around other Korean people, Brian felt that his roommate practiced what he referred to as "reverse racism" but which could probably more accurately be called just plain racism:

> He is absolutely against any other race but Korean, right? Yeah, he's like that. He won't hang around with any other race or— it's only Koreans. And I asked him "why?" and he goes "well, we have to stick together," you know, and things like that. And I just don't, you know, I just don't believe that. (June 21st, 1995, p. 10)

Brian confessed that he is very uncomfortable around other Korean people, finds that they tend to form closed groups, and he admits to having no close Korean friends. He prefers to spend his time with people from many different backgrounds, particularly favoring Italians and the cultural mix that he grew accustomed to in school. In a limited way, he displays the same kind of animosity toward other Koreans that Ariana felt for other Chinese, hating that "they" want to stick together, and having no desire to travel to the country or connect with relatives still living in Korea.

While in university, at age 20, Brian also began to understand his parents' situation a little bit more. He traveled to Israel with the SOREL program, a program first created by Israeli generals to bring the Jewish Diaspora from many different countries to aid in the building process. Living and working in Israel without any knowledge of the language[s] made him more sympathetic to what his parents had gone through in immigrating:

> It was just that when I went there, I was having so much problems just communicating, and I could just relate to how hard my parents probably had it, too, when they first came. And, that helped me to understand. I mean, it doesn't help now, but just to understand it, that might help a bit. (July 6th, 1995, p. 9)

Brian realizes that his understanding is late in coming, but he does feel that traveling to Israel made him more patient with his parents, and less critical of them.

And, finally, I asked Brian about other Korean language sources in his home while he was growing up. Did he remember any Korean books, or being told Korean stories, or watching Korean videos? He said that he didn't remember his parents ever reading to him, and certainly not in Korean. He remembers his father reading a Korean newspaper, but it has only been in recent years, with the immigration of larger numbers of Korean families, that they have begun to watch Korean programs and videos. Brian was spoken to little while growing up, didn't have other sources of the Korean language, and was encouraged to begin speaking English at home. It is little wonder that he lost his first language and that his brother, three years younger, never learned to speak it at all.

THE NARRATIVE CONTEXT

Brian was the youngest participant whose life story I chose to include. There are few narrative characteristics that I want to point out, but those few are particularly interesting to me. Early in this research project, I noted in my journal that the stories tended to divide naturally into what I will call microstories and macrostories. Microstories seem to be about isolated incidents, not necessarily tied together into a coherent pattern, sometimes, but not always, remembered in minute detail. Macrostories are those that frame a narrative in terms of history and cause/effect, giving it sense and coherence, but usually very little detail. In general, the younger the person, the more s/he seems to tell a series of confusing microstories, while the older participants seem to be more comfortable narrating macrostories. Therefore, younger participants tend to narrate often unrelated anecdotes, and older participants tend to tell stories that have a beginning, a middle, and an end. Brian, as the youngest life story-teller here, also tells the most "micro" microstories. Reading transcripts of our interviews is very difficult because he begins a story, then leaves it, sometimes coming back to it, sometimes not, sometimes using only hand-gestures or a kind of grunting sound to complete his thoughts. Brian's life story was the most difficult one to put together. It had no chronology of its own, being just a collage of images.

This is noteworthy because of the possible implications. The first thing I thought of attributing it to was an overall change in narrative patterns that could be occurring. Perhaps, I thought, in response to media and the evening news' "30-second sound bite," the form of narrative is changing. I began to think that, with our news-oriented culture, we have moved into an era in which getting something "quick and quotable" is the best way. Storytelling as an art form has gone the way of home-baked bread—something we admire and enjoy, but it is just too "organic" for the mainstream. Moreover, television and visual media often rely on juxtaposition of images to create their message. By relating to me a series of seemingly unrelated images, Brian could have been challenging me to put them together in the same way that television challenges its viewers, a narrative technique that he had unconsciously assumed.

The second idea that occurred to me was that narrative could be changing in response to changes in the way information is distributed— in interactive rather than transmissive modes. Although once teachers and other educators stood before a class and pontificated, although once we saw the sermon and the eulogy as an art form, we now engage in much more interactive teaching. Audiences are drawn into lessons, and are encouraged to think things through, rather than being told how to think. In fact, I have often found this trend to be upsetting when taken too far. Sometimes, particularly in writing or film that people like to describe as postmodern, the audience has to work altogether too hard to gain any meaning from it at all. Ambiguity rather than clarity seems to be the desired result. With his unfinished sentences and unfinished thoughts, Brian, I thought, was perhaps reflecting the fashionably postmodern, current "invitation into" his narrative that is reflected in classrooms, allowing me to finish the stories.

A third possibility was offered by my husband, who during a casual conversation about what I was working on, sent me running to my journal to write down what he had said:

> *Satoru said something that might be important about this. He said it's possible that they haven't really lived enough yet. I thought about that for a while and thought "yeah...it could be that younger people haven't reflected enough to be able to write the stories yet. They're still too close to living them."*
> (Researcher Journal, September 23rd, 1995, p. 33)

It is a very distinct possibility that narrative form itself isn't changing, but that it changes within individuals over time. As people age, perhaps they become more able to reformulate their stories so that all of the different threads of their lives tie in together and create a coherent pattern. Perhaps then, Brian's disconnected narrative was disconnected because he is still in the process of working so many of these things out in his life. Perhaps the story he tells in 10 years' time will be more reflective, less chaotic, and have a sense of roundedness and wholeness that it currently lacks.

Or, finally, Brian's disconnected narrative could be a direct result of his language experiences. Brian often mentioned during the interviews that he had trouble with putting his school essays and papers together grammatically. ·He said he often had to rewrite essays 10 or more times in order to get his point across. He spoke of needing to use a thesaurus at all times when he is writing essays because, if he doesn't do so, he will end up using the same limited vocabulary items again and again. He claims that this is not because he doesn't know any other words, but because he can't recall other words when he needs them,[3] a not unfamiliar experience for any of us. Brian claims that his grammar is quite poor, that he often writes run-on sentences, and he attributes these problems to his having once been an ESL student, implying that he still considers himself a nonnative speaker of English, even though English is his dominant, his only, language (and even though the 1996 Canadian census would list him as a native speaker of English). Perhaps then, his disconnected narrative is a result of being unable to find the right words, or to monitor his oral performance, or to formulate complete grammatical sentences in his mind. Perhaps the false starts that are a hallmark of his interviews are symptomatic of more than just temporary losses for words. It is possible that monolingual development in one language, followed by a complete shift and monolingual development in another language, did leave some linguistic confusion. Because so many of the younger participants in this research project followed a similar pattern with the same narrative results, it is hard to find comparisons. This would be a fruitful line of inquiry in future research.

ENDNOTES

1. This was surprising because he wasn't even sure about his ball-park figures. He thought his dad was in his 50s, maybe, and that his mom was still in her 40s. He guessed that because he assumed they were in their 20s when they immigrated to Canada.
2. Brian's story was not, therefore, given a "member check." As with all stories that were not "member checked" however, he did receive copies of the transcripts so that any mistakes could be corrected.
3. Notice again the similarity to Lara's feelings about vocabulary recall.

9. BRIAN'S STORY: NOTHING TOO DEEP

My parents came to Canada probably about 3 years before I was born. I was born in 1973. They came here for opportunity, definitely; that's the main reason I think. They still talk about Korea and how they miss it, but when I ask them "Are you happy you came?", they definitely answer "yes." When they came here, everyone was moving to Canada. My dad's whole family—his brothers and sisters—all moved to here. I almost don't know any relatives in Korea now because most of them ended up moving here. I only knew my grandmother when I was little. She was pretty instrumental in actually teaching me Korean. All my grandparents died, except for my dad's mother, before I was born, so I knew only one grandmother for only maybe 5 years or 6 years. I don't even remember that much of her. We didn't[1] really keep in touch with her. My dad still remembers her, like, he still holds the Korean ceremony every time, whenever the anniversary of her death is.

On my mom's side though, I think she is the only one who moved here, so I have a lot of aunts and uncles in Korea [whom] I've never met. I think it has been hard on her. My mom is pretty shy to begin with, and her English didn't improve as much as my dad's because my dad went into school to improve his English, but my mom didn't. She stayed home and was a housewife, so her English is still not too good. For example, I went traveling last summer and she wrote to me twice. I couldn't understand her letters at all. She can speak some English, but when it comes to writing she has none of the fundamentals of grammar.

I know my mom sometimes wishes she was back in Korea just because her English is so bad and she can't do the things that she'd like to. You know, she'll read my university calendar and she won't understand any of it. She lost a lot of her confidence because she can't speak the language. My dad's English is okay. Grammatically, it's not that good. He'll read and he'll use the wrong tenses and things like that but he'll get his point across and he has a pretty large vocabulary, but he's a pretty confident person in general.

To be honest with you, the only remembrances of my first language [I have are] what my parents have told me because I don't have a clear [recollection of] speaking Korean at all. I know I used to because I was a former ESL student. To my parents, I spoke Korean fluently. It was the only language that they knew; they [had just come] from Korea about 2 years [before] so it was completely a Korean household, and all our friends were Korean, and that's where my culture and my language [lay]. So, I guess [the loss of my first language] started out in preschool. There's that Korean hard-work ethic, so I started school really early. When I was 3 or 4, [my parents] put me into preschool. [That] was okay because [preschool] didn't revolve completely around languages—there <u>were</u> a lot of arts and things—and so, I think it was Grade 1 or 2, Grade 1 probably, when I was first sent to an ESL teacher.

I had a lot of troubles when I started school. I was really shy, so that didn't help in making friends, and that, [<u>coupled with</u>] moving out for half my classes to an ESL class, it—it was sort of tough. When I was in the preschool, in Grade 1, when they were trying to teach me English—I was just overwhelmed, really. I can remember starting to cry in the classroom, and wanting to go home. I just didn't want to learn really at that point, so I think that was the main reason—it wasn't anything too deep, I don't think. But, I adapted pretty quickly. I don't think I had that tough a time actually. In terms of discrimination, my parents put me into a lot of these summer camps, and you know kids, right? They're cruel, so of course I had some problems, but it wasn't that bad actually for me. Probably because I was the only Asian kid, they didn't gang up on me or anything. So, I don't think I had a tough time growing up.

I was probably in ESL for 2 years. When the other students had their regular English class, and even after school sometimes, I'd be sent off there. I was the only Asian in that ESL program, and the other students in my ESL class were mostly Italian; I think there were some East Indians in ESL too, but in the general class altogether there were actually quite a few East Indians. Maybe there were five of us in Grade 1 ESL, but [the others] had been living here a long time and they had been speaking English most of their lives, so they were quite well off already. We were put all together, and we had to get to know each other just because we were all there together and because we couldn't speak English so well. We sort of bonded together; I kept in touch with some of them throughout the years, and some of them are still my good friends.

I remember my ESL teacher was an East Indian woman, and she was very nice. It was probably easier for me to interact at first because my ESL teacher and Grade 1 and 2 teacher were visible minorities. My ESL teacher is probably the person I have to thank for my language abilities today. I think the ESL teacher especially helped me, not only with my language, but with the customs and traditions of the western, Canadian life. I eventually gained the language pretty fast, but, because I was still speaking Korean at home, it sort of hindered my movements up. My teacher told my parents not to speak Korean at home, to speak English as much as possible, and I guess that's when I first started to lose my language. It was because I wasn't improving too well in English in school. I think that, when I started out especially, my parents were pretty protective of me, and they didn't let me hang out with other friends quite a bit, and because of that, I really only talked to my parents, for a while anyway. I think maybe that was one of the reasons; if I could talk to my parents just in Korean, that wouldn't have helped. I would have just learned English at school and then come back and [spoke] Korean [at home]. Because I was exposed to so much Korean, my ESL teacher told my parents to try to speak English at home and that's when I started to lose it. After that, my English improved pretty fast. Most of the Italians still spoke Italian at home. They've actually kept their languages. Because they had some English already, the ESL teacher didn't have to say "Don't speak Italian at home" because their English was a bit better than mine, and that was because I was just speaking Korean all the time. It was probably better for her to say "Don't speak Korean at home" so that my English would improve.

By the time I was in Grade 3, I actually was in the top reading group. There were three reading groups—beginner, intermediate, and the advanced—and I was in the advanced reading group. I don't think I really belonged there; I think [my participation in that reading group] was mostly because the teacher liked me and she thought I would do better in it. She thought [my] being in there would maybe improve my English even more. But, I know I didn't belong there because we used to have school tests. I was in the first reading group, no longer in ESL, and we would have these standardized tests. Usually she'd read out the names of people who failed, ones who didn't do well, so they'd have to write it again, but I remember one time when I didn't pass and everyone else in my group did pass, she read out everyone else's name but, I guess, spared me the disgrace. I would have been pretty upset if I heard just my name as a failure. She did that a couple of other times, too, and I think that was pretty good of her. Every time I would probably do the worst of everyone in the tests, and when she called out the names of those who passed and failed the test, she would never call out my name and say I was the only one who failed; she'd call out the name of everyone who'd passed, just so that I wouldn't feel bad. Just to be singled out for failure, I don't think that [would have been]—. But I knew I didn't belong.

In Grade 4 with a different teacher I was put back down into the intermediate level. I think it helped because I was with more people who were at my level and I worked hard at it. When I was a kid, I was pretty polite and really hard-working and—actually it's a shame I grew up really—so I moved on to Grade 5 and 6 and 7, all at the intermediate level. My marks improved just because I knew the English. I could understand what they were teaching in science and art and music and history.

When I was in Grade 7, my Grade 7 teacher thought I would be someone who could introduce a new girl from Portugal to Canadian life, I guess because I used to be an ESL student. But, I couldn't help her. When he made the seating arrangement, he made us sit together. I mean, I got to know her quite well, and, I mean, she still didn't interact well with other people and [make] friends, just because a lot of people still made fun of her. They didn't really give her a chance, which I thought was pretty sad. They would make fun of her accent constantly. They wouldn't...whenever she would say something, they made fun of her, so, of course, she was discouraged, and so her English didn't improve too much in that sense. But, she was an ESL student also. When we had our English group sessions, she would usually be sent to the ESL room downstairs, which was the same thing that [had] happened to me, too. But, she moved away, so I don't know what happened to her.

By then, I had completely lost Korean. I can still understand some of it because my parents still, when they get angry or they want to say something in a hurry, they'll speak in Korean, but, in terms of speaking it, or reading it, or writing it, or even understanding native Korean speakers, I have no clue; it's absolutely gone. Of course, I don't understand everything [my parents say]. Commands mostly. Just "hurry up," "get this," "go there," things like that. I can't say them. I couldn't even repeat them, but I can completely understand those things. I just don't even think about it. I don't know why; it's just in there.

I think it's sort of sad that I don't understand Korean because we have a lot of relatives who come over from Korea—they knew me when I was little when I could speak fluently—and when they find out I can't speak Korean anymore they get pretty upset. They don't get angry, but they can't believe it; they can't understand why I lost it that fast. And every year my parents say, "Oh, you should start learning Korean again," and even I want to, too.

I've had a lot of trouble communicating with my parents, especially since now I've lost Korean. My parents tell me all the time "you should try to understand Korean." They say that over and over again. They'll try to say something to me in Korean because they don't know the words in English, or they want to say it fast, or they're angry, or something. When I don't understand, they'll get so frustrated and I'll get so frustrated too, because I want them to be able to speak it and I want to be able to understand it—but I can't. Almost every week there's an incident like that. Right now, I absolutely wish I had kept the language. I think it would come in so handy just being able to travel, even for jobs, but, just generally, I wish I had kept it because I think it would have helped so much more in understanding my parents. Since I was born here, I have a totally western mind-set. They don't.

At the beginning, my parents were absolutely intolerable, in my eyes. When I was in high school, and elementary school, I had to come home right away for 2 hours of piano practice, whereas my friends would always go, "Hey do you want to play floor hockey?" but I never could because I had to be home. If I was just 15 minutes late, I would get in so much trouble. I wasn't even allowed to get a job in high school because they didn't think it was right for me to work when my dad was working. They thought that if I ended up working, I'd be more concerned with money than school. Eventually, just seeing how other families worked helped my parents slowly change. Because I was the oldest one, I ended up teaching them a lot of things too, so I think in the end they slowly changed. My younger brother, he's been lucky. My parents were more westernized while he was growing up.

And, it wasn't just the mind-set. I don't really think I really talk to them about things like [social or emotional issues]. I still talk to my friends mostly about things like that and so, when my parents and I do talk it's mostly "the weather's nice" and things like that. I mean it's not that shallow, but in terms of social things, it's mostly with my friends that I discuss stuff. My parents are very private people, even with us. They haven't really told me about their childhoods, and things like that. To tell you the truth, I don't even know their ages. I would guess they were 20-something when they came here, so they would be 40-something now. I think they're older than that maybe; I think my dad's in his 50s. I think my mom's in her 40s. Sometimes they include us [in family decisions], but [*those discussions* are] always in English. It wasn't [a situation] where I would have any say in it. They would decide and they would do what they were going to do, so I wasn't going to add anything to help them, so, you know.... I don't know if that's just the Asian way or language trouble.

So eventually, I entered high school. I had, and still have, a lot of problems with my English. I have a lot of pronunciation problems. There's still a lot of words that I pronounce wrong, or that I won't even use because I don't know how to pronounce them, even though I understand them—like do you say "taciturn" or "takiturn." I have a lot of problems with that still, and names, especially western names, are a problem. I used to collect baseball cards in high school and I'd go, "I'll trade you a Mike Blower's [blow-ers] card," when it's actually pronounced "blowers" [flowers]. When I talk with my friends, they will correct my pronunciation or whatever. Maybe it is just because I am in [the university] setting, but I think generally Canadians don't have pronunciation problems like I do. I find that anyways, when I talk to them. I just have so many problems like that.

In Grade 8 in high school, I guess more people were concerned with just being cool and things like that and I was still working hard, so I was at the top of the class in Grade 8. My teacher recommended me for English 9 Honors. I took that and I think it totally helped me. Just being put in an environment where everyone is so good that I have to catch up to them, I had to work so hard, and most of the literature I was reading was challenging. I had been forced to read a lot of books because that's one way the ESL teacher thought that I could improve my English and so I just read every children's book out, but that was the highest level that I got to. I didn't improve. I didn't read anything that may be considered "good" in any way; I was still reading *Black Stallion* stories or the *Hardy Boys*, even in high school. So Grade 9 and 10 introduced me to a whole a new world of literature. I studied a lot of Canadian literature and really good Shakespeare. Then I went on to English 10/11, which was 2 years in one, and that even improved me even more. I studied so much literature, and I finally understood a lot of words, and it was really good. Then, in Grade 11, instead of taking an English course, I took an English literature course, and that helped me even more.

But, creative writing in the English classes was the hardest for me. What I mostly [would] do, just because I didn't have a lot of words to use,...I'd use the same words over and over again. And I think I did that all throughout, up to Grade 5 at least, it was constantly using the same words, especially, I remember, the word "then." Even now, when I write essays, I use the thesaurus quite a bit just to make it sound different. Personally, I find it hard to come up with words, different words, and I still have to use a dictionary just to write essays; it's not completely on my own. I still don't think I'm a good writer. I have to proofread many times for my essay to sound decent, but sometimes my content is what stands apart I think. I remember in English 12, it wasn't that my essays were well-structured; it was mostly my content was good and that's why I got pretty decent marks. Maybe I'm just that kind of person. I'm not sure really. But, I think it maybe has a bit to do with losing Korean and learning English late.

Of course by [the time I was in high school my] Korean was absolutely gone. I didn't even use it at home. I'd speak to my parents in English and they'd speak to me in English because their English had improved so it was almost an English household by that time...English-speaking anyways. Then, I entered English 12 honors, advanced placement, and that was probably my best course in Grade 12. That was how much I'd improved by then. I mean, even compared to people who were here all their lives,[2] I could read literature and finally understand it, you know, I could understand it on a high level, and I think that's sort of a breaking point[3] for me. I didn't do as well in first-year university English, but I don't think I really tried that hard. I don't think I worked that hard in first year because it was my first year away from home and I didn't concentrate at all in English.

I don't really know anything about the Korean culture. If [*my parents*] hadn't told me all these years, I wouldn't even have known that I spoke Korean, so it's strange, in a way. I don't think they really ever read books to me in Korean, not even children's books. I don't think I've maintained it too well except for food and that's just because that's what my parents eat at home. In fact, I don't think that [my parents have] maintained it as well either. They don't practice the religion that they grew up on. They don't really wear the clothes that they used to wear[4]— that probably wouldn't be practical here—and they're not really into hanging out with Korean friends and so, in that respect, probably my parents too [have lost the culture]. I don't really follow the culture, but I don't think I've followed it to a great extent. I don't think I've totally ignored it either because I do read Korean books and things like that—in English, but just on Korea. They're not anything deep or anything, they're not Korean literature, just maybe more like fact-based books on the country. Actually I don't pick them out myself. My parents make me read them. So, I don't really read them—not out of...[personal cultural interest]. But, it hasn't bothered me or anything, just because I can't remember anything of speaking Korean; it just [doesn't really bother me]. I don't have any feelings for it, for the loss—I haven't really thought about it much.

ENDNOTES

1. I found that Brian was not terribly comfortable with narration. I have made several editorial changes throughout. I did not correct all instances, only those where I felt the story was being interfered with; therefore, there are more changes at the beginning of the story when clarity is essential than toward the end when the context is supplied. When I added words or phrases, those words are in brackets. When the changes were to clarify a pronoun reference, the words are in italics. When the changes are to correct grammar, the words are underlined.
2. This comment is particularly interesting given that Brian too has been here all his life. He seems to be establishing some kind of distance between himself and White Canadians, and establishing that "real" Canadians speak English at home.
3. Because *breaking point* has a negative connotation, I later asked Brian to define

what he meant by it. He replied:

> *I still wasn't really clicking in all through my high school years in English anyways; my marks weren't as high as the other people. But in Grade 12, my marks suddenly rose and were better than average, even though it was an Honors class...I think it was mainly because of my teacher, that did it, and I think, then, that's when I felt that I wasn't, you know, just hanging on sort of thing.*

4. I find this reference to Korean clothing very peculiar. During our interviews, Brian several times mentioned not even knowing what traditional Korean clothing, what his parents probably wore, looked like. It surprised me that he was unaware that Korean fashion is very westernized; he seemed to assume that the clothing worn in Korea was quite different from that worn here.

10. HELENA: INTRODUCTION

THE INTERVIEW CONTEXT

The first time I visited Helena's apartment, I admired it immensely. It was an older, two-bedroom apartment with hardwood floors, fairly nicely furnished, in a safe, high-rent neighborhood, and she shared it with a roommate who gave us a lot of space. I couldn't help but look around a little bit, wishing that I had had an apartment like hers when I was 25, instead of the urban slums my student budget had allowed. There were lots of windows, and even though we sat in the dining room, the furthest point from the windows in the apartment, there was still a lot of natural light.

We established a pattern with that first interview, one that I chose, and then grew to dislike. We would sit at the dining room table, on hard maple chairs, with the tape recorder in between us, and I would anxiously shift positions, crossing my legs, uncrossing them, sitting with my feet up on the chair, sitting on one foot, sitting on my hands, standing, and generally casting longing glances at the comfortable-looking sofa about 15 feet away. I had my back to the wall, and Helena would either sit directly across the table from me, or to my left. I preferred it when she sat directly across from me because then I could see her wonderfully expressive face, and see both of her hands waving wildly while she talked.

It soon became apparent, though, that just prior to my first visit, Helena and her roommate had cleaned the apartment in honor of Helena's impending parental visit. During each successive interview, I would find myself in a messier apartment, claustrophobically wedged into my chair against the wall by a hamster cage, several boxes and a large bicycle belonging to Helena's boyfriend. Remnants of Helena's recent 25th birthday celebration also festooned the dining room, as did several articles of clothing and the evidence of several hastily eaten meals. The funny thing was that I liked it. I, the person who, even after having broken my lower back in a gym accident, wouldn't lie still if I felt that the vacuuming should be done, the same person who would always start collecting dishes and bottles to take to the kitchen at *other people's* parties, and whose cleanser of choice is bleach served "straight up," no gloves, found myself completely comfortable in their home.

When I met Helena, she was at a kind of crux point in her life. First, she had celebrated her 25th birthday 1 week prior to our second interview, and therefore, as she said, "So, [participating in this research project] is like huge. It is like perfect timing because I've been so reflective for the past two weeks" (July 26th, 1995, p. 1).

Helena was reflecting about her Hungarian heritage, her culture, and, oddly enough, her language loss. She was already grappling with the question of whether she should just walk away from what she remembered of the Hungarian language, or whether she should pursue it and try to further her knowledge of it, thus keeping it. Helena felt very strongly that she was "on this line," that she had "to decide pretty quick," because her parents were aging and,

> *definitely when my first parent passes away that's going to be a very*
> *emotionally charging thing. It's going to really start hitting me that it's the*
> *end of having access to it.* (August 8th, 1995, p. 26)

Secondly, Helena was also in a reflective period in her life because her parents came to visit her between our first and second interviews. This meant that she spent long hours discussing her language loss with her parents when they were visiting, checking her stories and asking to hear other stories, about her language experiences, and theirs, which led her to comment to me that "it was a really good thing for you that they came" (July 26th, 1995, p. 9). Because Helena and her parents had not been particularly close for many years, their visit was especially important in this respect. Even prior to our meetings, Helena was trying to understand the role that they played in her life, and the reasons why their relationship had fared so poorly for so many years. When she read in the newspaper about my research project, therefore, she felt a strong pull that it was meant for her:

> *I mean, I really believe some things are fate because, I mean, I wasn't at work*
> *that day, and it was a matter of me going down and getting the paper and then*
> *flipping to it, and reading it, and going "holy smokes." And it wasn't even a*
> *matter of putting it away and later calling, or thinking about it, it was like I*
> *kind of walked to the phone and said "can I participate?"* (August 8th, 1995,
> p. 27)

Moreover, Helena's parents' visit was important to our interviews in other ways. First, Helena was able to ask her parents a lot of questions and discover things that she hadn't known. For example, until this visit, Helena had not known that her father didn't speak a word of English until she was two years old. Until that time, he had not had enough exposure to the English language to feel confident in expressing himself at all. She also found out that her mother had fallen into the same pattern, not understanding anything for the first 2 or 3 years and therefore being unable to speak English. While her parents were visiting, Helena was also able to go to a Hungarian restaurant close to her house that she had always been too shy to go to alone. She realized that she felt embarrassed and ashamed at being unable to express herself in Hungarian, and therefore she knew she would never go to that restaurant again.

Second, when her parents arrived, Helena had already completed one interview with me and felt that she had some understanding of what I might want to know. She found herself noticing things, because of my questions for her,[1] that she hadn't noticed before. For example, Helena realized that in her conversations with her parents, she was constantly being called on to understand a Hungarian word from context, and/or to supply the English word for her parents:

> And then my dad will say a word. I don't know what it is and then I'd listen to the context of the sentence, and I'd say "Oh you mean a whatever," and then he'd say "yeah." So I learn that word, and then the next time he uses it, I know what he means. And then I don't end up having to fix it for him, I end up just going "Oh, I know what you mean." And then,—and so somehow I'm learning all these words, but I don't use them myself, but for him to use it, I know what he means. (July 26th, 1995, p. 10)

Helena also found herself listening to her parents' speech more carefully. She noticed that, although she told me during our first interview that her parents always spoke Hungarian together, her parents actually code-switch even when they are speaking only between themselves, and "they throw in English words whenever it's just easier for them to now, so they're kind of losing it, too" (July 26th, 1995, p. 26).

A third thing that "emerged" during Helena's parental visit was actually noticed by her boyfriend. Helena's boyfriend, Lawrence, complained to her that he had to concentrate when he was trying to listen to her parents and to understand them. He found their conversations almost impenetrable because Helena, too, would adopt her parents' speech habits, and, as Lawrence said, her "vocabulary just went downhill" while her parents were around. Helena was completely unaware that this was happening. Not only did her vocabulary deteriorate, but Lawrence also pointed out that her language "totally declined while they were here, and easily about 3 or 4 days after they left" because she ended up "talking like they did." After 3 or 4 days, he said, she finally "climbed back up to be able to speak" (July 26th, 1995, p. 6). Despite the fact that Helena often commented how grateful she was to her boyfriend for constantly correcting her grammar and criticizing her speech, rather patronizing and inappropriate behavior to my way of thinking,[2] I think that there is an important point in this. Given that Helena's speech became nonstandard when she was around her parents, credibility is given to the argument that parents should not be encouraged to give up the first language in the home in favor of English, because the English that they model for their children will likely be nonstandard, reinforcing rather than correcting poor English-language skills.

But finally, more importantly for me, Helena, like Ariana, seemed reluctant to allow me to interview her parents.[3] Ariana said that she would talk to her mother and father about being interviewed, and then managed to avoid the topic whenever I tried to bring it up. Helena knew that there was only a short period of time when her parents would be available, and yet she didn't mention to me that they would be in town, so I didn't know until after they had left. She did not return my phone calls until after their visit, and even forgot one interview that was scheduled during the time they were to be in town. This was surprising, given that when she signed the consent form, she also signed the completely separate section that would have allowed me to interview her parents. Although Helena may not have mentioned the visit because she wanted to spend time alone with her parents, I became convinced that Helena, like many of the other participants, wanted to be the medium for the messages/stories they told, partly because I kept coming up against this phenomenon again and again, and partly because participants became somewhat skittish when it actually came time to schedule a parental interview.

Helena was also the first participant, after my difficulties with Ariana, whose life story I completed. I debated with myself about the idea of *member checks* not wanting to relive what I felt was a very stressful fiasco, but also wanting to be perfectly fair, and in keeping with a strong feminist sympathy in my research. In the end, I decided to give Helena a copy of the life story I had edited from her words, and ask her to read it through. We did this during a fourth meeting, over breakfast that I brought with me to her apartment. Helena read through the story, corrected two time-sequence errors, and then said "yep, that's my story," It was such a different experience from that with Ariana, that I decided to give member checks another try. However, I soon found it to be impractical for another reason. When I tried doing a member check with Lara, she became very distressed by the ragged quality of her oral prose and wanted to edit it into better English text. I realized that this issue might be one that would be brought up repeatedly, especially because many of the participants in my study were writers or communications specialists. I therefore decided to make member checks something I offered as an option, but did not specifically request.

Probably because I had already completed a number of life stories when I began interviewing Helena, an interview strategy that I adopted first made its appearance with her. When I noticed similarities between something that Helena had said, and something that I recalled from another interview, or when I wanted to engage in ongoing analysis, I often wanted to question her about it. Rather than asking a direct question, or making a statement that might be taken as judgmental, I began by saying "I'm going to say something, and I want you to tell me your opinion of what I just said." Therefore, instead of asking "Do you think that you had trouble with English in school because your parents were unable to help you with your homework?", I would say instead "I'm going to say something and I want you to tell me if you think it's an accurate statement. Sometimes when parents don't speak the language of school instruction at home, the children come home with their homework and, if they have trouble, they just can't complete it. But, the school makes the assumption that there's teaching going on in the home." By asking the question in such an ambiguous manner, I am inviting Helena to make it relevant to her life, or not. In this case, her reply was,

Yeah, because my parents could help me in math. They could help me in sciences. These are things that go across language, the concepts, but in terms of—they couldn't help me with the social studies project, or the language arts' project because they don't know. (July 26th, 1995, p. 15)

In this case, Helena both personalized the statement I made, and also made it a comment about language. It made me feel somewhat more confident that I was not putting words in the subjects' mouths, and indeed, I did find on several occasions that I would be contradicted. I also found this to be a more effective way of "asking" because it invited the participant to comment rather than to answer a question. This, in turn, would often lead to more storying.

THE LIFE HISTORY CONTEXT

Helena was born in July 1970, in a small city in southern Alberta, Canada, a second-generation Canadian on both sides. At that time, her parents had been married only a short period of time, her father having immigrated only in 1968. Helena's mother immigrated to Canada in 1963 when she was 16 years old, 7 years after her own parents had come to Canada. Helena's mother's parents considered themselves Hungarian even though they immigrated to Canada during the revolution in 1956 from a part of Rumania that had belonged to Hungary until the war. They worked in Canada, and, when they could afford to bring their five children to Canada, they sent for them.

Helena's father grew up in Hungary, trained as an engineer, and then discovered that he didn't share in the Communist dream. Having an uncle who had lived in southern Alberta since the turn of the century, Helena's father decided that he wanted to immigrate as well. He and a friend forged their papers, went across to Austria, and then applied to emigrate to Canada. Because of his mining engineering degree, he was given the option of moving to Timmins, Ontario, where he could work in mining, though not as an engineer, or moving to southern Alberta where his uncle lived. He chose to go to southern Alberta and to make his own experience. Helena spoke of how badly his having to make that kind of decision made her feel. Her father had to choose between following a career path, and living near his only family in Canada. Helena commented that,

> *He had to do whatever it took to make a living, and he had to throw away what his identity at that point had been, and what he had worked very hard to become, and almost for him I feel bad.* (August 8th, 1995, p. 21)

She went on to say that had he tried to become an engineer again after he had settled in Canada and learned sufficient English to pass the examination, he wouldn't have been able to because (a) he would have forgotten some things, and (b) due to advances in the field, he would no longer have been up-to-date.[4]

Helena's father was very disillusioned by his immigration experience. He felt that Canada was not as free as he thought it would be, that he had been sold a false dream. Although Helena joked that her father was a victim of insufficient research and that he should have known better than to choose socialist Canada rather than the more personal-freedom-oriented United States, she also explained that, to her father, Hungary remained the land of dreams. In fact, when her family visited Hungary in 1992, she and her brother were disappointed. They had expected a fairy-tale land, but found instead that their father switched allegiance and began talking about how wonderful Canada was in comparison with Hungary.

Having not spoken to Helena's father, I am not sure what caused him to glorify Hungary and then be disappointed by it. I can only speak from my own experience from living in Japan. When I first went to Japan, I was very disillusioned by the country and the people, but as I slowly became used to rules of social conduct and could function in the language, I became adjusted and happy. I never relinquished, however, my image of Canada as being more beautiful, more free, friendlier, less ethnocentric, less discriminatory, more open, more honest, etc., and I repeatedly told my husband about my wonderful country. It wasn't until I returned to Canada after 5 years that I realized my portrait of Canada had been naive. I began to reevaluate Japan in a new light, a painful process for me. It is hard to give up an image from childhood. It is difficult to realize that your beliefs have no foundation. It is hurtful to have those you love to you and say, "You lied to me about this country. Why?" So much of this I wanted to say to Helena, but I could only tell her of my experiences—which were not necessarily those of her father.

Helena's parents met while working at a macaroni factory, something that Helena finds quite amusing. All of the workers at the factory were Hungarian, and they communicated in Hungarian, while, she joked, they were making this "truly...Hungarian food" (June 22nd, 1995, p. 13). Helena's mother later began working for a soda company and her father worked in a slaughter house, until they got very frustrated by the lack of opportunity in their work. Helena's father took up the trade of carpet-laying, and, with his wife, chose to open a business in 1981. They slowly became interior housing contractors. Presumably, like many European immigrants (also see Lara), they were quite success-ful, as Helena mentioned that her parents owned several rental properties close to their own home in southern Alberta.

After Helena was born, she and her parents lived on a farm just on the outskirts of the city. Until she was 3 years old, they lived in the basement of the house, which belonged to her great uncle, and rented out the upstairs suite. She, therefore, did have English-speaking neighbors upstairs, but she didn't spend any time with them. She was surrounded by Hungarian friends and family and seldom exposed to the English language. In fact, the Hungarian community was so strong that Helena's great uncle, the first blacksmith in southern Alberta, spoke almost no English at all:

> He was like 97 years old, but like, he spent like 80 years in Canada, and still didn't really pick up anything. But, like I said, I guess in that area, the culture just stuck together so closely that they didn't have to. (June 22nd, 1995, p. 12)

Helena's family next moved into the city, where Helena began to meet other children and therefore she learned to speak some English outside of the home. She still spent most of her time with her family, however, so she wasn't exposed to English much until she was older. In fact, Helena credits television rather than neighborhood activities with being her primary source of English language experience:

Sesame Street really helped, I think. Sesame Street was huge. I really think Sesame Street taught me English more than anything else. And cartoons, I learned from cartoons. (July 26th, 1995, p. 16)

But, it wasn't only TV that helped Helena. Helena remembers loving "those stupid word books that my mom got for me as a kid" (July 26th, 1995, p. 16). Her mother bought her instruction books that taught her English language arts, and eventually also the math books and all of the workbooks that were on the market. Although Helena did talk about how her mother made school so much fun for her by incorporating such activities, I found it surprising that she didn't make the connection that her mother was teaching her English as a Second Language, probably in the only way she was able.[5] Helena later told me that she herself was very proactive in trying to better her English all the way through school, taking her essays and reports to her teachers and asking for extra help and more homework; she learned to be proactive, it seems, from her mother. Even after I pointed this out to Helena, she seemed not to realize its importance. Helena's response was that her mother gave her English workbooks because there was no point in giving her Hungarian workbooks because Hungarian wasn't necessary for survival. I realized that, while I was amazed by Helena's mother's resourcefulness, Helena took it for granted, part of her role as a mother.

Until Helena was in high school, she was very close to her parents, particularly her father. It is from interaction with her father that Helena learned most of her Hungarian language. She explained that she would be able to carry on simple conversations about cars or mechanics, or pulley systems in Hungarian because her father would explain to her how to fix cars, and together they'd go through some of his old textbooks from university. She would also engage in some political discussion, politics being a topic that she and her father are both passionate about.[6] Yet, medicine, business, law, things with which Helena is familiar in English, she would not be able to discuss in Hungarian at all. As she said, "it really depends on what kind of stuff my dad talked to me about as a kid" (July 26th, 1995, p. 9).

I was intrigued by Helena's story because most often in the language-loss literature, the degree of first language maintenance or loss is dependent on the mother, often correlated with her literacy or educational attainment in the L1, yet second-language success is sometimes linked to the father. In Helena's family, it is opposite. This is particularly surprising because she describes her father as the public relations and business partner in her parents' business, while her mother works behind the scenes, doing the accounting and technical support

work. Her father is more comfortable with speaking English than her
mother, and yet it was Helena's father who taught Helena to speak
Hungarian, and her mother who found a way to teach her English. Of
course, there may be little more to this than Helena enjoyed spending
time with her father more, and broached a wider range of subjects with
him, ones that he didn't have the English to discuss.

One of Helena's most hilarious (to her) stories was the one in which
she described her mother's attempt to discuss something with her that
she didn't have the language to discuss—menstruation. Before Helena
would be permitted to attend sixth-grade camp, she had to understand
menstruation, as did her Spanish-background best friend.[7] The two
friends each asked their mothers to explain it to them, but neither mother
was able to explain in English or their first languages. Helena told me
how she and her friend consulted medical dictionaries, ending up with a
great deal of technical knowledge, and absolutely no understanding of
women's bodily processes at all. Until she was older, Helena only knew
that "something happens" so that when you get married "something
happens" and then you have a baby. Helena and her friend "thought it
was hilarious," and they actually played with their mothers just "for the
fun" because they "knew that they couldn't tell us in *our* language, and
we also knew that they didn't know how to explain it, and they didn't
feel comfortable..." (July 26th, 1995, p. 22).

From a more mature perspective, Helena thought this was sadly
amusing, and, because Helena is a very resourceful person who was
finally able to understand menstruation on her own, I agreed with her. I
do find the implications somewhat disturbing however. What if Helena
needed to talk about something more serious, like recreational drugs, or
sex, or date rape, or AIDS and other STDs, or abuse, and she had been a
less resourceful person? Such things are seldom found in dictionaries,
and yet, a Hungarian-English dictionary was Helena's parents' only
resource when communication broke down in their family. When
children lose their first languages, parents can lose the ability to
positively influence their children, and to impart moral standards to
them. Helena may have finally understood menstruation, for instance,
but did she also develop the attitudes and ethics towards physical
maturation that her parents would have liked? When I asked Helena
about this, she merely said she just never told her parents if there was
anything wrong in her life. As it turns out, an abusive sexual
relationship was a part of Helena's entry into adulthood, but, by that
time, she had already left home and couldn't have talked to her parents
anyway.

As Helena aged, her relationship with her parents, particularly with her father, deteriorated. Her parents' scholastic expectations were extremely high: as she put it, "it's, like, there's this minimum requirement list and like everyone else's minimum requirement list is way down here, and mine is like way up here" (July 26th, 1995, p. 19). Helena's parents, unable to understand anecdotal reports, and somewhat adrift when trying to understand Canadian cultural norms, relied on letter grades and awards and their own 1950s Hungarian mores to interpret Helena's life. She was not allowed to date until she was 18 years old, but the first man she dated was supposed to be the man she intended to marry. When Helena got 68% on an exam that everyone else in the class failed, and the whole class had to have their test papers signed by their parents, Helena procrastinated until her teacher threatened to phone her parents, at which point Helena explained that she couldn't do it because "the issue would have stopped at the fact that it was 68, and anything that I would have to say wouldn't matter anymore, and there'd just be no way to get them to see it any other way" (July 26th, 1995, p. 20). The teacher insisted, and Helena was punished. She explained that, when the same situation occurred, it was actually easier for her to forge her parents' signatures and pay the consequences if she got caught, because her parents couldn't have gotten any angrier, and sometimes she got away with it. If she didn't get away with it, at least "it would just mean that many more months of freedom" (July 26th, 1995, p. 20).

At the beginning of her Grade 12 school year, Helena's relationship with her parents had broken down to the point at which she left home. After a few days at her aunt's house, Helena agreed to go home if her parents would go to counseling with her. They tried counseling but, because of language and cultural barriers, Helena became emotionally distraught and left home again. She first moved into a convent associated with her school, and then arranged to become a nanny in exchange for room and board so that she could finish school. For more than 2 years, she was unable to talk to her parents rationally. They would pressure her to accomplish her goals in life but to do it their way, and Helena's response was to stop talking to them altogether. She is justifiably proud of herself though because,

> They've seen—I proved a lot to them, that I did get to—they thought I wouldn't go to university, that I was just going to have my boyfriend living off me—and I still did go to university, and I got my degree. And every goal that I said I was going to accomplish, I did. And it was with zero help from them, and zero encouragement as well. (August 8th, 1995, pp. 1-2)

Helena feels that everything she went through was worth it, because she and her parents have a good relationship today. Yet, she acknowledges that the pain and anxiety both she and her parents suffered may have been avoided, if she had remained more closely connected to their language and their culture.

Currently, Helena is living in a large metropolitan center, where she moved because she had "high career aspirations." She works in marketing, but, being ambitious, she has expanded her role in her company to include in-house teaching and workshops, and various other duties. Although she and her parents have a good relationship now, Helena says that they still don't understand what it is that she does. They think that she works in accounting and advertising, because those are words that they understand in Hungarian, whereas marketing is a fuzzy concept, even in English. Helena found that, when she tried to explain marketing to her parents, they held her job in low esteem because they couldn't understand it. I found Helena's response to this refreshing; she thinks it's amusing. Helena feels that if her parents don't like her now, then they never will, because she is living her life the best way she knows how. Her mother, apparently, has really begun to show admiration for her daughter's accomplishments.

THE NARRATIVE CONTEXT

Helena is funny. She is not just a little bit humorous, but side-splittingly funny, and therefore a wonderful person to interview. The first time I met her, I came home and wrote in my journal that,

> [Helena] is really a treasure. She is brash and rebellious....She is loud and effusive and infectious and I can't imagine not wanting to spend time with her. (Researcher Journal, p. 23)

It is particularly noteworthy that I wrote so glowingly about Helena, given that the first time I met her I was ill. It would have been much more characteristic of me to associate the negative events with Helena and to have had a less enthusiastic journal response to her.

Yet, Helena claims that she is uncomfortable around other people, particularly around large groups of people, and has difficulty talking to them, a characteristic not normally associated with gregariousness and boisterous good humor. She explained that,

> I have a lot of ideas that I'd like to share, and I'd like, and I was very good at doing that one-on-one, and I can say a speech in front of 1,000 people, but to actually sit with a group of people, like I could never have been part of the popular group in high school because I didn't have the social skills to be with a large group of people who hung out together all the time....And I mean I really think that reflected how I felt in Grade 1, is that I didn't want to be with the

girls and boys. I had my one best friend in the neighborhood, and I didn't want to go play with the rest of them because it was "My God, there's so many of them, and I have to talk to all of them." And plus, I was just different. (August 8th, 1995, p. 14)

Helena's discomfort seems to stem from her language difficulties when she was younger, and her awareness that she was culturally different from her classmates.

I came to understand that Helena's self-deprecating humor and loud behavior, which she says her friends complain about, are a result of introversion rather than extroversion. While in school, Helena was never friends with other students of Hungarian heritage because she didn't maintain the language, nor did she learn Hungarian dancing or engage in the activities that other Hungarian families had their children participate in. Yet, she did not feel completely comfortable as "an English-speaking Canadian" either. She isolated herself from both groups, and, perhaps like Jay Gatsby in F. Scott Fitzgerald's (1953) novel, then "sprang from [her] own Platonic conception of [her]self" (p. 65).

And, Helena's self-directed satire was also very interesting to me, something that I ended up commenting on in my journal. I noted that Helena, Brian, Nadia, and, in later interviews, Hanna and Nellie, all told humorous anecdotes in which they were the butt of the joke, though "[Helena] does it to an extreme." Yet, Ariana, who was of approximately the same age, did not. I wrote,

In fact, I associate this kind of humor with humility (is there an etymological connection?) and integrity. I find other forms of humility uncomfortable and dishonest....I guess I don't expect humor directed at themselves from older generations, but from people my own age or thereabouts, I do. Perhaps that's why I sometimes felt [Ariana] was dishonest and/or a bit of a social misfit? (Researcher Journal, August 19th, 1995, p. 21)

I realize that I do have certain narrative expectations from my peer group that I don't have with older generations. I expect a certain degree of earnestness from people 10 or 20 years older than myself, and I expect a really cutting kind of pessimistic humor from people 10 or 20 years younger. I began to wonder how I developed my innate sense of what constitutes the "right kind" of narrative for each peer group, how those expectations are modified for nonnative speakers of English, and whether other people have similar expectations.

One of the other expectations that I hold is also demonstrated in Helena's speech forms. I expect people of approximately my generation to engage in what we long ago used to call "valley" speech, but what is now so mainstream that it commands little attention. This is very informal and direct speech in which there is a lot of mimicking of dialogues or internal monologues. For example, although older people might say, "So, I thought that he should get out of my way," using the past tense of the verb "to think," younger generations would tend to say "Like, I'm going 'move it'" using the present progressive with a directly quoted, present-tense verb to describe actions that took place in the past. Likewise, "And then I said 'please get out of my way'" might be replaced by "Like, I'm going like, 'move over man.'" "Like" is a filler word, used to replace "uhm," "and then," "something similar to," or any of a number of other low-meaning-load phrases. Also prevalent in this type of speech, is the acting out of entire, often fictitious, conversations, using only voice changes to indicate that different people are being represented. I have edited out this characteristic in Helena's, Brian's, and Ariana's stories because it tends to be confusing,

Helena, more than other participants, also displayed a lot of confusion in the tenses she used in her stories. She acknowledged frequently that she had always had trouble with English grammar and sentence structure, and that her spelling was also extremely poor. She attributed all of this to the influence of Hungarian. She tended to confuse word order, often adopting Hungarian patterns, and she also tried to spell phonetically because Hungarian is a phonetic language. She also mentioned that her parents' grammar was poor, as is her younger brother's, a familial problem which she attributes to their never having been taught the rules of English grammar. Helena feels that if they had just been formally taught the basics instead of being "cast adrift" in the English language, she and her brother would have learned standard grammar.

Helena's need for formal instruction and structure is a theme that runs throughout her interviews. She learned French quickly and well because she learned the rules. She was unable to understand computer programming until she realized that it was like learning a language, and she applied herself to the basic rules. Oddly enough, she claims not to have any grammatical difficulties in Hungarian with respect to the degree of linguistic ability she possesses, partly because she would sometimes try to teach herself the language from grammar-based books. On the other hand, her claim could be an entirely false one, born only of the higher expectations she has for herself in the English language.

A final note about the narrative context is that Helena was the only person in this research study who was born in Canada, and who had later visited the land of her first language. I thought that this would add an interesting perspective to the study, and, indeed, it did. First, I found that Helena always referred to "going back" to "the old country" instead of "visiting Hungary." She also talked about "our customs" and "our values" as opposed to "Canadian customs." Despite having been born here, she was very much imbued with a Hungarian mentality. Yet, she was also glad that she wasn't Hungarian. As she commented,

> *I was definitely glad that I wasn't born and raised there. My brother and I felt "wow, we are so lucky. It's great that we can say that this is here;" I mean, there are parts of it that were great, and I think it's a great place to visit, but I wouldn't want to live there. And, you know, looking back on the history of it, the history isn't anything to be too excited about 'cause they were always wanting to be Germans or being attacked by Turks and saved by the Germans after, so—and then, I learned about Attilla the Hun, and I go "he wasn't exactly the greatest guy in the world," ...and I'm, like, going "there isn't a lot to be really excited about, like they've got some neat customs and everything, and so I really like it there, but it wasn't a great experience."* (August 8th, 1995, p. 25)

It seems that, when she has located herself and her story in Hungary, Helena talks about "their" Hungarian customs and "their" Hungarian history, but when she locates her stories in Canada, she talks of "our" Hungarian customs and "our" Hungarian history, while "their" refers to Canadianisms.   In this way, Helena's identity is very much geographically determined.

Yet, it also seems to reveal more than that. First, Helena positions herself outside whatever geographical context she happens to be in. She thereby demonstrates a very conflicted identity, something that was quite common among the research volunteers, though more common among visible minority participants. Helena attempted to articulate what it meant to be different, and yet not to be visibly different:

> *I remember reading about...someone writing about what it was like to be a first-generation Canadian, and I sat there. I'm like almost in tears about the whole thing, because he was right. You didn't look any different. You didn't sound any different. But, you were different, and no one knew why. And he was talking about—like he came from a Ukrainian background or something where your last name wasn't the same—you didn't eat the same things, you didn't necessarily do the same things, but you looked normal, but you're not. And it was just like—it was like hidden, and people just thought you were weird, but they didn't know why you were different. And you're just kind of just wishing that all of that stuff would just go away.* (July 26th, 1995, p. 31)

Helena also explained that her current boyfriend is a 13th-generation Canadian, and she feels that she cannot relate to his family at all. She said that she would often sit in her boyfriend's family home thinking, "that is so foreign to me," and she frequently gets frustrated that he "will never understand what I had to go through to get where I am today," nor can his family fathom the amount of envy she has because they are "just

Canadian," whereas she is a "Canadian Canadian-Hungarian" (July 26th, 1995, p. 29).

Second, Helena has taken on the Hungary of her parents rather than the Hungary that exists today. The Hungary that Helena knows and understands is, like Lara commented, one that is based on Hungarian norms from the late 1950s and early 1960s rather than current Hungary, one that has been fashioned from textbooks, and one that has been transplanted to a Canadian context. For example, Helena claims that, after her trip to Hungary, she is able to use "everyday peasantry talk" (July 26th, 1995, p. 8) for discussing the weather, or what she wanted to eat, or what she wanted to do that day, but she wouldn't be able to discuss anything technical or business-oriented. It is odd that Helena would identify this as peasantry talk when her family is now, and always was, an urban family. It is also, I think, indicative of her adopting her parents' image of Hungary embellished by textbook reading on Hungarian *peasants*, a word that is no longer used except in a colonial manner, or to talk about the past.

Finally, I asked Helena to speculate about why she said "going back" to Hungary rather than "going to," and I pointed out a couple of other instances in which she seemed to regard Hungary rather than Canada as the land of her birth. Although at first she assumed that it may have been the result of adopting her parents' speech patterns and cultural attitudes, she later clarified that,

> *it's something that's a part of me, that's there, that I have a connection to, and to go back to it is to go back to something that's a part of me, that is hidden inside of me, and that's where so much of everything that has always been thrown in my face, that is a part of me, that, even if they didn't say it is, I know that's where it comes from.* (July 26th, 1995, p. 30)

Helena, too, is somewhat of an outsider looking in. Having had her differences "thrown in her face" all of her life, she is unable—or unwilling—to refer to Canada as her birthright, reserving those kinds of references for a Hungary that no longer exists, if indeed it ever did.

ENDNOTES

1. Although I had asked few questions at this point, I had given Helena a list of the types of questions I might ask in later interviews.
2. If this were a dissertation on antiracist and nonethnocentric thought, rather than on language loss, I would analyze the language that Lawrence used to describe Helena's speech, pointing out that her language could be viewed as "richer" rather than "poorer" because it was flavored by Hungarian words and

phrases, and also pointing out that she may not have "climbed back up" to be able to speak, but instead may have climbed back down.

3. A separate part of the consent form asked if I could interview parents or other third parties. Although Helena and Ariana signed this part of the consent form, they later seemed hesitant to introduce me to their parents. Possible reasons for this are discussed later.

4. In Canada, after World War II, engineers were very much in demand. Trained engineers from European countries were able to write an examination, proving their knowledge, and would then be able to join the Professional Engineers Association, and work in Canada. This is no longer the case.

5. When Helena was older, her parents entered her in speech competitions at the Kiwanis festivals. She had to memorize and practice speeches that were performed in public. This, too, seemed to me to be a parental strategy for improving Helena's mastery of the language when her parents had little knowledge of it themselves.

6. Helena is very active in the federal Liberal party and would like to become an elected official.

7. It is interesting that Helena's best friend was also someone who lost her first language, especially as Helena was enrolled in the Catholic school system, which had no ESL program. Most ESL students in southern Alberta were enrolled in the public school system.

11. HELENA'S STORY: LEARNING THE RULES

I'll kind of be talking about my brother as well, as he influenced my experiences. My brother and I are 5 years apart, so he was born when I was 5, right before I started school. My brother actually had a lot more trouble when I started going to school, because I'd come home and speak English at home, but my parents still spoke Hungarian, so my brother didn't actually learn to speak until he was about 3 My parents associated that with the fact that he must have been very confused, not knowing which language was what. And, when he did begin to speak, it was like a big mumble of words.

My father came to Canada in 1968; I was born in '70. My mom immigrated in '63. My parents met here in Canada, and so basically my father's learning of English went along with my learning of English. I was born in Smallcity Alberta, and it's an interesting area because of the fact that there's well over 30 different ethnic groups there. Ethnic groups tended, at that point in time, to stick together, so my parents met while working and my mother always told me that there was, like, the Ukrainian people that worked there, the Italian people and the Hungarian people, and the Hungarian people just spoke to each other and just hung around together. So, they only spoke Hungarian—and so that's why she and my father never really had an opportunity to learn English until I came along.

At home we always spoke Hungarian. But, I think, probably because there was TV in the house, I also learned English. I really think *Sesame Street* taught me English more than anything else. So, I was learning English, but I wasn't really speaking it at home. We lived on a farm that belonged to my great uncle until I was about 3 years old, and so everyone in my life at that time was Hungarian. It was when we moved into the city of Smallcity that I started to meet other children. Because of them I spoke English outside of the home, but, looking back on it now, I realize that my English must have been really poor. When you're older, people tell you when they don't understand you, but little kids don't so much. I just know that I had to talk a lot, repeat myself a lot, and then I'd get teased about things that I would say wrong. At the time I didn't know that; I had friends, and that's all that counted.

At that point, most of my time was still spent with my family. My mother worked, and when she was working, I stayed with my grandmother or my aunt. I had a cousin who was 5 years older than me and an aunt that was 7 years older than me, so we all spoke Hungarian amongst ourselves. They were my two best friends. I only really had a couple of close friends in the neighborhood, so I didn't really speak much English until I started getting older and older. I don't think I really knew the difference between the two languages, I just knew that I was communicating with people. I know that I must have started losing some Hungarian when I was about 5 years old because that's when my brother was born and my grandmother from Hungary came out to visit us. I felt self-conscious talking to her in Hungarian, like I thought about it before I spoke.

I never got into any trouble whatsoever for speaking English, but when I came home I never did; I just spoke Hungarian. Once school started, I started to slowly speak English at home. I just think that's when the change occurred because our family contact went from me coming home with things to color, to me coming home learning about rights and responsibilities in social studies, and those are concepts that I couldn't talk about in the same way as I could about "So, what's for dinner?" "So, what's for dinner?" could stay in Hungarian, but "What do you guys think about these concepts?" and discussing things with them to get my ideas for a paper was completely different. The more complicated my thoughts became in English, the more my parents kind of had to switch. In daily life too, they had to start using English more and more, especially when they started their own business.

I was encouraged to speak English at home when the teachers noticed that I said my words backwards. I can see them saying, you know, "Helena's having a hard time. You should encourage her to speak English at home more," but it's an impression more than words. When you speak Hungarian, the words come out backwards to English words, so when I wanted to speak, everything came out jarbled [garbled] in school. So, instead of saying "I went to the store" it would be "store to I went" or "went I," so everything came out backwards. When I went to Grade 1, I'd be saying that. Instead of saying "I'm going home," I'd say "home go I." My friends just used to think I had a speech impediment, I guess. Perhaps that's why my grammar, to this day, is awful. My word comprehension is very high, but I still have problems with my spelling. Hungarian is very phonetic, and I do that with my English as well, but I'm smart enough to be able to figure it out. And, I know I can have my things proofread, but I still struggle a lot and that was always one of my weaker subjects in school, was English.[1] It's like I'm stuck in between two different worlds and I'm never going to have proper grammar in either section; I just don't know where I belong anymore.[2]

My parents were very encouraging of my speaking more and more English. At the Kiwanis festival, I always did speeches and poetry and stuff like that, and they'd coach me on that; they'd get me to memorize my things and I'd read it to them and they'd tell me how to do it better. Thinking back on it though, I don't know how they helped me. They always encouraged me to do well in my studies, even though they couldn't help me with my homework. The only way they could judge my performance was by my placing in a contest or by whatever my mark was. They could understand a percent; they could understand a letter grade; they could understand an award.

In terms of like language, I had so much problems. I could read—no problem. I could read like anything, but in terms of speaking, the words still came out completely wrong. And I had a hard time saying some English. I mean my emphasises [sic] were all over the place. Yet, because my mom made me like school—like she used to make a game out of it, so that I thought it was a good thing—I'd say "could I take some books home? Can I stay after school and learn this?" and they thought I was just being a real keener student, but it was just like kind of like my mom made it fun for me.

But, looking at my pictures of Grade 1, I can see that I was just petrified. I just hated the first day of school. Grade 1, I guess, was the hardest. I had a hard time understanding instructions. I hardly think I ever got over it. I remember in Grade 2 we were learning how to use a dictionary and how to read the headings on the top of the pages. The teacher wrote out examples of what we were supposed to do first. She gave us words to look up in the dictionary and we had to list what the word headers were at the top. Well, I just kept writing the same word over and over again because I didn't understand her instructions.[3] I also remember adding and subtracting—I could do it, but I just couldn't understand the difference. When she said *subtraction*, I thought *addition* and vice versa; I used to get them mixed up.[4] I used to get opposites always mixed up and I just couldn't understand instructions for some reason. It was—always got mixed up. Exact instructions I never really understood. I remember one instance in math class. I didn't really understand the concept of subtraction, which was strange because I knew how to count and add and do multiplication; I just didn't know what they meant when they wanted me to do something.

I liked doing work that I didn't have to speak; like math I just loved. But, anything that was spoken I didn't like, which is absolutely bizarre now because my friends know me as talkative. Later, one of the things I definitely always got in trouble for, was I'd talk too much in class and I'd talk too loudly, and even to this day people say I talk far too loudly. Like they'll say, "Why are you so loud?" when we're in a restaurant, or when I get excited about something. That's something that annoys me more about Canadian culture than anything. 'Cause they're going "I don't like it," I feel I have to be pulled back. I still talk with my hands. I just talk with my hands and when I get excited my voice gets louder and louder. I know that when my family gets together our table is going to be the loudest one. When my family goes out for dinner, we're real loud, and the whole restaurant knows we're there because we have a great time and we are speaking really loudly. Hungarian is such a harsh language that people think we're fighting when we're having the best of times, and it's just because of the way the language sounds. And so my friends— like some of them that come from like a British background—and they'll be like "You're talking really loud" and I'll get like 'the nudge.' So that's been a big cultural barrier that I carry through to this day, is people saying "calm down, calm down." It's emotional. I feel like hitting them and saying "speak up, speak up."

But, usually, I just felt odd. I was really actually ashamed for a long time about being Hungarian, and all I really wanted in life was to have a North American last name. I wanted to be a Smith or a Johnson, or anything. Even today, everyone I've dated pretty much has had a nice Anglo-Saxon name. I'm not doing it on purpose, honest. And even my first name—I just wished it was like Sue 'cause there was a million Sues in my classroom and I just hated my name. And I was embarrassed about my parents' accents and that they couldn't speak English very well, and that everyone else's parents could and I was ashamed of the whole thing that I didn't speak like everyone else; I didn't have the background that everyone else did.

I still find myself today when I go to a store with my mom, talking for her, without even realizing it, because everyone always asks her to repeat everything and just—when she starts, I'll finish for her. Now it's an unconscious thing, but before I always spoke for my parents. And they gave me a lot of responsibility to make phone calls for them because people had a hard time understanding them, so I spoke for them. I never realized that, 'til now. I was ashamed for a long time. When I was 10, I had a friend whose mother was Spanish, and we had a lot of the same feelings about it. We were embarrassed; we didn't want them to talk; we didn't want them to go out with us and our parents were wondering why we were shutting them out. Like, I remember my mom explaining menstruation to me because they had to tell it to you to go to Grade 6 camp. Me and my Spanish friend Alina went to the park with our notes they had to sign, and we just started to howl thinking about this. They couldn't tell you in technical terms because they wouldn't know in English. We just thought it was hilarious, because we knew that they couldn't tell us in our language, and we also knew that they didn't know how to explain it, and they wouldn't feel comfortable. My parents wanted to be very much a part of my life, but I pushed them away and I gave them as little information as possible.

In fact, a lot of times I would just say the word that I knew would make the most sense to my parents, and there was a lot of things actually that I think that I always gave them the best answer that they would understand as opposed to saying the truth about something. I used to pull the wool over their eyes all the time because if they couldn't understand something, I had the power to explain it however I wanted. Like, I knew I could tell them that black was white and they'd probably believe it because if they didn't know any different, that would be it. If my dad asked me what a word was, I could tell him something completely different and he would never know until someone else told him that he was completely wrong. If they didn't understand what I was doing or something, or what a specific activity was, I could make it be to whatever I thought that they wanted it to be, but make it in such a way that it was partially the truth, and then just expand upon it, so whatever I originally said wasn't a lie, but it really was when I started out telling them.

When I was in Grade 7, my grandmother passed away. Before that, I would go after school to her house and I'd translate what was going on on TV to her 'cause she didn't understand any English. After she passed away, I didn't have that anymore. The same year, my aunt that used to take care of me also moved away, so after that, there was no reason for me to have to speak Hungarian. I became a latch-key kid who went home and was babysat by the TV. So, my influence was really taken away from home life and family, and that's when it slowly started to decline. I was starting to spend a lot of time with my friends and taking a lot of lessons outside. And, my parents were encouraging me to speak more and more English, so by the time I was in junior high, I was probably no longer really speaking Hungarian at home.

My paternal grandmother passed away when I was 10, and a lot of times we had planned to have trips to Hungary but we never did them. After she passed away, my father wasn't really keen on going back there. But after that, it really started to decline. That's also when—my best friend was from a Spanish background, and we both started to rebel against the whole culture thing, and our language thing. We were embarrassed about it all, but we had each other to lean on because we just both decided we hated that fact and we just wished we were Canadian. Then, during my adolescent years, I just hated the whole culture. I just wanted to be English and I just wished everything was English, my food was English, everything.

It was kind of a cultural thing as well because up until probably I started school, our house was like being in Hungary. And, as I started going through school, changes were introduced. I remember when I was about 10, I went to a friend's house and we had tacos. I had to come home and there was no way to explain tacos because there isn't any such thing as a taco, so we had to go out and experience that. I had to explain things, until now my parents are a lot more English than they are Hungarian. The more Canadian my parents became, the more we'd lose things off and then that part of our language would also leave, because I didn't have to express it anymore and because there weren't any Hungarian words to express what we were now doing.

In our school, whenever people came from different cultures, they'd put them in the classroom and they'd make me be their friend, figuring that somehow I would understand them. I'd say like, "Do you understand Hungarian?" in Hungarian, and the person would be like "No" and I'd be like "Well, this is pretty futile." But, I have the patience to talk slowly. It's not that you have to talk loudly, just talk slowly and they'll probably understand you. And so that was probably the only benefit that I ever gave these people that came to our school, that I would listen and was patient with them 'cause that's what it was like at home.

It was different for my mom because when she came to Canada at age 14, they threw her into Grade 1, because she was like "I'm not stupid; I just don't understand English." So, like everyone was thrown into Grade 1 class regardless of their age. So, she left school pretty much when she was 16 because she was like, you know, "I'm in Grade 3 now, but all it is is English that I don't understand." She's just so smart though, and I wonder what kind of opportunities she could have had if she had been given a fair shake in the beginning. Throwing her into Grade 1 was just retarded. And then basically following how everyone else did, she got married. She met my dad and then she basically followed his way, but she really pushed me without even really realizing it. Like a lot of the things I do, it's more for my mom sometimes I find, without even consciously thinking about it, but I just know I've been given a lot of breaks and she hasn't—but she's smarter probably than I'll ever be.

I guess, too, formally learning a language makes a huge difference. Having someone teach you the rules and how to do it, and correcting you all the time, makes a huge difference from being stranded—"figure it out for yourself"—like my mother was. I got mad a lot of the times when I'd hand in an assignment and I'd get like a 70 on it because the grammar stunk. Like the concept I'm getting an "A" on it, but because every line had a red line through it, I'd lose marks, so I'd be like totally bitter. What

I ended up doing was going to another teacher and saying, "Okay, I'm having problems. Can you proofread everything?" I've always been very proactive in everything that I did, so in that way I may have gained a lot of respect from my teachers. I knew what I wanted to do, and I knew I could do it, but I was never actually just sat down and taught grammar. It was in my last university course that I had a teacher who was very, very strict about all of this, and gave me back my assignment and gave me, like, a 60 and called me illiterate. Part of his concept was that the process of writing is rewriting, and there were three steps for our final paper. There was the proposal and then we had to do the first draft, and I must have rewritten that paper about 20 times because I wasn't going to let myself get a 60, but just seeing how much my writing improved and seeing that first draft to my final draft, I said, "You're right. I didn't know how to write until now." I can make the concept flow, knowing that this is how you bring the person in, fill in the blanks in the middle, and then you try to bring them back, wrap it all up at the end. And so that's why I never had a problem getting my thoughts across because it's been in a logical manner, and it works and that's the only reason that they will let me get away with as much as I have over the years, but when it comes right down to the little things, I just get killed. It's amazing all the things I've figured out now, and I'm having to go back to really elementary-level stuff, but they just assumed you knew it all. I think I started learning, about in Junior High, about putting in *the*; instead of saying "put it on TV," saying "put it on the TV."

We went back to Hungary for the first time about 3 years ago, 1991. We spent about 6 or 7 weeks there. When I first got there, I still understood everything, but I couldn't speak. By the end, my language had changed. I only learned Hungarian up until I was a child, so when I spoke in Hungarian everyone laughed because I sounded like I was a kid. After a while I'd remember more sophisticated language. I was so proud I was learning all these big words. When I had no choice, it all came back and more. Like I started learning on top of what I did. After 2 weeks of intense headaches of not understanding, like overload, all Hungarian and no English, I was communicating with everyone and learning big words. And so it changed then, and now I'm more conscious of it. Every so often when I'm on the phone with my parents, I'll initiate speaking to them in Hungarian. I think maybe just because of the fact that I'm older too, I'm more worried about it. Yet, I really think because my foundation is so strong that I wouldn't have a problem learning it again in 6 months.

At this point, I couldn't speak in terms of business, but everyday talk I guess I can manage. I don't know anything technical, but I can talk about the weather. I can talk about what I want to eat, what people are doing today. I wouldn't be able to talk about meteorology and cumulus clouds or anything, but I would be able to say "It's a cloudy day." In reading, because Hungarian is a very phonetic language, all I have to do is sound everything out and I know what I'm reading. Like it's funny when I'm going through the process, like I'll be reading the word and I'll start sounding it out, and I'm saying it wrong, and then I go, "Oh, this is what that word is," and I'll say it correctly. That's what happens with every word. When we were in Hungary for example, and I'd be walking down the street, I'd be like a reading maniac. I was just like a little kid absorbing so much information, and I'd read every sign that was around me, and I was excited when I knew what it meant. In terms of writing Hungarian, I'd be learning my ABCs in primary school. In terms of reading, I could manage a Grade 3 or 4 level of understanding, but you could put anything in front of me and I'd be able to sound it out and maybe tell you what it meant, but it would take me a lot longer. I wouldn't be able to read through it and translate.

When we took French in school, I think I could pick up French a lot easier, even though the languages are completely different. Because of Hungarian being so phonetical, and because you can make almost every sound except a "th" sound in Hungarian, when I took French, picking up the accent was really easy. I found learning French a lot easier because you say things backwards in French too, like a lot of the thought process was already there. So, my French marks were great in school, and learning other languages became a lot easier for me. When I took French, I didn't have the same problems that I did with English, and that's why I understand it well, but when it came to English I didn't learn any rules and so I had the worst time with grammar. Just because of the fact that I want to communicate in French, I learned the rules that had to go with it, but I figured I could already communicate in English so what's the big problem? Why should I bother to learn the rules? And I guess I really didn't want to admit that there was a difference between spoken English and written English, that I would have to do things differently, either.

I moved out during my Grade 12 year because at that point there was such a cultural difference between my parents and I. I had become independent partly because I had gone and done my exchange to Quebec for 3 months, and I came home and they were going back to the old rules again, that I had definitely outgrown by that time. My dad was like ultra-strict. At first I was able to stay with friends, and then I began working as a nanny to earn my keep. After about 6 months and throwing every theory in the air about all the reasons I may have moved out, my parents realized that "No, she just doesn't like us." And it wasn't that

I didn't like them; it was just their rules that I didn't like. My dad gave me this book of poems and things after that 6 months, and he wrote some lovely things in it that crushed my whole heart into a million pieces. He tries to say what he means, and even when I read what he wrote, I can think "No wonder my sentence structure stinks," but I knew then that a lot of times they wanted to say things, but they just don't know how, and I didn't always know how to listen to what they were saying.

When I was 21, I realized that Hungarian was something that I probably wasn't going to be able to carry on, so I started focusing my attention towards French. I realized that was an official language here and if I was going to have any second language it was going to be French. I still wanted to be able to say that I knew three different languages. Just because my parents can speak so many languages, I wanted to be able to speak more languages. I had tried to learn German but I did it through correspondence during high school, so that was impossible. Because a friend was Spanish, and I had another friend who wanted to learn Spanish, we kind of did that together but it was a lot like French and so I thought I'd just stick to the French thing. In fact, I did the French exchange to Quebec for 3 months in Grade 11, and so I actually got to the point where if I wanted to speak in Hungarian, the words weren't coming out in Hungarian anymore; French words were coming out. And I really had to stop and concentrate and it actually started to scare me that, well, before that I had just always assumed Hungarian would be there, and then it wasn't.

Now I have more an initiative to try and keep some of my Hungarian, but I know I'll probably never get it back because I don't see myself finding a Hungarian husband. I know my children, unless they have this big cultural search initiative, will probably never know the language and will wonder why grandma and grandpa speak funny. I'm kind of sad about it really, but one of the things my mom always said is that we came to Canada to become Canadian; we didn't come to Canada to continue to be Hungarian. I don't have a problem with that, either. She asked me if I ever wanted to take, like, Hungarian dance, but she never pushed like some mothers that we knew did. Now many of their kids speak and look, and everything, and my parents never did; they always tried to get me to become part Canadian.[5] And I guess part of my attitude when other groups come to Canada and I see that they don't want to, it kind of upsets me. When I go to Richmond and I see that they have all the Chinese signs, I'm like, "I can't understand a word that's in there and I'm Canadian here." It's not like I expect to go into a Hungarian store and be able to just read Hungarian signs.

And, it makes me sad because I'd like to have a really enriched life and have lots of different aspects too. Knowing that I can't experience those Hungarian things means I'm losing it. Down the road no one else is going to understand. It's going to be just my memory. And my husband will never understand that memory. My children will never understand that memory, and the only time that any of them will is when they go into my parent's home.

Since I've moved here to this city, I've gone to a few flea markets and when there are Hungarian-speaking people, I turn around. But, I'm very self-conscious about speaking Hungarian and I don't know why. With French, I have no problem, even if I make mistakes, but for some reason I have this pride issue, and that's why I don't want to go speak Hungarian. I feel extremely self-conscious about speaking Hungarian because I hear it and I understand it, but when I speak, my mouth and my brain are doing two separate things; they just don't connect. I can sit in on a conversation and I understand unless they start talking about something really in-depth, but I couldn't speak if my life depended on it. My mouth just doesn't do what it's supposed to be doing, like the words just don't come out. I have to just sit there and I dig and I dig and I dig and then a word comes out, and it doesn't come out like my head says it. It's just like when you talk to other people who are learning English and you know it's all coming out wrong—I know that's what's happening with my mouth. I have so much empathy for these people learning English because I'm sitting there thinking how I would be in Hungarian. I'm thinking "I know in your head it's working; you're speaking fluent English but your mouth is doing something completely different," and I just wonder where it gets lost from my brain to my tongue.

I toyed around a few times with the idea of going to the Hungarian cultural center so that I don't totally lose it. I'm not sure if I should have kept it, but I almost wish that my parents still didn't have it or that I didn't have people in my family who still had it, so it wouldn't be, like, in my face. Keeping Hungarian really isn't going to get me anywhere next to a nice hobby on the side and people will say "Isn't that nice? She kept her language and she goes to her classes at night." There's just no place for me to use it at all, except if I go to the flea market. I don't have any friends that speak it. It's almost like some romanticized idea to speak it? But once my parents pass away....

I didn't really realize until my parents came to visit that my dad, if he can't think of something, will say it in Hungarian and I'll figure it out, I'll know what it means. I didn't realize I was doing that. So, our conversation goes in and out of Hungarian and English all the time with my parents, and I didn't even realize that. If my dad can't think of something, he puts it in Hungarian and somehow I understand; it's almost like, even when you're reading in English, there's lots of words in a novel, you don't really know what it means, but because of the context of the sentence, you figure out what it is. So, I learn that word and then the next time he uses it, I know what he means, so somehow I'm learning all these words, but I don't use them myself. But, for him to use it, I know what he means. It's not going to come out of my mouth; I'd have to turn to my dad and say, and then the exact same process would come back the other way, and I never really realized it until now that we do that. So, I think that's why I've kept up knowing some Hungarian, is because my dad talks in Hungarian that way.

ENDNOTES

1. This is kind of backwards by Helena's description. It is also reminiscent of the way she tacks phrases on the ends of sentences, constantly qualifying rather than actually producing run-on sentences. This seems to be a very eastern European tendency in the interviews that I have completed to date in this study—Hungarian and Finnish (summary of Researcher Journal, August 23rd, 1995).

2. Note the dissimilarity between Helena's comments and those of Richard (or of Bhabha, 1994). Instead of feeling able to draw from two cultural traditions, she feels unable to draw from either.

3. This is particularly interesting given that several students in a course that I have been teaching reported the same kind of thing happening with their ESL students. This implies that it is a fairly standard strategy for students who don't understand what to do, perhaps making them feel more in control, less obviously isolated.

4. I wonder whether Helena was actually mixing up addition and subtraction, or if it was the complex language used to express the two that was confusing (e.g., "take away from," and "take away" express opposite functions in mathematics).

5. This is a very curious way of referring to her cultural identity. Helena was born Canadian. Yet, perhaps because of an odd Canadian custom of asking people "where are you from?", meaning "from what heritage does your last name derive?", Helena, like many other people including myself, feels excluded from the "real" Canadian culture. It is necessary to keep in mind that, prior to the 1980s, very few immigrants from other than European countries were admitted to Canada. When Helena was young, as when I was young in Canada, discrimination was often practised on the basis of last names. Eastern European names, those from countries that either were Communist or bordered Communist countries, were the most targeted.

II. DWELLING IN THE BORDERLANDS

Borders

If you're an exile—which I feel myself, in many ways, to have been—you always bear within yourself a recollection of what you've left behind and what you can remember, and you play it against the current experience. So there's necessarily that sense of counterpoint. And by counterpoint I mean things that can't be reduced to homophony. That can't be reduced to a kind of simple reconciliation.
—Edward Said (in Marranca, Robinson, & Chaudhuri, 1991, p. 43)

I remember as a child sitting in a small, white motor boat, fishing in the early morning hours, in Active Pass where the ferries passed close enough to see the lips moving on the passengers on deck, whispering to friends of my father's so as not to scare the salmon away, trying to appear mature and worldly, and being frustrated by a series of jokes that to my adult mind now appear to be variations on a theme:

Q: If a plane crashed in the middle of the border, where would the survivors be buried?
A: You don't bury survivors.
Q: If a rooster laid an egg on the peak of a roof, which way would the egg roll off?
A: Roosters don't lay eggs.
Q: If winds were blowing on a peanut tree from the north, the south, the east, the west, from below, and from above, which way would the peanut tree bend?
A: There is no such thing as a peanut tree.

One would think that, after having heard the first joke, I would have been prepared to answer the other two when I heard them. Such was not the case; I kept trying to logically analyze the problem and come to a reasonable conclusion.

These three jokes kept coming back to haunt me while I was interviewing, analyzing, synthesizing, and writing, and I kept wondering how they fit in with the rest of the paradigm. I finally realized that I, like the children the language-loss storytellers had been, had searched for a simple choice among two, three, or four alternatives, when the questions themselves were misleading. Similarly, most of the case studies in this book are characterized by a tension and struggle between two or more competing cultural identities, in which the protagonist believes that s/he should choose one or the other. Frustrated by popular discourses that represent the negotiation between two cultures as an either/or binary, or perhaps a continuum between two competing factions,[1] they were unable to recognize their own syntheses of their multiple identities. They were therefore unable to celebrate their unique sociocultural positions that both differed from their parents' (multiple) cultural identities, and from a generic assimilated *Canadian* identity. They were not applauded for,[2] and therefore could not applaud themselves, having worked through the dominant discourses (see Crawford, 1992a, 1992b) to achieve their own unique hybridities.[3]   In fact, Woolard (1989, cited in Ben Raphael, 1994) argues that the cultural hegemony dominating our thinking, which I take to mean the view of languages and cultures as bounded and fixed, may lead to the death of subordinate languages. Trying to maintain a "pure" form of the minority language, resisting the influence of the dominant language, may be less effective than a working *corruption* of the minority language, allowing for adaptation to the dominant language. In fact, Woolard believes that such language change may be a condition for survival. By extension, viewing two (or more) cultures as distinct, and trying to live within one or the other, rather than living within both and allowing other cultural traditions to bleed in, may ultimately be detrimental to the emotional and cultural survival of people having multiple cultural backgrounds.

> Q: If a child was born into one language and culture, but grew up within a different language and culture, which language and culture would s/he belong to? If a Korean child becomes a Canadian citizen, does s/he become the adjective or the noun in the phrase Korean-Canadian?
> A: There is no such thing as living in the space of the hyphen; a hyphen is just another kind of border.

ENDNOTES

1. See, for example, academic discourses around living in the space of the hyphen and/or hyphenated identities. While working on this research, I found myself frustrated by such discourses, prompting me to write in my journal that:

   [A colleague] feels that there is space in the hyphen. I don't. I was thinking about having two languages and two cultures in this context, and I realized that even my marriage doesn't "dwell in the spaces" between Japanese and Canadian, but in a third place that we have to create together. You can't compromise between cultures when they aren't on a continuum, and how can cultures be opposed on a continuum? Our children will not be Japanese, nor will they be Canadian, or White, or Asian, or whatever, so what does it mean to have kids living in the spaces in between? I don't want my children living in the space of the hyphen. I want them to create something new and different and dynamic, and other. Living

in the space of the hyphen still recognizes a dichotomy, and I don't want that for my family. They will be mixed-race. They will be living the mixture of races.....I can live in the hyphen because I am White...My children won't be able to do that. I don't want them to play in the hyphen—it's such a minimal and bounded space, not even as wide as a typewritten "m." Maybe that is what creates the discomfort and dis-placement, not having enough room. (Researcher Journal, September 30th, 1995, p. 36)

2. As Bretzer (1992) has pointed out, "Monolinguals often feel both excluded and diminished, believing that bilingual code-switchers are drawing a verbal circle around their terrain" (p. 214), and thus "Language...is audible evidence of loss of power for non-Hispanic Whites [in Miami]" (p. 215). In other words, fearing the power that bilinguals enjoy, monolingual English speakers have focused on language usage as the marker for defining inclusion in the cultural community of Americans; thereby, heritage language use becomes one of those "nonessential charcteristics to be relinquished for the sake of assimilation (Bretzer, 1992, p. 215). The Canadian dominant ideology of language is not noticeably distinct from the American (see later), except that in some regions of the country, inclusion is based on the usage of French and/or English.

3 I would very much like to thank Dr. René Galindo for putting into succinct prose the point I was trying to make in this section. I have borrowed his clarity, and in some cases his phraseology, in order to more fully explicate this idea.

12. DWELLING IN THE BORDERLANDS: INTRODUCTION

When I think about the word *borderland*, I realize that it refers to the line demarcating the boundary between two landscapes, like the 49th parallel that runs between us (Canadians) and them (our southern neighbors). However, because I am a Canadian who has grown up on a diet of American television, when I hear the word *borderland*, I do not think of the lush, green wetlands which characterize the frontier between western Canada and the Pacific Northwest, nor the fields of wheat and clover straddling the boundary between the American midwest and the Canadian prairies, nor the rolling hills, the farmland, and the seacoast that run from the Maritimes down into New England, but instead I have images of a barren, arid land, of dust rising from the empty, unpaved streets between clapboard buildings, of lonely, haggard, kerchiefed grandmothers wringing mops off their front stoops (though I have only the vaguest notion of what a stoop is), and of skinny dogs strolling listlessly through the evening heat. It's not a place I want to live. It's not a place where visitors can find a comfortable hotel.

So, who lives there? When I think of this borderland's inhabitants, I do not think of people who freely chose to live there. Instead, I imagine that the in-dwellers of that landscape have somehow been consigned to that life because they do not fit in the fertile, active, dynamic lands that lie to the north and the south. Yet, I also know that they remain for a reason, even if I cannot fathom what that reason may be.

Perhaps, because you have read the previous chapters, you have been able to see that the wasteland image represents what it means to live between two cultures, belonging and yet not belonging to both, between two languages, which are constantly engaged in verbal battles over you and through you, between two homelands, neither and both of which are home to you. The first borderland represents many different and equally rich potentials, healthy living, and vital creativity—what might have been for the inhabitants of the linguistic borderlands (and what has been for Bhabha [1994]). The second borderland represents worry, stagnation, and discomfort, nouns that describe where the residents of the linguistic borderlands have, at least for a time, found themselves living.

INHABITANTS

It is important to introduce, briefly, all of the subjects who participated in

153

the present research study in order to honor the time and energy that they contributed to our understanding of first language loss.

> Er that I ferther in this tale pace,
> Me thinketh it accordant to resoun
> To telle you al the condicioun
> Of eech of hem, so as it seemed me,
> And whiche they were, and of what degree,
> And eek in what array that they were inne:
> (Chaucer, *The Canterbury Tales*, General Prologue, lines 36-41)

Nadia

Nadia was the first person to volunteer for this research project, completing her interviews before the call for subjects was published. A registered nurse, Nadia came to my home to collect urine samples when my husband and I purchased our life insurance. We talked a little bit about our respective professions, and, when I explained the subject of my research, Nadia became excited and said that she would love to participate, because her first language was Ukrainian. Nadia was, in essence, a pilot study. With her, I discussed not only the subject of language loss, but also the best ways to both ask questions and aid people in their struggles with narrating large sections of their lives.

Nadia was born in a small town in Manitoba into a unique linguistic situation, one which left her alone and often lonely. She and her family were Ukrainian-speaking Catholics in a town that was predominantly German and Mennonite. She therefore had to travel outside the town to go to church, and was isolated from many activities. She remembers some German teaching in her school, even though the linguistic norm was English. Nadia also remembers having several reserve First Nations' schoolmates who spoke English as a second language, but she didn't notice their cultural difference when she was very young, and they had largely dropped out of school by the time she was in high school.

Most of Nadia's memories of speaking Ukrainian in childhood revolve around food and ceremonies. This was understandable, given that holidays and festivals were occasions for her family to travel and to visit with other members of their family and their church. As she also explained, "I jumped around and started talking about my culture and stuff. I see many languages associated to a culture, and so, also, when I did family things, that's where Ukrainian was" (June 13th, 1995, p. 30). At the time of our interviews, Nadia was enrolled in Ukrainian lessons through her church, hoping to recapture enough of the language to participate in family conversations, and to surprise her parents on her next visit home.

William

William was one of the subjects who didn't really fit into the parameters of the study, but I chose to interview him because he was able to articulate so well the relationship between language and identity. Born and schooled in Wales, he grew up in a family with strong and proud, nationalistic and cultural ties to the Welsh language, his "language of the hearth" (November 28th, 1995, p. 1). In his family, the reciting and writing of Welsh poetry, and the ability to speak and write articulately and symbolically were highly valued (one of his uncles won the Bardic Chair), yet he remembers being scornful of the less-melodic English language that he was forced to learn at school. He also remembers overhearing family conversations stressing the need to use Welsh, and of being told of his father's experiences of being beaten for speaking English in school. He mentioned a film that I wanted to view, but could not find, called *The Corner is Green*, in which children who spoke Welsh were given a placard inviting other students to ridicule them; the only way for them to get rid of the placard was to hand it on to another child who accidentally spoke Welsh on the school playground. At the present time, the situation in the villages has changed so that, as William explained,

> But I wouldn't dare go back to Wales and speak English for a sustained period of time. It would be absolutely wrong because it...the signal would be..."oh, he thinks he's better than we are. That he's now graduated from the Welsh." The neighbors, whoever, would think this, that he's above it all. You see, there's a strong tradition that people would go away to universities from the village on to Oxbridge or somewhere, and they'd come back at the end of the semester, first term, and they'd have feigned accents, Oxbridge accents; it's the worst thing in the world you could possibly do. It was considered so insulting, and so bad. (December 12th, 1995, p. 9)

Of course, when he went away to the city to university, William did find himself looked down on by the "ignorant monoglot" (ibid., p. 14) English boys, a contempt that ran both ways. Moreover, as he was explaining his choice to study biology in university, he gave evidence that the Welsh language is still under attack:

> ...at what we call the O level, the age 15 exams in the UK, one was obliged not to do Latin, because the timetable was so structured that one did either Welsh or Latin in the timetable. If you proceeded with the Welsh language and Welsh literature, which I did,...then one wasn't able to do Latin, and one's access to, for example, Oxford or Cambridge, or to medicine, was automatically gone because you had to have Latin. (William, November 28th, 1995, p. 7)

Furthering one's knowledge of Welsh, then, remains incompatible with elite professions and elite universities.

After university, wanting to escape the successful but confining life that would have been mapped out for him in Wales, he immigrated to Canada to take a teaching position. He said that his first impression of Canada was that it "must be the biggest pencil box in the world!" (ibid., p. 4), because of the aroma of cedar which greeted him when he landed—and he has never recovered from the wonder of falling in love with this country. Yet, he is nostalgic for a time and a place to speak his language, finding that most of the people who claim to speak Welsh in Canada really don't know it at all. William was moved to tears describing to me a chance comment from his brother-in-law that he, William, must feel really kind of like a fish out of water because he didn't really belong here linguistically, in this "bi-semilingual country masquerading as a semi-bilingual one" (ibid. p. 14).

Dhiet

Dhiet was a young man I tutored in my neighborhood. Under normal circumstances, he would not have volunteered for this study because he didn't read English well enough to read to the newspaper, nor would he have cared to "contribute to knowledge on first language loss," nor would he have appreciated my research, but, by getting to know me slightly, he came to value all of these things a little bit more. Dhiet was extremely difficult to interview, being defensive and angry, and also speaking English with less than native-like fluency. Dhiet was born in Vietnam, and immigrated to Canada through the refugee camps; he therefore spoke pidgin Cantonese and had lost all but the most rudimentary Vietnamese. Dhiet and I communicated by using dictionaries extensively. He explained to me that, prior to their escape from Vietnam, his father had been a prisoner, where he had been forced to violently rape a woman prisoner for the pleasure of the guards. When a child resulted, and the woman died, his mother adopted the child into their own family. When his father was finally released from prison, the family bought passage on an illegal boat. Dhiet explained to me in all seriousness that, on his boat, there was nothing very serious like rape or murder, the passengers did engage in cannibalism. Dhiet's view of the sanctity of human life and my own were somewhat different. His family was involved in business dealings which, although I took care not to ask about them, sounded as if they might be slightly less than legal.

Dhiet considered himself an English-speaker, although he was aware of his limited English ability. Dhiet had an older brother who was fluent in both Vietnamese and English, and two younger siblings who were fluent only in English. He and his younger siblings had been taken away from the family by their social worker because of suspected child abuse, which Dhiet claims was untrue in a Vietnamese sense. Dhiet and his siblings wanted to go home, but they were not allowed to return, even though they ran away from foster care many times. Dhiet finally was able to return home when he turned 16, but his siblings were not allowed to return because they no longer spoke Vietnamese and Dhiet's parents spoke no English. When I met him, Dhiet was very angry because he had to watch his parents struggling to learn English in order to regain custody of their children, when he felt that the children should never have been put in a position in which they lost the language. I don't know how the story ended; Dhiet was arrested and detained in juvenile prison.

Greta

Originally, I wanted to tell Greta's story as one of the five major narratives in this book. Eventually I changed my mind because (a) her complicated situation(s) resulted in too much potential for "explaining away" her language loss as the result of singular, confounding, family problems, and (b) her familial situation could be considered one of adoption or fostering, conditions which I had decided to exclude.

Greta's father, a Dutch Jew, had roomed with a family in a major Dutch city during the war while she and her mother lived in the countryside. After the war, Greta's father left her mother for the woman who ran the boarding house, and Greta's mother had a nervous break-down. After she recovered, her mother carried on an overseas courtship with a Canadian man although Greta wasn't sure how they met or corresponded. (Greta later asked her mother, and found out that the man had lived next door to Greta's mother's sister, and the sister had acted as a correspondence go-between). Greta's mother decided to marry him, and therefore Greta immigrated to Canada from Holland when she was 6 years old, fluent in Dutch. Greta remembers the time onboard the ship, during which, one of the few children, she was the focus of much attention. She remembers arriving in Canada, and traveling by train across the country, she and her mother banding together with other Dutch-speaking passengers to compare under-standings of how Canadian currency worked, and what different food items contained. She remembers finally, arriving in British Columbia, meeting her soon-to-be stepfather, and spending her first night in a cold, dark, strange hotel room, completely alone for the first time in her life.

The household was not a particularly happy one. Greta's new father forbade (with physical reinforcement) the use of Dutch in the home, and, as backup, Greta's stepbrother, approximately the same age as Greta, was entrusted with policing their language usage when the father was not at home. Greta's mother internalized her husband's attitude toward the Dutch language also, telling her daughter that Dutch wasn't a nice language. Greta's mother never learned English well, but she continued to speak only in broken English with her daughter as long as Greta lived in that household. Greta even now is filled with anger directed at her stepfather:

> *I was really resentful that my stepfather could force that situation on me; I mean, I probably would have lost that language quite quickly anyway, but I sort of pinned it on him that I did because the minute I did feel badly for losing, I think I blamed him, maybe more than I had to, but the blame is certainly there.* (July 12th, 1995, p. 9)

At the time I met her, Greta had, in one sense, reclaimed her Dutch heritage. She had married a Dutch-speaking, Canadian-born man, and had developed a very close relationship with her in-laws. She spoke often of how much she admired the way they had kept both cultural traditions alive in their family, and how they had ensured that their children spoke the Dutch language. I really loved Greta. I loved her company, her manner, her way of speaking, her home, her family, her sense of style. I really enjoyed spending time with her, and getting to know her.

Alexandra

Alexandra asserted many times that she was unaffected by the loss of the German language which she had spoken until she was about 9 or 10, that in fact, the loss of German had been extremely beneficial to her.[1] She insisted that the only loss she felt was the loss of opportunity to speak a second language. She told me these things so many times, and so forcefully, that I stopped believing her.

Born on the prairies, Alexandra was the youngest of six children in a German-speaking household. Her mother was her father's second wife; her three oldest siblings were half-brothers. When Alexandra was 10 years old, her own mother died and her father couldn't manage both his family and his farm. Her three oldest brothers, aged 16, 18, and 20, moved out on their own, while the three youngest children became wards of the state and were placed in foster care with families who did not speak or understand German. When her family split up, Alexandra did not maintain contact with her father because she felt betrayed.

Instead, she considered the family that she lived with and grew up with to be her family, and she never even discussed her former family with her foster family. Although she had some desire to maintain contact with her siblings, because she felt no *need* to see them, and because her foster parents would have found it difficult to accommodate her desire to see her former siblings, she seldom had any contact with them.

She remembers speaking German at her brother's wedding 4 months after her family broke up, but that is the last recollection she has of being in a German-speaking environment. At this time she doesn't remember any German words at all; in fact, she says she can't even count to 10 in German.

Kuong

Kuong immigrated to Canada from Vietnam when he was 3 or 4 years old, and first lived near Windsor, Ontario because his family's sponsor lived in a small town there. He attended school there for Grades 1, 2, and 3, and, because he was instructed in both French and English, believed the two languages were just different dialects until he moved out to British Columbia in Grade 4. He remembers absolutely nothing of his primary school classrooms, although he can remember the walk to school, and the fear that he felt when he heard little children screaming in the principal's office. He thought maybe he didn't remember the classrooms because he never understood anything during his primary schooling; his first recollections of instruction are from Grade 4 when he was finally able to understand some of the things the teacher said.

Kuong has an older sibling attending college who is fluent in both Vietnamese and English, and whom he envies, and an older sibling attending a School for the Deaf who signs and lip-reads only in English. His younger brother is in jail; apparently there was some confusion about his date of birth when the family immigrated, so the Canadian authorities believe his 16-year-old brother to be an adult, and have imprisoned him accordingly.

Kuong's parents don't speak very much English. Because Kuong got mixed up with drugs and crime when he was still in elementary school, he has been in and out of group homes. Because he has therefore been predominantly in English-speaking environments, he doesn't speak Vietnamese, yet he also knows that he has serious difficulties in reading, writing, and expressing himself in English. Kuong feels that he will never be gainfully employed in Canada. He doesn't have the grammatical skill necessary for white-collar work, and he doesn't have the physical strength (because of heroin addiction) for blue-collar work.

His parents have offered to buy him a fishing boat if he finishes Grade 10 (he was 18 years old at the time of the interviews in 1995), but he doesn't speak enough Vietnamese to communicate with other fishermen. He thinks he'll probably only live another 10 years because of his lifestyle and because of how he earns a living; however, he reasons that, if he limited himself to legal employment, he wouldn't even be able to survive for 10 years.

Kurt, Cameron, and Julian

These interviews were a family affair, and provided a lot of interesting insights into family dynamics and language loss. Kurt, the father, was a political refugee who had spent almost 9 months in prison in Poland under martial law, and who arrived in Canada as a single man in 1983. Six years later, he returned to Poland to visit and became reacquainted with a former university friend who had been widowed. They married, and, in 1990, she immigrated to Canada with her two sons, aged almost 7 and almost 5. Kurt contacted me because his sons were losing their Polish and I think he hoped that I could offer his family some advice. He also hoped that my research would result in educational change, and that his sons would not then lose Polish. I interviewed Kurt and his two sons individually. Because their immigration and subsequent loss of Polish is so recent, they were all able to relate stories of incidents at school and in the community. Although the boys first thought that coming to Canada was a joke and that they would return to Poland, they later realized that they were here for good. They now are both trying to relearn Polish because they want to go back to visit friends and relatives.

Alex

Alex is a borderlander who is also the son of borderlanders. His mother was born to Russian immigrants in Chicago, but moved to Russia when her parents returned there after the Revolution. She moved into a border town that had once been the southwest part of Poland, just north of the Ukraine, but which had become part of White Russia. Living in such a linguistically diverse region, Alex's parents spoke Polish and White Russian (a dialect) and standard Russian, depending on the situation. When Alex was born, they adopted Polish as the home language. They moved to a vibrant Polish-speaking community in the United States when Alex was 3 years and 3 months old. They later moved to northern Canada where several of their relatives lived, and where they were able to communicate in Ukrainian, another language spoken by both of his parents.

Alex remembers beginning school, and he remembers the day when his Polish first name was changed to Alex so that his teachers could more easily pronounce it. Like Kuong, he has no recollection of Grade 1 and 2, though he has clear memories of Grade 3 and following (after he could speak English) and of playschool and kindergarten (when he played and had fun in Polish). While Alex was growing up, his parents relied on him to translate English into Polish for them; his father worked in a foundry and did not require English, while his mother stayed home. When I met him, Alex could speak only a little, broken, Polish, and could follow a very basic conversation in Polish. He remembers being much more fluent, and he feels like he is losing Polish bit-by-bit, day-by-day.

Naomi

Naomi guesses that her language skills are roughly equivalent to that of a 6-year-old Japanese child. I would approximate them somewhat earlier. Born in an internment camp in "what was called a hospital" but was "basically a barn" (October 19th, 1995, p. 1), Naomi spoke only Japanese until she was 6 years old, at which time her monolingual Japanese grandmother died, and Naomi started school. She remembers watching the other children to see what she was supposed to be doing in the classroom.

Naomi's situation is unique because she was not only a visible minority, but also a ridiculed one, belonging to a cultural group that was despised after World War II. She remembers being called a "dirty Jap," and she also recalls wanting to learn English as quickly as possible. She recalls that "it was more that the Japanese language was sort of *driven from* us, because we wanted to fit in so badly, and people would stare, say that we were plotting things, or whatever, and that's where, in my age group, and for a lot of the older people, I think that's where a lot of language got lost" [my emphasis] (October 19th, 1995, p. 8). Like Ariana and Greta, Naomi uses violent language to describe the loss of her language.

Naomi adapted, and even married a Caucasian man in the days of few mixed marriages. They have one daughter, who "thinks nothing of going up to someone and saying 'Oh, are you a halfie?, what halfie are you?'" (October 19th, 1995, p. 18), which Naomi feels is a positive reflection on her daughter's generation. Only recently, Naomi has begun to study Japanese conversation in a language exchange situation. When she began, she was upset to discover that she couldn't even express the most basic of sentences without making mistakes, despite assuming that she was still able to "get by" in conversation. Yet, she feels that she has internalized the Japanese value system, and many concepts for which there are no English equivalents, and, for instance, is always badgering her daughter to work hard at school so as not to bring "haji" (shame) into the family. Naomi herself has internalized a lot of the prejudice she experienced as a child, and she explains that "I probably try harder to be the perfect parent, because I don't want her friends' parents to say "Oh, [Janice] is the way she is because her mom's a Jap"" (October 3rd, 1995, p. 11).

Hana Kim

Born in Korea, Hana Kim came with her parents on a temporary overseas assignment to Canada when she was 4 years old. Because they were planning to return to Korea in 3 years, her parents did not expect the children to speak Korean, but instead let them "do what came naturally" (June 20th, 1995, p. 1), going to English playschool, watching TV, and speaking English at home. At the end of 3 years when her parents had decided to immigrate, Hana Kim was still able to speak Korean, but she began losing it when she was in Grade 2. By the time she was 11 years old and they returned to Korea for a visit, she was almost unable to communicate. She returned again when she was 17 years old, and was able to understand some basic things, but was unable to say what she wanted to say. Oddly enough, Hana Kim returned to Korea once again when she was in her late 20s, and, at that time, many of her relatives commented that her Korean had improved. She mused that,

> I think as I've gotten older—I think maybe I'm concentrating more, and I understand how the language works more, because you're more mature, and I think that's allowing me to speak it a bit better. (June 20th, 1995, p. 2)

Yet, accustomed to being a very articulate speaker (Hana Kim works as a television broadcaster and anchorwoman), she felt frustrated by her inability to communicate her ideas and comments. She was also frustrated that people in Korea would "see that you've got a Korean face" and then "they kind of expect you to be able to speak Korean too. If you're White it doesn't matter; they don't have those expectations, you know" (June 30th, 1995, p. 7).

Even were she to still speak Korean, Hana Kim would likely have become a broadcaster. As a child in Korea, she used to mimic the broadcasters on the radio from the time she began to talk. On the other hand, she also feels that growing up speaking English to parents who couldn't speak the language also contributed to her choice of profession because she had to learn to speak slowly, deliberately, and carefully, and to constantly evaluate the difficulty of her vocabulary. She therefore didn't have to change her speech habits in order to train as a news reporter.

Minette

On the day the call for subjects for my research study was published, my telephone rang at 6:45 a.m. It was Minette. A professional writer, Minette had lost her husband a few months previously, and had been reflecting on her loss of her native French after receiving letters of condolence from her relatives in Belgium. She spoke of sitting at her desk "trying to acknowledge them with my pen in one hand and my French/English dictionary in the other, and piece together pidgin French to try to thank them, and try to tell them what this loss has meant in my life" (June 19th, 1995, p. 2).

Minette immigrated to Canada when she was about 3 years old, but began school speaking with a heavy European accent because, although her mother spoke eight languages, English being one of them, she never acquired native-like pronunciation. Minette remembers being helped with her pronunciation by her Grade 1 teacher, and she recalls that it took several years before she was able to speak like others and become "truly assimilated and...one of the gang" (June 19th, 1995, p. 4), perhaps because she came home and spoke with a European accent, not wanting her mother "to know [she] was engaged in this process" (June 19th, 1995, p. 14). Even now Minette feels more comfortable speaking English with a European accent; she feels like her Canadian accent is artificial, a "layer of veneer...[that] has been deliberately applied" (June 19th, 1995, p. 3), the way I feel when I try to speak like an Australian English speaker, or a Texan.

Because she makes a living from wordcraft, Minette was able to describe language loss to me in metaphor. Describing the process, she explained that,

> ...it's kind of like an old pair of underwear slipping down I guess. The elastic goes and goes and you're not really conscious of it. It's not as though it snaps and then your drawers are down around your ankles. This is just a loosening of the bond.... (June 19th, 1995, p. 4)

A reflective person, Minette was also able to offer the best description I have ever encountered of learning to love a country after immigrating to it:

I suspect, initially when you come to a country, well, it's like a marriage. You can't expect total devotion and very deep feelings for the first year or two. You don't understand. You think you're getting it, but you don't understand the depth that comes with years and with maturity in a relationship. And, you can't be expected to understand that. (July 11th, 1995, p. 12)

Nellie

Nellie remembers that she really didn't want to come here from Hong Kong when she was 6 years old, and she remembers saying "I don't want to go there; I don't know how to speak the language" (October 6th, 1995, p. 1). At first, she was really quiet in class, and she'd spend time on her own during recess, and eat lunch alone, because she was too afraid to talk to anybody, but she remembers also feeling confident during math class because her math skills were so far advanced. After her first year (Grade 2), which she spent in an ESL class with six other students from different grades and different first languages, she began to feel more confident in English, but she sometimes slipped in Cantonese words when she got excited, and then she became fluent, and then she began using English at home. Her parents even commented to her that "it's good that you learned English, but when you're home, we'd like you to speak Cantonese" (October 6th, 1995, p. 2). But, there was no one in her school or her neighborhood who spoke Cantonese, and she was able to speak to her siblings and her parents in English without being punished, and so that is what she did. From that time forward, she remembers being quiet whenever she was immersed in a Cantonese-language environment.

The pampered baby in her family, Nellie found that language loss did not really affect her relationships with her father or sister, but it did make her relationships with her mother and her brother more distant. As her brother was never able to become comfortable in English, he chose not to respect her language abilities, refusing even to slow his speaking pace, or adjust his vocabulary, in Cantonese. Nellie speaks of him with coldness. Her mother now admits that she really disliked Nellie when Nellie was growing up because her mother was unable to understand her.

As a teenager and young adult, Nellie had a long-term relationship with a Caucasian boyfriend. Her parents, particularly her mother, were extremely upset by the relationship, even moving to Toronto in the hope that she would forget about him. Their plan backfired; Nellie instead refused to leave Vancouver, and moved out on her own. Over time, and with the evolution of her relationship, she decided to move to Toronto, but, by the time she announced her decision to her parents, they had already made arrangements to move back to Vancouver. Nellie was also frustrated by Chinese cultural standards. Whereas she was an above-average student who didn't drink, smoke, or do drugs, who never got into trouble, who didn't date until she was 16, and who took on responsibility in school, she didn't meet the criteria for a "good" Chinese girl. Only over time, when Nellie was in her mid-20s, and with Canadianization did her parents come to appreciate her in Canadian terms.

Michael

After immigrating to Toronto from Portugal at the age of 1 or 2, Michael didn't learn to speak English until he began Grade 1. When he started school, it became obvious to his teacher that Michael couldn't speak English very well, and so she encouraged his parents to speak to him in that language at home. They tried, but by the time Michael was in Grade 3 and able to function well in school, they reverted to Portuguese in the home. The pattern was well-established however, and Michael continued to reply to them in English.

Apart from his language difficulties, Michael doesn't recall much of his early years of school except that he was in trouble a lot. He "spent a lot of time in the corner" (November 17th, 1995, p. 1), which he attributes to "language issues," and to the fact that he didn't get a lot of support at school. Later, his language issues were multiplied when, during puberty, he simultaneously returned to Portugal for a visit, and also began having speech difficulty when his voice started changing. According to his speech therapist, he began using his false vocal chords; he began feeling very self-conscious using the English language. When he visited Portugal during the summer vacation, he began to feel more comfortable around the Portuguese language, and, at the same time, he stopped using his false vocal chords. It is a chicken-and-egg question whether he feels more comfortable with the sounds and rhythm of Portuguese than with English because his language difficulty was solved in Portugal, or if his language difficulty was solved in Portugal because he felt more comfortable with the language. Either way, it is a moot point; he can no longer speak the language, even having difficulty in retrieving single words.

Charles

My husband met Charles in a course he was taking and brought him home, demonstrating how life has an impact on research, and research on life. Charles was at a period in his life when he was trying to recapture his "Japanese-ness" and so he sought out a relationship with my husband. My husband, happy to be befriended by a "real Canadian," soon realized that Charles was one of the people I was describing in my research. It is odd how their perceptions of each other embodied mutual need.

Born in Vancouver to a Japanese mother and a Japanese-speaking Taiwanese father, Charles was an average student who grew up speaking Japanese until the advent of *Sesame Street*.[2] By the time he was in kindergarten, Charles was speaking English to his siblings and Japanese to his parents. At the present time, he mixes Japanese and English together, but English forms the basis of his sentences, while Japanese nouns and phrases are thrown in. His Japanese is therefore subjected to Anglicization. He would describe himself as Japanese-Canadian (emphasizing the adjective rather than the noun because he feels that "Japanese" is a racial descriptor while "Canadian" is not), but is quick to point out that this is a misnomer as he is more Canadian than Japanese. "Canadian-Japanese" sounds funny though, he thinks.

Charles attended a high school that was more than 80% Asian. The majority of students were Chinese, but, because he was physically indistinguishable from the Chinese students, he was lumped together with them as the "high-achieving Asians." He recalls experiencing a lot of racism from Caucasian students who thought of him as Asian, and also from other Asian students who recognized him as "other."

∞∞∞∞∞∞∞∞∞∞∞∞

Now that a few of the more salient characteristics/aspects of each of the borderland's inhabitants have been brought forward, it is time to hear what they have to say about dwelling in the borderlands. Borderland life profoundly affected the inhabitants in terms of five "umbrella" categories: (1) family relationships, (2) self-image and cultural identity, (3) school relationships, (4) school performance, and (5) the meaning of "loss." They are presented here in hierarchy, beginning with the most prioritized and most prevalent, family relationships.

ENDNOTES

1. I have come to be very suspicious of such claims, which are often used to contradict research directed at heritage language maintenance. Through this project, after close questioning of subjects who initially said similar things, I have come to realize that they do not mean they are glad to have lost the first language, but rather that, if they had to be monolingual, then they are glad to be monolingual in English rather than in some other language. I have not met

any person who has said "I am glad I don't speak that language anymore," though that is not to say such people do not exist.

2. This one television program came up in interviews over and over again. It seems to have had an extraordinary impact.

13. FAMILY RELATIONSHIPS

Perhaps the most common familial consequence of first language loss is the subsequent "loss" of extended family. Many of the subjects explained that they did not maintain contact with grandparents, aunts, uncles, or cousins who either remained in the first language country, or who immigrated yet never learned to speak English. Sometimes this was a source of anger and frustration, while at other times subjects simply reported that they never contacted their extended families again:

> I have a loss that I kind of wish, "Well, I wish that I could write a letter in Polish, however simplistic", or for example to my Russian relatives who I haven't talked to—I don't think I've ever talked to them since we moved to Canada in '68.... (Alex, December 5th, 1995, p. 18; see also Brian's story)

Oddly enough, anger and frustration seemed more common in Asian families than in European families, though European language groups also expressed frustration with the inevitability of language loss. Although language loss was something they knew about and sought to prevent, they still were unable to halt the process, and instead learned to understand and accept why it happens:

> I think there are close to 40 million people living in Poland and 10 million Poles living abroad, but people make jokes of people living abroad, forgetting their native language, speaking pidgin Polish, making funny mistakes, speaking with American accent in Polish language and, when I was in Poland I couldn't understand—"Why do you forget your native language? It's so obvious you should cherish"—all that stuff blah, blah, blah. When I came here and I realized the adaptation process is very difficult and you have to make up your mind do you want to live in Polish ghetto and be only among Polish friends, or do you want to assimilate and be successful here? It's a little bit different perspective. And my wife, her cousin I think lives in Toronto, and they were an elderly couple, I think they are in their 60s, 70s now, and their sons who are successful engineers, and one I think is lawyer, second generation, they don't speak Polish at all. And they were an object of big condemnation in Poland: "Oh, they went to Toronto and they left after Second World War and now their children don't even speak Polish"—my wife wouldn't understand it. When I visited Poland, she told me about that and she thought it was outrageous. After a few years, we had a discussion about this couple, and it's completely different perspective, well it's not so easy. Now I can see from the other side, now I can understand it. (Kurt, March 6th, 1996, p. 8)

Moreover, the younger subjects seemed more willing to accept the familial breakdown than were older people. Once subjects had faced parental decline and mortality, they seemed to realize that their link to the heritage language and culture was about to be severed, and they often reported trying to contact family members, even struggling to relearn some of the heritage language in order to write letters and arrange visits. For Minette, the trigger was the loss of her husband and the wish to reply to the many letters of bereavement she had received from family in Belgium. For Michael, a persistent desire to see the land of his birth finally prompted attempts to write to relatives in Portugal. For Hana Kim, a postmarriage trip to Korea instilled shame and a renewed commitment to relearning the language to pass on to her children. For Nadia, the realization that her parents were aging caused her to become determined that familial Ukrainian language use would not end with her. Of course, for others like Lara, the loss or impending loss of their parents made them aware that attempts to regain the language were futile. Unless her children opted to study the Finnish language and try to trace their roots, she felt she had to accept that the language was gone with her generation.

The loss of family communications sometimes resulted from a deliberate rejection of the first language, followed by a growing reluctance to spend time with non-English-speaking relatives:

> It just wasn't fun to speak Chinese anymore because I was, now I was practicing the English language and I was having a lot of fun because I was now mastering it, and I started speaking English with everybody. I mean, you know, it didn't matter whether it was my mother or my sister or anything, and my grandmother, at the time, she doesn't speak English, and when I went to visit her, I would speak broken Chinese, a lot of it with English in there. And she used to get really mad at me, because, you know, she used to say "I don't understand those words, so you're going to have to say them in Chinese," and, pretty soon I felt that my relationship with my grandmother kind of suffered because I didn't want to speak Chinese anymore.... (Nellie, October 6th, 1995, p. 2)

> And then my maternal grandparents, my grandmother, used to always scream at us in Ukrainian [because we couldn't speak it]. And...she'd just surprise us because she'd be nattering away in Ukrainian the whole day and then all of a sudden the Hog report would come on and she'd turn it on and listen to it in English, and she'd be nodding away, and we're going like "Mom, how does she understand; she won't speak English?" (Nadia, June 8th, 1995, p. 2; see also Ariana's story)

At other times, it was while spending time with relatives that subjects first became aware that they had lost the language. Although they had been able to communicate with their parents in the L1, they were then surprised to learn that they could not communicate with other people. This led to a sudden realization that (a) their parents had adjusted their L1 linguistic output to their children's level of L1 ability, or that (b) they were only conversant with one register of the language. Michael explained that,

*I'm comfortable with their accents and their pace. I find it more difficult when
[other people]...come and celebrate festivities with us, and I find that some of
the language they use is hard, a little harder for me...and it's not technical
language or anything; it's still just personal conversation, but they use words
that I guess my parents don't always use....* (November 17th, 1995, p. 4)

One of the most dramatic stories was that told by Christine during a
pilot interview in November 1992. Fluent in Cantonese until beginning
school in Canada's Maritimes, she completely lost her L1 while still in
elementary school. She told of watching home videos in which she was
interacting with her mother and grandmother in Cantonese—and of
being absolutely unable to understand a word that she herself was
saying in the videos. She had no recollection of ever being able to speak
to her non-English-speaking relatives until she had viewed the videos.
Similarly, Greta (like Lara in the previous story) had no recollection of
the language she was speaking, although she knows she must have
spoken it on occasions that she can recall vividly:

*I do [remember speaking Dutch]. but that's a funny thing because how can
you remember speaking if you don't remember the actual sort of soundtrack in
your mind? I mean the soundtrack is not there, or I would remember the
words, but I remember always talking and people, and I was an only child at
that time, but I remember always having neighborhood friends [in Holland].*
(Greta, July 12th, 1995, p. 8)

In cases where the parents didn't learn to speak English fluently, the
loss of family moved closer to home. It became difficult for the parents
to be influential in their children's lives, to guide them, to nurture them,
or even to encourage their learning at school by helping with their
homework or discussing the day's events. Kuong explained that,

*I didn't write too fast, and just we do stuff like for one day, and like next day
was different stuff, different stuff. You have to finish the work in one day and
stuff, and I, I take homework maybe once a week to try it out, and like, I need
help. Like the stuff, the spelling and stuff, and all that, vocabulary, and I can't
read when I was little, right?* (September 9th, 1994, p. 6)

But there was nobody at home who could help him; he recalls being
asked to read aloud in Grade 7, and being unable to read any of the
words at all. In fact, he claims that he didn't learn to read until Grade 8,
when he was given individual instruction, when a teacher recognized his
inability, then took the time to teach him.

When parents were unable to speak English, the situation also often
led to an inversion of family relationships. Children became the
designated English-speakers, the contact person for schools, banks,
stores, and other social institutions. They often had to deal with complex

matters without fully understanding the context, and without fully being able to understand what their parents wanted them to do. They reported that their parents lost self-confidence, and, in many ways, lost the ability to parent, because, as both Alex and Nellie put it, "I can speak English; it's something I have *over* my parents" (Alex, November 16th, 1995, p. 12). This was much more prevalent among younger, and more recently immigrated subjects, many of whom alternated between feeling sorry for their parents on the one hand, and admiring them for their determination and their willingness to take on any kind of employment in order to support the family on the other.

And, because they didn't speak English, many university-educated parents were only able to gain employment as salespeople, unskilled laborers, restaurant workers, cleaners—though it is testimony to some parents' determination that, even with limited English abilities, they eventually became self-employed, starting businesses ranging from construction contracting to owning a pet store. Not all parents were able to "escape" their language difficulties, however. Greta, for instance, explained why her mother couldn't afford to leave her abusive husband, even though a social worker advised her that he could likely be committed to a mental health institution:

> You know, "how would I live?, how could I support?, and he told me that I would lose all the children if I left." You know, he would tell her all these things just to keep control, but one of the things was language, and she just didn't feel that she could make her way, speaking such broken English. So it was a real tie, that it was like a chain that kept her there. (August 2nd, 1995, p. 16)

Moreover, non-English-speaking parents tended to have a different set of cultural standards than their children, still holding onto the values and mores of the first language culture, while their children adopted Western cultural norms. This was exacerbated by the parents' inability to "keep up with" changing cultural values, in the way that parents are often called upon to do, either in the L1 or in the L2:

> They were 1950s Finnish, that culture, and, for the most part, when we moved into [small town, Manitoba]. I think that they maintained that same era in their way of thinking about society as a whole, and I don't think they ever really felt secure....And you have to realize that people in Finland moved beyond that and were now 90s people, or 70s, or 60s, or whatever, and my parents never really integrated and adopted the North American and the [northern Manitoba] culture, if you want to call it that.... (Lara, August 7th, 1995, p. 9)

> To explain to my parents what rock and roll is and why I like it, was difficult

because in Poland when they left, at that time, there was no rock and roll. They would hear the music and all that, and they would ask me "Well, what do you like about this noise?", and it would be difficult for me to explain to them, why did I like it? I'd say "It makes me feel alive," and tapping my toes, and my dad would say "Good, go mow the lawn." (Alex, November 16th, 1995, p. 11)

And, realization that their parents couldn't always understand what they were involved in, led to frustration. Alex spoke of his difficulty in trying to explain to his White Russian-speaking parents what he wanted to do for a living. He became a computer programmer and analyst, something he was never able to explain to his parents. They had immigrated in the days before computer use was widespread, from a rural area in Poland where their Grade 7 education was considered excessive to their needs, and they had never learned to speak English with any degree of fluency. Alex, for his part, never mastered any but the most basic White Russian or Polish, and could not explain his choice of courses, of career, nor even the necessity to study hard, to them in any meaningful way:

And my mother was—she didn't—she was happy about it too, but she didn't really understand the concept, I mean, she couldn't really understand "why are you spending so many hours? Why is it that four times a year you seem to be buried in your books for nights on end and your eyes look terrible?" She couldn't understand the concept whatsoever. That's a good example. Language barrier; I could not explain to her what it is I'm studying like, computers—totally no way you could explain it to her—no way. I never explained it to her—she just assumed that I knew what I was doing, and I used to say "Don't worry about it. For me to explain it to you, I'd literally have to teach you it, and I'm learning it myself right now, so—" (Alex, November 16th, 1995, pp. 15-16).

Alex told me that both his parents died without ever understanding what he did for a living, without ever realizing that he had been successful in Canada in academic, social, and economic terms, that he had, in fact, fulfilled the dreams that they had had for him, and for which they had chosen to immigrate.

Other subjects told me how they were able to deceive their parents because of the inability to communicate. In her story, Helena explained at length how she would knowingly lie to her parents and then cover up her lies by incorporating her lie with the truth when her parents confronted her; fortunately, Helena was a good student who never got into any serious trouble. Even so, lack of communication eventually led to her leaving home in anger and having to struggle to complete school and continue to university. Many other subjects also talked about their ability to deceive their parents about school activities or report cards, about the price of things they needed to have for school (inflating both

the price and the need), about the courses they were taking in high
school, about the precise gender mix, location, and nature of parties,
about relationships, about drug use.

The frustration and disappointment in losing an L1 often manifested
itself as a kind of anger toward the parents, best described by Nadia:

> I think a lot of times I blame my mom and dad. If my grandmother could still
> scream [at my parents for not teaching us Ukrainian], I'd probably scream with
> her now. (June 13th, 1995, p. 20)

Although the subjects realized that their parents did the best they could
with what was available to them, they often felt residual resentment that
their parents had not forced them to continue speaking their first
languages, or worse, that their parents had encouraged them to pursue
English because it would be more instrumental in their careers, but later
criticized them for being unable to speak their first languages. They felt
that their parents, or their teachers, should have foreseen the loss of the
first language and done something to prevent it because, as Greta explained, children or teenagers themselves wouldn't understand the
importance:

> When you're a teenager you have so many other concerns, and, it just sort of
> slipped away and I didn't realize what I had lost until it was gone. (Greta,
> July 12th, 1995, p. 3; see also Richard's story)

To the good, not a few of the subjects in this study told me that their
participation had helped to mend broken family relationships. They
explained that many of the questions I had asked triggered their own
curiosity and they then questioned their parents about things they'd
never before discussed. The parents were often pleased that their
children were expressing an interest in their heritage cultures, and felt
encouraged to tell stories. To me, this was the most gratifying part of
this research project. Minette discovered that one of the many books her
father had written in Belgian French about his war experiences had been
translated into English, and she chose to read it. Michael had always
blamed himself for the change in his family language patterns (which
resulted in all of his siblings also losing Portuguese), believing that his
teacher had asked his parents to speak English at home after she realized
that his English skills were not improving. He found out instead that his
parents had followed the standard advice given to Portuguese parents in
their school district, that he wasn't individually to blame. Greta discovered that discussions focused on language were a nonthreatening way
for her to speak to her mother about her biological father who had

deserted them in Holland, and her mother's choice to become a Canadian war bride, resulting in an abusive relationship.

I wish that I could report that all parents were pleased that children were participating in this research project, but unfortunately, there were some misgivings as well. Of all the parents I could have potentially interviewed (excepting those who volunteered their children for the study), not one actually met with me, despite my repeated invitations. I'm not entirely sure why this happened. In some cases, I think that there was reluctance on the subjects' part to have the parents interviewed. I felt that many subjects preferred to be the link between me and their stories, perhaps because they feared contradiction, and perhaps because the relationship we developed was special to them, not to be shared. As I wrote in my journal,

> I am becoming increasingly hesitant to try contacting parents and other relatives in this research. Although a number of people have signed a release for me to contact their relatives, after several interviews I have the distinct impression that they'd rather I didn't, that they'd prefer to be the mediators for me. I can understand this; they have struggled to give me a truth, and sometimes the things that they remember give me knowledge that could hurt them in terms of their familial relationships. They respect me and they fear contradiction, which might culminate in my losing respect for them. They have not tried to mislead me; instead they have been brutally honest I feel, but I sense they fear being doubted. (Researcher Journal, October 11th, 1995)

Other times, I suspected that parents didn't want to be interviewed because they feared that their English wasn't good enough, but they were still hesitant to speak to a translator. I thought perhaps too many parents feared the nature of the interview, worried that they might be forced to realize that "they did something wrong" and that they had caused their children's language loss. In any event, although third-party interviews with parents had been part of my original plan, I chose to forgo those interviews because they seemed to cause distress. Instead, if I had questions I wanted answered, I asked the subjects if they would mind asking their parents about it, and they almost invariably came back with second-hand accounts, which they relayed to me orally or in writing.[1]

It has become apparent to me, in exploring the complexity of family relationships when language loss is involved, that there is a lot of shame, anger, frustration, and embarrassment attached to the loss of a first language. Researchers such as Extra (1989), Hakuta and D'Andrea (1992), Folmer (1992), and Grosjean (1982, cited in Harres, 1989) have described a gradual, smooth process, in which each succeeding generation speaks and understands less of the L1. It is quite clear that this picture is overly optimistic. There are first-, second-, and third-generation Canadians involved in this study who have lost their first languages, and, in each case, it has been the individuals in one generation that have lost the language. It is they, and their parents, who must bear the stigma and feel the shame and disappointment at losing a part of their cultural heritage.

ENDNOTES

1. Moreover, I concur with the argument that "interviewing multiple family members, asking about specific events poses an ethical dilemma, since it requires revealing parts of previous interviews from other persons in the family" (LaRossa, Bennett, & Gelles, cited in Fischer, 1983, p. 38).

14. SELF-IMAGE AND CULTURAL IDENTITY

I think the one thing that I find, I guess, the most—I wouldn't say repellent, but I would say antagonistic—for me is identity. The notion of a single identity. And so multiple identity, the polyphony of many voices playing off against each other, without, as I say, the need to reconcile them, just to hold them together.... More than one culture, more than one awareness, both in its negative and its positive modes.
—Edward Said (in Marranca, Robinson, & Chaudhuri, 1991, p. 43)

Perhaps the most complex issues raised in this research concerned self-image and cultural identity. A negative self-image seemed to be highlighted in virtually every aspect of this research study, whether because subjects hadn't been able to receive positive reinforcement from their relatives and immediate family, or because they blamed themselves for their language loss—as Nadia explained, she was frustrated with herself because "I just see it as a freebie, and I missed out on a freebie, and now I have to pay for it" (Nadia, July 21st, 1995, p. 10)—or because they assumed that stupidity must be a factor in language loss:

> *And I don't understand how I could have lost it. I wonder like, what—is there something wrong with me that I lost this language? I mean, I'm not stupid; why, why did I suddenly lose it? And that my parents spoke it—ahh, it baffles me, too* (Hana Kim, June 20th, 1995, p. 5),

or because they had absorbed the myth of a singular unified identity and couldn't reconcile that image with their own experiences. In fact, during many interviews, I found myself in a counseling position, assuring the storytellers that language loss in no way implies any kind of innate inferiority, or reinforcing their defensive claims that they could not possibly be stupid, given all of their accomplishments.[1]

Most disturbing to me, in terms of negative self-image, were subjects who had adopted a very negative view of their own cultural heritage or race.[2] This took two forms. When their negative views turned inward, they felt shame about their heritage, and often tried to adopt other cultural norms. Helena talked of how she always wanted a nice *White* name, and joked that she had never dated any men who did not have simple Anglo last names. During the course of my interviews with many of the Asian subjects, I heard the old chestnut that they were "bananas," by which they meant that they were yellow on the outside, but white on the inside. Richard, a Cree spirit,[3] described himself as an "apple", in this case, red on the outside and white on the inside. Although none of them seems ashamed to connect themselves with fruit in this manner, I felt uncomfortable. I wondered whether it was one of those things—it's okay to call yourself a banana, but it is not okay to call someone else one. And, what kind of fruits are we, those of us who are white on the outside (or rather, beige), but we don't feel that we fit in with "White culture" on the inside?

The negative view was sometimes turned outward, particularly with the subjects I would uncomfortably refer to as "visible minorities." In this form, negative self-image translated as racism within a race. Although the most pronounced manifestation of it that I encountered was in Ariana's story, I met up with racism against one's own race many times, in many contexts, and to many degrees:

> *I find that people who speak Cantonese are very loud and I think it's an ugly language; I mean the sounds that you make are really ugly....I think Cantonese—it comes across a lot of times as rude almost because at times—the tendency to speak very loud almost, and the sounds that you make, and so I, I just don't tend to associate, don't want to really associate with people like that?* (Nellie, November 3rd, 1995, p. 4)

> *And I get really embarrassed if I, if I, if there's a group nearby.—I don't want people to think, "Oh yeah, she's one of them, you know, and that's the way she is, too." And I just find it very offensive. I just don't like it.* (Nellie, November 3rd, 1995, p. 4)

> *We wanted to forget we were Japanese—[laughs] because we were still the enemy after the war.* (Naomi, October 3rd, 1995, p. 1)

A more subtle form of racism against one's own race is found in many subjects who wanted to differentiate themselves from more recent immigrant groups:

> *And, I, like, I think if I walked into a room full of Chinese people, I would almost be tempted to use my English just to have them know that I—I'm better in some ways because I have access to both languages.* (Nellie, October 6th, 1995, p. 11; see also Brian's story about his Korean roommate)

Yet, even more subtle indications of, if not racism, then bias, could be found. Nadia, for instance, constantly referred to speakers of Ukrainian as "nattering" (June 8th, 1995, p. 2) or "blabbing" (June 8th, 1995, p. 9) or "babbling" (June 8th, 1995, p. 18), or "screaming" (June 13th, 1995, p. 8) or "rattling" (July 21st, 1995, p. 8) in the Ukrainian language, making the language sound childish or immature, its speakers nonsensical and annoying.

Also very common among these subjects is an uncertainty about their own identities, manifested as an inability to identify with either the heritage culture or the dominant (English) culture. I was struck by the number of times Ariana, Brian, Naomi, Nellie, Alexandra, and others referred to themselves as "Canadianized" rather than Canadian. When I questioned them about this curious usage, I was told that, indeed, they were Canadian citizens, but they were "not permitted" to be Canadian, particularly when they were in a group of White Canadians, so they were Canadianized.

> *You don't know, are you really Canadian, or are you Chinese? Are you Chinese-Canadian or are you Chinese? You don't know. It's this identity crisis.* (Ariana, June 22nd, 1995, p. 5)

> *I see myself very Canadianized....I—if someone asked me what nationality I was, or what are you?, I wouldn't— I don't know if I ever said it once that I was a Canadian, but I've always said that I'm Chinese.* (Nellie, October 6th, 1995, p. 17)

Soon, I began asking the subjects to describe themselves in terms of their cultural identity, whether they considered themselves "hyphenated Canadians," or something else. Often the reply was that they rejected the hyphenation, because they didn't speak the first language, but they didn't consider themselves fully Canadian either:

> *Well, I just feel that I'm not really Chinese, because if I were Chinese, how come I can't speak it?* (Ariana, July 13th, 1995, p. 7)

> *I will say that I'm of German descent. I'm Canadian, more Canadian, but...I do consider myself German because both parents were. And there was German in the background there, yeah, for sure.*
> So do you ever describe yourself as a German Canadian?
> *No, no. I don't think of myself that way. If I could speak German I might. But I don't.* (Alexandra, March 1st, 1996, p. 12)

Heritage language ability and cultural identity are inextricably linked, it seems.

Such identity crises are particularly striking in juxtaposition to the words of Edward Said that open this chapter. Said speaks of the antagonism of trying to reconcile himself to a single identity rather than holding a multiple of voices/identities together. When this is a difficult task for those people who belong to, and are brought up within, the dominant culture, how much more difficult it must be for those who begin to develop their (cultural) selves in one language and culture, and then continue their development in another language and culture. I am reminded of F. Scott Fitzgerald's (1945) words that I believe are from *The Crack-Up*, in which he describes the mark of true genius as being the ability to hold two opposing thoughts in one's mind at the same time without going mad. Perhaps something similar can be said for the ability to hold two (or more) cultural selves in one's mind and body at the same time—especially when one of those selves may hold a racist bias against the other. Is a unified, coherent self more sane?—or less? Is it something to which students should aspire? Is it a product of our western culture that we impose on such students, this desire to reconcile a unified self?

For ESL teachers, some frequently given advice is that we should make our classrooms a English-speaking places and help our students to choose new English names to go with the new English-speaking identities that we hope they will assume. I have always found it to be an uncomfortable exercise, particularly given that I loathed having my own name mispronounced or changed just to make it easier for others in Japan. Moreover, my husband has a beautiful name in Japanese, but he has been assigned two "English" names during his 6 years in Canada, because people have been unwilling to try to pronounce his real name.[4] The first name was "Sam," which I objected to because that was my nickname. The second one was "Matt," a one syllable, lackluster (matte), boring, and flat (mat) name.

Several of the storytellers in my research project also sported English names. I was not surprised that the Chinese women had English names; from my own teaching practice, I know that it is standard practice for some groups of Hong Kong Chinese to give their children an English as well as a more traditional name.[5] I was surprised that Brian did not know his own Korean name, nor did Charles know his Japanese one. Alex explained that his name had been changed to an English name, which approximated his Polish nickname by his school principal because it would be easier for the teachers to pronounce. I was surprised by how important even little name changes can be:

> Oh, now there is my one little point where I did feel resentful. We were in Grade 3 and the teacher asked us to spell our names. We had written down our whole name and I wrote down Elisabeth with an "s" which is the way it is on my passport and she corrected me. And I wrote down "z" and I felt really angry and I've never forgotten, but I never wrote it with an "s" again. I thought "okay,"—I don't know what I thought. Who knows, but I just never have forgotten that—that's a really sharp memory and at that point, yeah I guess if you were to say at what time do you really feel that you lost your language, I think I'd say that time, where they took my name away. That was Elisabeth, the Dutch one, was traded for the Elizabeth the Canadian one, or the English one. (Greta, August 2nd, 1995, p. 19)

Greta also had her last name changed, though for a different reason. Her stepfather assumed (or, at least, he claimed to assume) that as soon as he married her mother, Greta, too, would take on his last name. She therefore used the last name Johnsen after she immigrated to Canada, yet, when she went to get married, she discovered that her last name had never been changed, that she was still Greta Van Beneen. She said that "I felt really cheated when I learned that I had been signing Johnsen all those years when I could have been signing Van Beneen. I felt so awful that I had, that that name had been taken away from me" (August 2nd, 1995, p. 19). As Greta went on to explain, "Your name is your identity" (August 2nd, 1995, p. 19).

And, in his story, Richard gave us a clue to how important language can be to identity. Although he spoke of what it means to lose a language, he truly connected that loss to a sense of self. From all the stories I heard during the course of this project, his words are those that most remain with me and haunt me. They bear repeating:

> It's like losing half the man you are, you know, the man with whom—not to lose the language makes me twice the man, so the loss of the language is the loss of the soul I think for an Indian person. It's a loss of the essence of the soul, not to know the language, because you never know how beautiful you are until you know the language. Because you can only be described in a foreign tongue, right? (Richard, September 19th, 1995, p. 6)

Richard's words help to give me some understanding of why Michael claims to feel more at home with some European languages than he does with English—even though he can no longer speak his native Portuguese—and why Greta feels some kind of "innate cultural recognition" (July 12th, 1996, p. 19) that makes her feel more comfortable when speaking to European people. Perhaps they are able to find the essences of their souls in the cadence of romance languages.

Another recurrent theme concerned the feeling that the language was still trapped somewhere inside—if only the subjects knew how to reach it. They wondered if "there's some little area of your mind that if you just could sort of open it up, you would see it all just sitting there and it wouldn't be hard to just dredge it out" (Greta, July 12th, 1995, p. 10). Oddly enough, those who felt that way usually seemed to specify 6 months as the length of time it would take them to recapture the language if only they were immersed in it again.

My speculation about this 6-month immersion-to-fluency ran in three directions. First, I began to make a list of the characteristics that participants making this claim had in common. Participants who felt this way liked their first languages, feeling some affinity for speakers of that language. They reported following strangers down the street, trying to screw up enough courage to speak a word or two:

I'm basically a very shy person. I don't speak to strangers often. I've heard
someone with a very heavy Dutch accent and "Oh, are you from Holland?
What part of Holland are you from?" And I would just never do that in any
other context. (Greta, July 12th, 1995, p. 19)

or listening in on conversations:

I'd go up and listen to them. You know, I'd like pretend I'm not listening
when I am, but I don't go up to them and say anything. No, I think I'd be more
like the eavesdrop person. (Nadia, July 21st, 1995, p. 11)

They also found that they would find ways of working their ethnicity
into conversations "even if the context is maybe not there" (Greta, August
2nd, 1995, p. 19), Minette often finding herself saying "Je suis de
Belgique," and Helena starting up conversations with other Hungarians
at festivals or fairs.

Subjects making this 6-month claim have also maintained some
receptive understanding, being able to understand certain words and
phrases used by their parents or others. Probably related to this, they
lost the first language later rather than earlier, when they started school
as opposed to when an older sibling started school. Also related to this,
their parents had to continue using the first language dominantly in the
home, and, almost invariably, the parents had very poor English
language skills. Most of this seemed to confirm common sense. More
surprising was that a larger number of women than men seemed to feel
this way, and, almost counter-intuitively it seemed more prevalent
among older participants than among the younger ones who had
immigrated more recently.[6] This may have been due to a change in
demographics, a change in the types of education minority first-language
children receive, or, perhaps, it may be due to the stronger ties to the
home that women and older generations feel.

I next wondered whether this claim had any basis in fact and, if it
did, what that meant about language learning and language loss. If this
were true, would it mean that we never really lose any knowledge, but
just lose track of it, or would it mean that our brain acts like our muscles,
taking less time to relearn a skill than it originally took to learn it?
Several of the participants expressed an interest in taking time off work
to be involved, if I could get funding, in experimentally testing their
intuition. Although I cannot conceive of a research design that could
possibly in/validate their claims, I am intrigued by the possibilities they
have raised. Why, for instance, did each of the participants who
mentioned relearning the language independently choose a 6-month
time frame? Why did they all specify immersion? Is it just that some

second-language learning strategies have become common knowledge and common sense?

Finally, I began to suspect that this belief was more symptomatic of an unwillingness to give up ownership of the language than it was of fact. When I was asked to join host Cecilia Waters on the Canadian Broadcasting Corporation's (CBC) phone-in show *Almanac*, one man did phone to tell me that he had relearned French in about 6 months, and then he proceeded to mix French and English for the duration of our conversation. A good friend later told me that the man's French was not terribly accurate. Moreover, Richard, the Cree spirit, relearned his language at the age of 30, and claimed that if he had not done so he never would have been able to tell me how much he had lost. He told me that, despite being comfortable hearing the language again within 2 seconds, he was unable to appreciate the full beauty of his language for about 5 years. This is particularly remarkable given that Richard never completely lost the language, rather, in his words, it just "went to sleep"[7] for a little while, and then was so happy to wake up.

I have no scientific basis for refuting (or supporting) the claim that certain subjects would be able to recapture the language more quickly than if they had never known it, but I would like to follow up on my suspicion that their belief it would take 6 months, comes more from an unwillingness to let go, a refusal to give up ownership, than it does from fact. On the other hand, perhaps people who feel they could be fluent again in 6 months have a different definition of fluency than Richard and me. Perhaps they equate fluency with the ability to get by in ordinary conversations. In any event, I know only enough to raise a few more questions—next time.

Also interesting was the language that subjects used to describe the feeling that they could relearn the language. Not only did Richard and Minette explain that their first languages would "wake up" if they were immersed in the culture for 6 months, but also Naomi felt that immersion would "rejuvenate [her] language" (Naomi, October 3rd, 1995, p. 6) abilities. Such words speak to the living nature of language, and consequently to the need for researchers to take an embodied approach to the study of language acquisition and loss.

I found myself wondering too, how much changing policies are responsible for some aspects of negative self-image. The subject with the most strongly expressed negative self-image and cultural identity, Ariana, explained in her story that she began attending school in the days before the advent of multiculturalism, at a time when assimilation rather than balanced biculturalism was the order of the day. In her present job as an ESL adult educator, Ariana is confronted daily by students who are being encouraged to keep their first languages and first cultures, which frustrates her retroactively. Adding to her frustration is the fact that her school and some of her students expect her to participate in multicultural events by explaining things like Chinese New Year's, or by teaching a few common Cantonese words. Ariana isn't able to participate; as she said "Hey, I've assimilated very nicely, thank you, and I've forgotten all my Chinese" (June 22nd, 1995, 1, p. 3), and this has left her feeling doubly deprived. While, as a child, she felt ashamed because she could never be White enough, she now, in the days of multicultural policy, feels ashamed that she isn't Chinese enough. It was little wonder then, to me, that her interviews were articulate, yet angry.

Ariana's sentiments were echoed by another visible minority, Naomi. Recalling that "it was not pleasant being Japanese-Canadian after the war" she explains that "that's probably why I lost it very quickly" (October 3rd, 1995, p. 3). Naomi's reactions are confused; on the one hand she feels that she was forced to assimilate, that her language was "driven from" her, while on the other hand, she feels that more recent immigrants should not be treated any differently. On the one hand, she feels that if Japanese immersion were available, she would enroll her daughter in it, on the other hand, she feels that she worked harder and became a better person because of the pressure she felt to be as white as possible:

> I guess my recollections of probably being young—the strongest recollections are unpleasant recollections of racial slurs and things being said, and so I guess it colours the way I look now when there's articles in the paper about people yelling that there's racism at new immigrants. I think those things they are yelling at you are nothing compared to what was yelled at me——I survived. I'm sure you will too. So, I think it slants, you know, the way I look at the problems that people feel they have. And I feel that they shouldn't speak their own language, Taiwanese, Cantonese, or Mandarin, because I couldn't speak my language, and I was better off for it. (Naomi, October 3rd, 1995, p. 3)

And Nellie, despite her frequently repeated regret that she lost her first language, and her embarrassment that her 7-year-old niece speaks more Cantonese than she does, reacts to Mandarin or Cantonese or French immersion with the simple statement that "I don't believe in it" (Nellie, January 20th, 1996, p. 8). There are strong feelings throughout these interviews that some immigrant groups, or some generations of immigrant groups, should not have more opportunities than others:

> Yeah, I firmly believe that when you come to Canada you should speak the language. And I have a great deal of difficulty with people who come and don't speak. Like my former hairdresser, she's from Peru. She's not teaching her

children English. "She'll get it in school," she says, "they have ESL," but I gather there are a lot of people that only speak their language in their home, and their children are not learning the language, and I mean that's wrong. Their children were born in Canada and then we have to pay for it. I think they should be charged for it. (Alexandra, February 14th, 1996, p. 7)

In the interviews, I found frequent support for the idea that new immigrants have it too easy, that they are a drain on the public purse, that they should be put in separate schools and forced to pay to learn the language of public instruction (and, indeed, one of the current recommendations for a new immigration policy is that immigrants should have to speak one of Canada's official languages). There seemed to be even more antagonism toward paying for ESL among former non-English-speakers than there is in among the general public—and if recent media reports of support for a local Member of Parliament's attempts to have ESL excluded from public education are any indication (British Columbia Television early news report, February 25th, 1997), there is widespread antagonism toward paying for ESL in the general public (see *Discordance* for quotations). It seems that the subjects in this study felt bitter resentment at paying taxes so that other people could receive benefits that they themselves did not receive. They seem to feel even more resentment than do those people who would never have benefited from ESL instruction.

Nadia had a different reason for putting new immigrant students together in separate schools where they could be educated through their first languages until they had learned enough English to go to public school. Having taught public health courses in the schools, she spoke about the difficulties she saw new students struggling to overcome:

I really kind of felt sorry for the kids because they didn't know a word of English, and there was always one child in a group of Chinese kids, and the other kids would get that really good child to translate for them. I feel really sorry for her. She's not really learning; she's working. And the other kids aren't learning; they're missing out....I think those kids will have really bad feelings about school because it wasn't fun. It was really hard. (July 21st, 1995, p. 21)

Nadia did, however, feel very strongly that first language schools should not be publicly funded, but should be paid for by immigrant families. Even after we spoke at length on several occasions about this issue, she maintained that she lost her first language, and that now she has to pay for the privilege of learning it again; therefore, Nadia sees no reason why immigrant families today shouldn't pay for first language education combined with ESL.

ENDNOTES

1. It is easy to understand where these attitudes may have developed. At one point in this research project, I considered including the stories of students who were enrolled in high school. I telephoned the principal of a very progressive high school with which I had personal contact (teaching and volunteering in one of their alternate school programs) and with which our university department has a close research relationship. I wrote about our telephone conversation in my research journal:

   > He assured me that no one in his chool would fit [my] criteria. He asked me what reason there might be for losing a first language, and I mentioned several—early immigration, parental bilingualism, etc.—and he replied "well, they're just stupid." I said that absolutely stupidity had nothing to do with it, that the people who were involved in my study were highly intelligent, including well-known city people, university students, college professors. He said "and I guess you think that professors are intelligent!" He repeated that language loss is correlated with stupidity, and when I disagreed, he said "oh no, you couldn't possibly write that in your research now, could you?"....He was implying that I was involved in some big language loss cover-up, that of course I couldn't state the real reason for it, but we all knew....Obviously, if he believes only stupid kids will lose their first languages, he is not going to be open to heritage language maintenance programs, despite the more than 75% enrollment of ESL students in his school. (Researcher Journal, February 3rd, 1996)

2. Note that, with the exception of Charles, hybridity in this context refers to an immigrant and a heritage culture rather than to mixed heritage.
3. I have been struggling with how to refer to Richard. Although I am aware that he would normally be referred to as a Cree man, he seems to me to be much more. I needed to find a word that would capture his essential other-worldliness, his personal power and vitality, his spirituality, and yet one that would somehow not attribute undue importance to his gender.
4. Most pronunciations of Satoru (no syllabic emphases) are atrocious. He is usually called (and often written to as) Sa*turo*, while my daughter, Hanika (no syllabic emphases: Huh-knee-kah) usually has her name pronounced *Hæ*-nick-ah.
5. On the other hand, we are all familiar with the common ESL anecdotes, such as the story about a teacher naming his Chinese student "Marlborough" after his favorite brand of cigarettes.
6. Please note that with such a small number of participants, I cannot make any claims as to this being statistically valid, especially given that with some participants the subject just never came up.
7. This is a metaphor that Minette also used. She felt that her French language ability was still somewhere inside her, asleep, and that she needed a period of immersion for it to wake up.

15. SCHOOL RELATIONSHIPS

One of the most important issues, if not the most important issue, for children at school is the desire to "fit in" with the rest of the students, to have friends, to be respected, to be the same, or, at least, to be different in an admirable way. Inability to speak English works against this desire. Wong Fillmore (1991) asks us to consider the questions:

> Consider what happens when young children find themselves in the attractive new world of the American school. What do they do when they discover that the only language that is spoken there is one that they do not know? How do they respond when they realize that the only language they know has no function or value in that new social world, and that, in fact, it constitutes a barrier to their participation in the social life of the school? (p. 325)

The answer that Wong Fillmore gives, and that this research project has found support for, is that children refuse to speak their first languages either at home or at school. They want to learn English quickly, as quickly as possible, even to the point of becoming hooked on school-related activities that help to develop English skills:

> I remember the one thing that I really liked was having electronic Speak and Spell. It's this hand-held electronic game that you can do a whole bunch of word games on there. You can do hangman on there, things like that. I just loved that game; I wouldn't put it down. And I remember our second Christmas there I wanted to have one for Christmas and my parents, at that point they hated me speaking English at home so much that they wouldn't buy it for me anymore. They said "No you've had enough. You've learned enough, you'll be fine. You don't need it now. What you do need is practice speaking Cantonese." And I guess it just progressed from there. (Nellie, October 6th, 1995, p. 5)

If they did not learn to speak English, they often found themselves alone. Nadia remembers going to school and sitting alone on a heated rooftop watching her classmates "because none of the people played with me; it was always hard to have friends" (June 8th, 1995, p. 18). Greta, too, remembers vividly what it felt like when language difficulties arose and she found herself left out of an activity:

> This girl my age, we ended up in school together. I can't remember which summer it was, whether it was the summer before I started school when I met her, or that first summer after Grade 1, but there was a church camp or something, and I remember thinking I was going to that—I'm not sure why I thought that—and I remember my mother and I packing and I was trying to decide what I would need, and I remember being out on the road waiting to be picked up, and nothing ever happened. No one ever came. Now there had obviously been some language difficulty, that I must have missed

something....She must have been telling me about her going, and asking me if I wanted to go too, but it just didn't happen like through the adults to make it happen....but I've never forgotten just how confused and awful that felt, and that must have been a real language difficulty. (Greta, August 2nd, 1995, p. 18)

Even 40 or more years later, Greta still feels the pain of not knowing how or why she was excluded from church camp.

After having learned to speak English well, many subjects were reluctant to then associate with newcomers from the same cultural and linguistic background. Although in extreme cases, this would develop into a kind of racism against their own race such as that manifested in Ariana, initially it was a reflection of how much children want to fit in with their peer group. Once in, they had no desire to do anything that might again set them apart. Kurt, the father of one young subject, explained that,

And it's funny because they have another Polish guy in Julian's class right now, and Julian has no patience for him because the other guy does not speak English, and "He is dumb. He is stupid. He does not understand the word. He speak Polish all the time in the class". And it's very interesting how this over time this has turned over 5 years he was in exactly the same position 5 years ago. Now he cannot understand the other guy's position. He is not an enemy of the other guy, but he has no understanding or patience. (Kurt, March 6th, 1996, p. 3)

Something that I found surprising because of the anger it generated, was the many stories of students being asked to sit with new ESL students after they had managed to learn English and to fit in with their classmates. Helena, of Hungarian background, talked of being "given" as a special friend to a new classmate from Germany, and her confusion at what possible benefit she could be to this student. Not only did she feel somewhat resentful of this forced friendship, but she also felt extremely inadequate, telling me that she felt her only contribution to the new student's comfort was that she spoke slowly. Brian, too, was curious about why his teacher chose to seat a girl from Portugal with him when his first language was Korean. And even when the classroom newcomer was from the same cultural and/or linguistic group, this practice caused anxiety. These were, after all, students who had lost their first languages and who were no longer able to communicate in their L1s. Moreover, they had struggled to assimilate, yet even after they'd successfully fitted in with their peers, they were still being treated as different, and then singled out for their difference by the classroom teacher.

That desire to fit in also extends beyond the classroom door. Many of the subjects in this study expressed embarrassment about inviting friends over to their houses; Naomi, like Brian, in fact, could not recall ever having a friend over to her house for dinner, a not uncommon recollection. Sometimes they explained that the food they ate at home was different from that of their classmates, and they didn't want to call attention to yet another difference. Others felt that their parents were embarrassed at having little to say in English, and they felt mortified when their parents would "talk funny":

> *Everyone wants to have cool parents too, like everyone. Like you know your mom and dad are so cool, but you know when my dad can't say... doesn't say "moguls," like I mean I laugh at it now, but he says "humpity bumpities," and he's telling his ski story and you're like going "Oh, my God," and your friends are laughing and you know... but you're going "My god, my dad looks like a complete idiot." And thinking "Therefore, I look like a complete idiot and I see no humour in this", and then you get mad, and then you have a fight, and then no one is...everyone's miserable.* (Helena, July 26th, 1995, p. 17)

Nellie was embarrassed for a different reason. She told of having her high school boyfriend invited to a family gathering. When they were all seated around the dinner table, her relatives carried on a conversation in Cantonese that neither she nor her boyfriend could understand.[1] She felt mortified that she and her boyfriend were not welcomed into the conversation, even though several of her aunts and uncles could speak some English, and she felt that they were deliberately making themselves appear as different and as inscrutable as possible in a kind of cultural defiance. Although she was able to understand the general gist of the conversation, she could not understand enough to translate for him, nor would she have been willing to translate something of the anti-Western rhetoric for him.

> *I've had boyfriends who don't speak Chinese, and when they go out to family dinners with us and my whole family is speaking Cantonese, I find that very rude. You know, and I try to say to them, "can you say that in English," or I would almost feign ignorance and say "I'm not sure what they're saying either," you know, just to make them feel better, just to make them feel that they're not the odd man out....I just say "what does that mean?"* (Nellie, November 3rd, 1995, pp. 4-5)

What Nellie seems to be pointing out is the racism within her family toward people in their country of adoption, or perhaps more rightly, a reaction to the racism which they had experienced, yet at no time during our interviews did she acknowledge it as such. Racism to Nellie was something that happened *to* people of Chinese descent.

Another disturbing lesson for me was the realization that even now, in an age of enlightened multiculturalism, at a time when all teachers need to be culturally aware, at a time when we are supposed to be promoting bilingualism, there are both covert and overt forces at work on students, forbidding them to use their first languages in the school. I expected to hear such stories from subjects in their 30s and 40s and older; I was unprepared to hear, perhaps because of my own involvement with the field of TESL, first- and second-hand accounts that such things were still going on. I was told of students who were unable to find the cafeteria, who were denied privileges offered only in English, or who were unable to use the bathroom because they didn't know how to ask properly in English. Hana Kim had what I consider to be a worse bathroom story to tell:

> And my mom says that the preschool teacher...was worried that because I couldn't speak English that I'd wet my pants or something by not being able to request that I wanted to go to the bathroom, and so my mom discovered that she had put all this toilet paper in my underwear, I guess so that I wouldn't pee my pants; I thought that was really weird. (Hana Kim, August 14th, 1995, p. 1)

As a parent, I would be horrified to discover my child had been violated and humiliated in this way, whatever the teacher's good intentions.

Kurt also told of the time his older son was at school, feverish, and wanting to call home. Even though he showed his teacher a quarter, mimicked dialing a phone and holding the receiver, and was obviously sick, his teacher apparently didn't understand what he wanted. When I interviewed Kurt's older son Julian, he excused her behavior, taking her failure to understand at face value:

> Well, my teacher was kind of like—I guess she was just—it was new back then; right now she's been in school, teaching kids, for like 9 years, and she was relatively new back then, and she didn't really know too much about new students. (Julian, March 6th, 1996, p. 2)

Kurt's younger son told of a similar situation that he had faced in his ESL classroom, one in which the teacher wouldn't allow any of the children to leave the classroom for any reason unless they could ask in perfect English. He, too, took her failure to understand at face value, attributing her difficulties to age:

> And [the teacher] yelled at you....Because she couldn't understand. She was in the school district for like 36, 50 years, and she didn't understand what I was saying. She retired last year. (Cameron, March 6th, 1996, p. 4)

Many of the other subjects were scared in school, and, like Brian, began crying when the teachers directed questions to them. Although Nellie said her teacher then only asked her to answer a question if she put her hand up, others said that their teachers would continue to prey on them, with the full knowledge that they would cry:

> *In school I have a couple of memories of being in the corner...and crying when I couldn't understand something, but that's about it for those 2 years.* (Michael, November 17th, 1995, p. 5)

Kuong even reported that his teacher screamed at him when he didn't understand his homework, and therefore he began cheating and copying other students' homework:

> *And every time I come there, right?, don't have my homework, they harsh like screaming, and I don't like that. I don't like class stuff, so I took cheating stuff.* (September 9th, 1994, p. 4)

They felt alone. They felt stupid. And, they had no one they could talk to.

More overt discrimination was also evident. Over the years, I have collected newspaper articles and letters to the editor regarding the treatment of ESL students in Vancouver schools. In those letters is ample evidence of a kind of right-wing backlash against immigrant children (see *Discordance*, later). Perhaps the most hotly-debated article was a claim from a city accountant of Chinese origin that Vancouver schools were not the welcoming places that teachers and administrators would have us believe. I was told many stories supporting his claim. As recently as 1992, one urban Vancouver school with close to 90% ESL student enrollment hung signs in the halls and classrooms and cafeteria reading "Speak English Only; En Français, s'il vous plaît."[2] According to Charles, the teachers then encouraged students to "tattle" on one another. In his words, this caused gang warfare. The different linguistic groups, including the English speakers, became openly hostile. They would report on each other for speaking languages other than English, and became increasingly distrustful of other groups that they thought might be talking about them in other languages, similar to the postwar fear "that [they] were plotting things" (Naomi, October 19th, 1995, p. 8). Nellie, too, confirmed this practice in other schools, telling me about a young Mandarin-speaking student that she tutors. Her student brought home a package of school rules, and "one of the rules was that they were not allowed to use a language other than English in the school" (November, 1995, p. 11), which, Nellie feels, exacerbates the differences in language groups: "It's just drawing more attention, I mean, all the kids who are going to the school will get this package, and it just makes them more aware of how different these people are..." (ibid., p. 11).

But, ESL classes and ESL teachers were universally loved by those students enrolled in ESL, meaning subjects under the age of about 25 who had grown up in urban centers where ESL was offered. Many students compared their situations to those endured by previous generations. Some older subjects, like Lara, told of being "shopped" from school to school, trying to gain admission. Students in recent years considered themselves lucky because they were enrolled in classes with students who were going through the same thing that they were:

> It was really nice to be there because it was dealing with people, even though I couldn't really communicate with those people in Cantonese because their first language wasn't Cantonese, it was nice to be there because we all had something in common, and I felt that they knew—they understand what I felt, and what I felt when I first came, and that was—I really like that part of it. (Nellie, October 6th, 1995, p. 5)

> It was just so much easier than having to learn it with all those other people who already knew English well enough, and I would lag behind, so you know, it was really good having a small class in the ESL class, and having a one-on-one thing, and yeah, just the people were really nice, and just helping each other out, and making good friends with them.... (Brian, July 6th, 1995, p. 2)

They considered themselves particularly lucky if their teachers had also learned English as a second language, and/or if they were visible minorities.

Perhaps the only noted drawback was that some teachers, ESL teachers included, with the best of intentions, recommended that their students speak English at home. Time and time again, I heard from subjects whose teachers had made this recommendation, and who were now ambivalent about that advice. Although, on the one hand, they reason that they learned English much more quickly and easily than they would have done, on the other hand, they feel that this (a) contributed to their first language loss, and (b) contributed to their continuing struggles with English grammar because they had learned from poor language models at home. In fact, one of the most prominent results of the switch to English in the home seemed to be that subjects would then become less comfortable with English for the rest of their lives rather than more comfortable. Michael was best able to explain this:

> I joke about English being my second language, you know, it's more than a joke because I don't always feel comfortable. That's the feeling that I'm not at home totally with it, and yet obviously it's the language that I'm most at home in. (Michael, December 1st, 1995, p. 2)

> I find that I don't have much facility for those things, like, it's things like "a bird in the hand is better than two in the bush" and those types of things...,

sayings that aren't easily translated into Portuguese. I guess if my parents—I learned most of my English from my parents—...and so if it wasn't said around there, I guess I didn't learn it. (Michael, November 17th, 1995, p. 6)

Michael was by no means alone in feeling this way. Self-consciousness about speech patterns, grammatical usage, nuances, pronunciation, and humor were the norm among the storytellers, even when they might not be able to explain what, exactly, distinguished their speech from that of others:

I do know I have a rather idiosyncratic way of speaking English; it goes on and on and is a bit tortuous and all that. And, perhaps it has some signatures on it that indicate that's my second language.... (William, December 12th, 1995, p. 12)

ENDNOTES

1. Some important information here might be that Nellie is 10 years younger than her next oldest sibling. Her brother and sister therefore continue to speak perfect Cantonese, and they both struggle with English.
2. During a course on the education of immigrant students that I taught during the winter of 1997, several of my students reported that languages other than English were forbidden in their practicum schools. This can be, in some cases, understood, given that some schools in the Vancouver region have majority cohorts from one L1 background other than English, that is, the majority of students may speak, for instance, Mandarin. In such cases, L1 parents may support the enforced use of English and the exclusion of the L1 from the school. Moreover, the advice to use French is moot, despite it being an official language in Canada. Native French-speaking students constitute less than 1% of the school district's population, and very few teachers, apart from those who teach in specialized programs, speak the language.

16. SCHOOL PERFORMANCE

In the previous section, I referred to past practice in which students were demoted to a lower grade, not because they were stupid or even uneducated in their L1s, but simply because they didn't speak English. I had been assured that this no longer happened by many graduate student colleagues who teach in the public school system. Yet, the family I interviewed provided evidence to the contrary. Originally from Poland, the stepfather, Kurt, immigrated to Canada as a political refugee in 1983. In 1990, he was permitted to return to Poland for a visit, where he met a widowed university friend, married her, and returned to Canada with her and her two sons. The elder son, Julian, had completed Grade 1 in Poland at the top of his class. When he reported to his new school in Canada, he was put back a year, into Grade 1:

> So, they sent me back into Grade 1, and it was only in Grade 4 that I went up to my normal level. I skipped Grade 4....In Grade 4,—I don't know what I learned in grade four because I was in a 3/4 split when I was in Grade 3, so basically I was doing sort of halfway in between Grade 3 and Grade 4 in there. That's when my mom saw the chance [my emphasis] to make me move back to my normal age level. (Julian, March 6th, 1996, pp. 2-3)

I am curious about Julian's assertion that his mother saw the chance for him to be promoted to his age level. Although I do not doubt the way he views this incident because his mother works as a multicultural worker in the school district and is very much involved in her children's education, Julian's mother is the one family member I did not have the opportunity to interview.

I also heard second-hand stories about recent immigrants who were put back a year or two in school because they couldn't speak English. This is especially problematic when elder siblings were demoted to their younger sibling's grade level, particularly in some Asian families when the elder son was placed in the same grade as a younger sister. Although I must admit that I am not familiar with the unique reasons for continuing this practice, I am dismayed by it, given the lingering effects that it has on children whose only impediment to learning is insufficient command of the English language. I cannot think of any instance in which demotion to a lower grade level would speed English acquisition; I question how much motivation children have to relearn concepts they knew in mathematics or geography or physical education in a second language, and I wonder about the long-term consequences of social isolation from their peer groups.

On the other hand, I did find some anecdotal evidence of Cummins' dual iceberg metaphor for language learning. Although I question the motivation to *relearn* concepts, this theory holds that concepts can be *transferred* from a minority first language to the second:

> *I must have been 8 or 9 when we suddenly started on something called the essay, the essay form, preparing us. I couldn't get what the hell—this was all about. How the hell was I supposed—? So, I write this essay, I write this piece of prose in English, and it didn't have a structure to it that satisfied the teacher or whatever, and then I remember him telling me, "Look, 'caiswere' in Welsh," which is "attempt"...and I suddenly made this connection. "Oh, yeah. Okay", because it was the essay...I don't know what you would call it in a technical sense, of transferring this structure and idea of what I was able to do in Welsh into this new language structure, even though I had the words and everything, I didn't have an essay structure in my mind....There was some kind of migration of structure between the two languages.* (William, November 28th, 1995, pp. 11-12)

To me, this explanation highlighted the need for teachers to be able to access concepts in classroom first languages, and for children to have at least initial access to bilingual education programs. Because William's teacher was able to give him the Welsh equivalent, William was spared a lot of frustration and feelings of ineptitude. Moreover, making this connection inspired him, and enhanced his self-image, not to mention that it saved valuable classroom time.

Familiar with prior research studies, I was prepared to hear that the subjects were always good at math and sciences, but that they had struggled with English. Indeed, a number of the storytellers mentioned that they were still concerned with their English abilities. Lara, a computer communications' consultant, explained that she admired articulate people and always felt inferior around them. Helena, who worked in communications education, said that she was aware that her grammar was "atrocious." and her spelling was "awful, awful, awful," and that her professors considered her "on the verge of illiteracy" because she was the "run-on sentence queen" (Helena, July 26th, 1996), and that therefore she really didn't know where she fit in, in terms of language. She knew she didn't speak Hungarian well, but felt that Hungarian was still somehow hindering her by adversely influencing her English ability. Nellie explained to me that the hardest part of being a teacher for her was having to speak English aloud:

> *I just ramble on when I speak in front of a group, and then I have no idea what I'm saying, and then I really panic because I think that I don't know what I'm trying to say. And I'll try and think of the exact words I've used to see if I've made a mistake. And lot of times when I make grammatical mistakes when I'm speaking, I get really embarrassed, because I feel that nobody else does this. I'm the only one who does it all the time....* (October 6th, 1995, p. 14)

What they seem to be saying is that when their speech "monitors" are engaged, they are aware of their mistakes, but still feel unable to correct them because they are unsure exactly where the errors occurred.

I was also prepared to hear that the subjects were particularly interested when studying their first language culture at school:

> When I went to school, I would always get everything on Holland from the encyclopedia, you know, I tried to learn as much as I could, and I was always very interested, and every time Holland came up in the new, I would always read that first, and I still do that. (Greta, July 12th, 1995, p. 18)

Although Michael was somewhat uncomfortable when they began looking at Portugal's colonialist practices during their period of empire-building, he was also proud:

> I remember feeling proud in school when we heard about Vasco de Gama and people like that....I was a little ashamed at the time about some of the ways that, that things were done to the native populations in the name of religion, in the name of the powers that be. (Michael, November 17th, 1995, p. 9)

Similarly, Helena felt it difficult to reconcile her father's nostalgic portraits of Hungary with what she studied in class about the atrocities of Attila the Hun.[1]

What did surprise me, however, was the number of subjects who felt that their struggles to learn English had made them fall in love with the English language, and who followed that dream to become journalists (Minette, Hana Kim), writers (Greta, Richard, Minette), teachers (Ariana, William, Nellie; Naomi volunteers for a language school), or otherwise involved in communicative professions (Michael was formerly a minister; Nadia is a nurse). While I realize that strong communicative skills are likely highly correlated with the willingness to volunteer for this kind of study, I think it is noteworthy that so many subjects attributed "falling in love" with the language to their earlier struggles to master it, their words echoing Hoffman's (1989) confession that,

> I've become obsessed with words. I gather them, put them away like a squirrel saving nuts for winter, swallow them and hunger for more. If I take in enough, then maybe I can incorporate the language, make it part of my psyche and my body....I have to add a bottom to the language that I learned from the top. (pp. 216-217)

While Greta, William, and the other subjects in this research, engaged in oral narration, did not have the reflective time to craft their explanations, similar sentiments, passions, struggles, are hinted at in the stories they tell:

You know, just really thinking about words and what they did, how people communicated. I just really remember always being very aware of that. And I think that's partly having to deal with the language at that age. I think it did a lot for my skills with language, even though I lost the language, I don't think I ever lost that interest in what words can do for you. (Greta, July 12th, 1995, p. 5)

William, too, described this love relationship with English, a rapture which stemmed from deeply permanent rupture in his life:

I've described it now and again as falling in love with the language. I absolutely love it, and I've been reading and writing poetry, and the whole bit. It's almost as though emotionally I've taken it on. (William, November 28th, 1995, pp. 9-10)

He went on to explain that his love of English really only began with the death of his eldest son in a car accident 10 years previously. Searching for solace in poetry and literature, and having no access to Welsh texts,[2] he finally turned to books in English to seek resolution. After years of living with the English language, he was able to find the grace and texture in English when texts in that language became his "lifesaver" (November 28th, 1995, p. 10). English became the language of his grief and, holding within it the experience of such a primary emotion, it became a homeland, a language not merely of vocation but of evocation as well.

But, school performance concerns were not limited to worry about grades or standing on the part of the students. I encountered also some evidence of questionable classroom practices and questionable teacher practices. Ariana, in her story, told of being recommended for ESL instruction, despite being born and raised in Canada. That Ariana continues to be angry about, and hurt by, this incident even 20 years after the fact indicates how much teachers must guard against making judgments based on stereotypes.

I was also surprised by the story told by Kuong, in which he explained to me how he "realized" he was stupid. It is important to note in this story, that Kuong did not question the teacher's practice, but rather he felt bad about his own performance:

I just sit there and listen. I didn't really raise my hand up, like there's some special calendar right? like through the whole year, through that whole year, like you get points for it. You get something right, like points and stuff. It's all a chart, your name, everybody every students be in, and then he ask you, like, no, he won't ask you, but he'll say "You write on the board this word" and you have to raise your hand up for everybody could tell whats the word is, and you get points for doing that right? People have like hundred and something, people have like fifty, and I have like five. I was like the lowest marker. I was the lowest of everyone through the whole thing. (September 9th, 1994, p. 7)

Kuong explained that he worked diligently during elementary school, but that it was just too hard, and he was constantly made to feel stupid, and so he eventually gave up working hard and began cheating instead. Even when he was cheating, he tried to figure out the answers on his own, but when he found that he still didn't understand, he started hanging out at the mall, stealing, and doing drugs. When his parents got angry about that, and beat him up, he left home and began living on the streets. After he was arrested and sent home, he went back to school, but he didn't think that he had the ability to graduate, even from Grade 10. Kuong's inability to understand, coupled with a lack of individual attention, therefore led to social problems and low self-esteem.

ENDNOTES

1. This does point out the need for classroom teachers to take a nonjudgmental position when classes are studying such subjects.
2. I found some indications, though I would hesitate to make any claims about them, that some more profound emotions, like grief, are experienced in, or in some way associated with the first language. I say this because it is often extreme emotion that leads people to search for their roots and to try to recapture the language.

17. THE MEANING OF LOSS

The meaning of a conversation is most accurately heard or perceived through a door slightly ajar, when you're sitting in a room next door to the people who are having the conversation;...the real elements of the conversation are best perceived when one can't hear the individual words....
—William (November 28th, 1995, p. 5)

In this chapter, we will sit by a door slightly ajar and try to hear, through the voices of the subjects, the echo of first languages resonating. Although Richard explained to me that he would never have known what it was that he had lost if he hadn't gone back and relearned his language, an argument that I can appreciate, it is also possible to hear echoes of what might have been if the subjects had never lost their first languages.

First, it soon became apparent that the subjects in this study all had different ideas of what it meant to lose a language. For some, like Brian, Michael, Lara, Alexandra, Ariana, and Greta it meant a complete loss of any language ability at all, which resulted in a loss of first language identity and a feeling of exclusion from their first language culture. Ariana describes it:

> *Well, I guess definitely losing the language was taking that identity away from me and what can I say? As I said before, it's really robbed me of my cultural heritage. As I said, if I wanted to get it back, it's going to be really difficult, and because of the way—and just the way my attitude has been shown in the [transcripts]—that I'm racist towards my own race—it's going to be an uphill battle. And, just having heard you say "[Ariana], this is almost racist what you're saying," and I'm embarrassed and I hope that you edit, well, that you can put that in your [research], but as long as you don't identify me. I'm really shocked. I—I don't realize these things until it's put down on paper and somebody objective can stand back and say "Well, look what she said. Here she is, herself Chinese, and she has this racist attitude toward her own race." And, I'm angry too....* (Ariana, July 20th, 1995, p. 4)

For other subjects, like Hana Kim, Nadia, Naomi, Nellie, Helena, and Alex, loss meant that they had stopped learning the language at an early age, had lost some aspects of the language, such as fluency or difficult vocabulary, or understanding of verb tenses, but had still been able to partially understand little bits of their parents' conversations. Oddly enough, all of the subjects who retained some aspects of their first languages had committed themselves to study of those languages at the time of this study. [1]

For Minette, language loss meant the complete loss of unschooled native French fluency and understanding, followed by years of high school French that left her with a perfect accent, good pronunciation, and perfect intonation, but poor communicative ability. For William, Richard, Helena, and Lara, language loss meant the loss of lyricism, vitality, and vibrancy, things they do not find in the English tongue:

> There are fewer words in the Welsh language, but this word next to this word, whereas these two on their own have a fixed kind of meaning, when these two come together, there is a third or a fourth element or dimension or meaning to the whole thing that's utterly different from the two separate words. (William, November 28th, 1995, p. 13; see also Lara's description of Finnish lyricism, and Richard's personification of Cree)

For Richard, and for William, both speakers of ancient tongues that have been subject to colonialist purges, language loss also meant a loss of ease with the language that resulted from leaving the language community. The loss of their first languages was not so much a loss, as a switch in dominant language and the language of greatest facility. For both of them, return to the language community would eventually result in fluency, but for William, the dominant language will forever be English, particularly troubling to him because of the prevailing Welsh attitudes (which he continues to share) about those who "go over to the other side," and become English speakers.

Both Richard and William associated language loss with leaving the language-speaking community. When Richard first volunteered to participate, he explained to me that he'd known Cree, lost it, relearned it, and then lost it again. During our time together, it became apparent that his understanding of loss did not mirror my own. In his story, Richard mentions that his language was in "abeyance," that it went to sleep for awhile and then woke up when he returned to Van River. He also explains that it only took him a few seconds to grow comfortable with hearing the language again, while it took him 5 years to be comfortable speaking it again. Richard's words were carefully chosen to explain exactly what he meant; what he meant, it seems, is that he lost Cree when he left the reserve, but, as he says, someone will always be there keeping the fire of Cree alive, and he can always go back and be warmed by that fire.

William's story is similar, and yet different. Coming from a family of Welsh bards and poets, he very much valued the lyricism of his Welsh language, yet he was also overwhelmed by it. Wanting to be his own person instead of always conforming to societal expectations in Wales, he accepted a teaching position in Canada after completing his degree. William has never lost Welsh, though he does admit to speaking English on the telephone with his Welsh-dominant sister now. To him, loss of the Welsh language meant a change in dominant language to English, and the loss of an immediate Welsh-speaking community. Although technically, William does not meet the criteria for language loss that I set out at the beginning of the study, I became intrigued by his story. William was one of several participants who cried when describing his loss, especially when he spoke of how he didn't fit in anywhere anymore because he would never be completely at ease speaking Welsh again. It was particularly painful, given that he is a very successful college professor, someone that we would not normally see as being adversely affected by language loss, given that he did not merely cry, but sobbed, and given that he felt he could never "go home" to his language again.

So, this leads me to believe that not only the meaning but also the definition of language loss needs to be explored. Narrative, paralinguistic, phonological, or other features of the first language may be retained by some people who have retained little or nothing else (see, for example, Schmidt, 1991). Language loss may also need to be associated with geographic location; indeed we know that language loss is tied to geography, just because loss is a consequence of immigration and the subsequent learning of a second language. Although I did not begin this research with these assumptions and therefore did not explore whether, or in what circumstances, they may be true, I think both aspects warrant further study.

From my initial analysis of the entire corpus of transcripts, I have seen a great deal of evidence that the younger the person who has lost the language, the more that loss is linked to marketability, increased employment opportunity, and economic advantage. For instance, Brian explained that there were many occasions when he "probably could have got the sale if [he] spoke Korean" (June 21, 1995, p. 3), yet others, like Nadia, cited the advantage of having a second language on a resumé—"I envied that guy—like that guy was my age—because he's gotten a lot of very good jobs because he spoke a different, a second language" (June 13th, 1995, p. 9). This may be because the younger people in this study tend to be from Korea, Hong Kong, Taiwan, Vietnam, countries from which there has recently been an enormous influx of immigrants, and therefore there is a high market demand for fluency in the languages that they have lost. On the other hand, loss of marketability and opportunity was also cited by Nadia and Helena, even though Ukrainian and Hungarian are not particularly marketable languages. Rather, given that some of the older subjects in this study spoke first languages such as Japanese, French, and German, also marketable languages, and given that these subjects mentioned that they would have felt the loss of opportunity were they still young, I think that this understanding of loss has at least as much to do with the time in their lives—when they are making career choices and are not yet faced with their parents' failing health—as with the predominance of certain languages in the community. I think it is also indicative of the economic uncertainty of the present time, in which speaking second languages is often viewed as having a needed edge up on the competition.

But, the older the subjects, and the further away they were from their loss, the more poignant and nostalgic were their feelings about language loss. From the comments of the subjects, I came to understand that after career and family matters had been taken care of, and after parental mortality or the realization of impending parental death had taken its toll, the subjects really understood that their last connection to their cultural heritage had been/was about to be severed. Although they had always thought that they would go back one day and relearn the language, they finally realized that that day would likely never come, as their last living links to the language are broken and the imperative to learn the language diminishes:

> It's kind of interesting because my father passed away before my mother did, and what I found was at that point in time, it intensified because, being an only child, all of a sudden I had to communicate with my mother a lot more....I found that I had to learn more or use it more....when my mother passed away, all of a sudden, there is,—it's gone. (Alex, December 5th, 1995, p. 19)

Moreover, they often realize that they have lost the opportunity to understand many facets of their parents' lives—as Lara questioned, "How do I analyze these people? Where do I come from?" (August 7th, 1995, p. 20). While Minette, herself a writer, felt deep regret that she would never completely know her father as a writer and as a subject in his books because he had written in French, Alex explained to me that his parents were unable to speak to him about many of their experiences. After both of his parents passed away, he was able to understand more about them by having their personal correspondence translated, and by speaking to other relatives in English. He was surprised to learn some things:

> They told me bits and pieces, but not much. For example, that I found out about 2 years ago, when my mother was in Russia, her village got taken over by the German army and she was responsible for burying the Jews they would kill...my mother always sort of had this hatred of Germans, which I never really could understand.... (Alex, December 5th, 1995, p. 5)

Minette was able to read one of her father's books in translation, but it was the only one that had been translated, and, though it held to the facts in the book, she knows that she is still missing the flavor of her father's prose.

Alex also commented on the expression *language loss*, a term almost inseparable from our romantic attachment to such literary works as *Paradise Lost*. After telling me that if I were to drop him in downtown Warsaw with a list of 10 items to find, he wouldn't be able to do it, he also explained that that task would always have been impossible for him. Alex reflected that,

> *It's not a case of once upon a time I used to be able to speak it, write it, and I was going to become another Mozart and do music with it, and whatever, and then we moved and then I lost it. It's not that case. It's a case I never really had it. We moved to North America and my development in the language and understanding of the culture and stuff, and that's tough. Loss is a very interesting phrase.* (Alex, December 5th, 1995, p. 17)

But Alex's commentary is particularly poignant because he may have become a musician or a poet or a shoemaker if he had continued to develop in Polish—but he didn't, and, as is the case with all turning points in our lives, he will never know. Would his life have been richer if he had continued to learn Polish?, would it have been poorer?, or would it have merely been different? Alex will always live with regret, a regret that his life may have been bigger somehow, a regret powerfully described by Minette and by Lara:

> *I think there is always a low-lying—now that I've experienced profound grief, due to the loss of my husband, now I understand grief, and my grief at the moment is like a low-lying chronic sadness. That's the way I can also describe the loss of a language. It is a loss, there's no question of that, and there is, on a much lesser level, a very low-lying sadness that is always there. It's a regret. I can't find a word. I think there's a more precise word, but I can't put my finger on it right now, but it's like a—what might have been. And that has always been there because it's a lost opportunity....It's an unfulfilled—it's just—it's funny, it's a sense of incompletion. It's perhaps like it's maybe the sort of feeling of—I don't know how to phrase this, but not nostalgia, but you want something. Maybe the kind of feeling that an adopted child has for the biological mother?* (Minette, July 11th, 1995, p. 18)

> *When it first dawned on me that I'd lost my language, was that there was a sadness, a disappointment, and a sense of tragedy. I think the tragedy is still there, and over time my attitude toward it has changed....there's still a sadness and a tragedy, but it's not as deep as it was.* (Lara, August 30th, 1995, p. 6)

And, the term *first language loss* describes, appropriately, the loss of something too deep for words. Struggles to explain can never fully describe the impact of the loss of the first language. The loss seems to be felt in a kind of first language consciousness which cannot be described in a second language, that cannot be translated to a foreign tongue.

Now let us stop eavesdropping. Let us tiptoe away from the door slightly ajar, and I will gently close it behind us.

ENDNOTES

1. This may have been a consequence of retaining part of the language, or they may have volunteered for this study because of their renewed interest in their first languages, or neither, or both.

Discordance

Reading over this manuscript, I am anguished by the rage which seems to jump from these pages, burrow beneath my pupils, and which then, traversing the optic nerve, lodges itself first in my throat so that muted, breathless, I cannot articulate concurrence, and which then penetrates the esophagus and is digested into my gut where it manifests a vengeful, hideous, and yet somehow sensuous nausea. Yet, countering the rage of these subjects, is rancor directed at their experiences by a frightened public who, manipulated by a tradition of long and tenderly-nourished immigrant alarms, responded in letters to the editor of a Vancouver newspaper without compassion for the children, or for their own forebears:

- Despite Canada's major economic problems, it is still a reasonably good country to which to be privileged to come. Doesn't that justify making some financial contribution to harmonious assimilation? (Sohm, 1994);

- The burgeoning costs associated with ESL teaching come at the expense of kids who were born and raised here (McInnis, 1994);

- "Then I read in your paper about people on unemployment insurance being allowed to bring in whole families of relatives from India and I got so angry and frustrated....I'm really fired up. Sooner or later people will stop paying taxes with this sort of bullshit going on" (Ogar, cited in Farrow, 1994).

- Of the 52.5% of kindergarten children identified as ESL last year in Vancouver, 78% were born in Canada. So for 5 years, their parents have made the choice *not* to have their children learn English. All of a sudden, they enroll in school and it becomes the taxpayers' problem that they do not understand the language of instruction! (Coward, 1994);

- Nowadays it seems most newcomers are using Canada as a hedge, to be abandoned if things go better in their old country, to insist on services in whatever happens to be their first language, and to enjoy the social benefits we provide. Why ever have we allowed this rot to set in? (Dean, 1994)

- The generosity of our immigration policies...is beginning to backfire on us. It is most noticeable in our schools, where the fully-funded teaching of English as a Second Languge (ESL) is threatening to bankrupt our ability to teach the academic basics to anyone (Boyd, 1994).

- Learning the language—at least a modicum—is the first reponsibility in order to ease the first months after arrival. Learning about the country, its history and government is also the onus of the immigrant. I suggest Ms. Ullman's mother neglected her parental responsibility

207

by expecting the school system would do the job of instructing and accommodating her child. (Winfield, 1994)

To these people, and to those who, like Judge Samuel Kiser in Amarillo, Texas, ruled that "speaking only Spanish [at home] amounted to child abuse" (Pellerin, 1995) in his words, "if she starts first grade with the other children and cannot even speak the language that the teachers and the other children speak, and she's a full-blood American citizen, you're abusing that child and you're relegating her to the position of a housemaid" (Kiser, 1995, cited in Pellerin, 1995), I offer the words of Hoffman (1989):

> It's not that we all want to speak the King's English, but whether we speak Appalachian or Harlem English, or Cockney, or Jamaican Creole, we want to be at home in our tongue. We want to be able to give voice accurately and fully to ourselves and our sense of the world....Linguistic dispossession is a sufficient motive for violence, for it is close to the dispossession of one's self. Blind rage, helpless rage is rage that has no words—rage that overwhelms one with darkness. And if one is perpetually without words, if one exists in the entropy of inarticulateness, that condition itself is bound to be an enraging frustration....Anger can be borne—it can even be satisfying—if it can gather into words and explode in a storm, or a rapier-sharp attack. But without this means of ventilation, it only turns back inward, building and swirling like a head of steam—building to an impotent, murderous rage. If all therapy is speaking therapy—a talking cure—then perhaps all neurosis is a speech dis-ease [sic]. (p. 124)

Hoffman did not lose her first language, but she lived most of her life in her second.

18. CONCLUSION

NOT A FINALE: A DECRESCENDO

It is tempting, in closing, to go beyond my data and write propaganda. I shall instead try to follow Wolcott's (1990) advice to review what has been attempted, what has been learned, and what new questions have been raised (p. 56), that is, to close with a summary, and implications arising from the research. Also in keeping with Wolcott, I follow this with personal reflection on the research.

Summary

This research project attempted to look at first language loss in a new way, from a personal, narrative perspective. Instead of working from a conventional ideology in which the researcher controls and directs the research, I have briefed the subjects about the foci of this research in an initial meeting, and then tried to allow them to set their own objectives and to choose how to meet those objectives. This, I believe, takes the subjects' accounts of their lives and their experiences seriously, as they were lived, rather than treating them as illustrations of my own agenda.[1] This is not the same as allowing the subjects' stories to speak for themselves, but instead acknowledges the importance of their individual intellectual reflexivities in the construction of knowledge.

This project also attempts to fill a gap in existing research by beginning with the question "what does it mean, in individual terms, to lose a language?" Rather than beginning with the assumption that first language loss is a negative experience, this book tries to examine whether, and in what manner, language loss has had negative repercussions in the subjects' lives. It also begins to reveal, from an insider perspective, which must not be confused with "truth," how first language loss happens, why it occurs for some individuals and not for others.

It seems to be fairly safe to assume, after all the stories have been told, that first language loss has indeed been a negative experience, one having far-reaching consequences for the individuals and the families involved in this study. Although this book reported on only 21 cases (and those 21 cases may have been atypically negative[2]), the large number of people who volunteered to expend time and energy talking about their experiences implies that language loss is a powerful individual experience. If I were asked to identify one noteworthy aspect of this research project, I would have to cite the number of people who wanted to tell their stories—the number of audience members who, when I was interviewed on the radio show *Almanac*, phoned to tell of their own language loss; the number of friends who, on hearing the topic of my research, responded with their own stories, or those of their relatives and friends; the number of teachers who, when they heard some of my comments on language loss, said that they had seen this happening, or had perhaps contributed to its occurrence themselves; and the number of colleagues and peers who, even while steeped in their own research and writing, took the time and the care to draw parallels to their own research, and to encourage me.

It also seems fairly clear, at least from the point-of-view of someone who has steeped herself in all of the stories here, that neither the home, nor the school, nor the community could have single-handedly ensured first language maintenance for the subjects in this study. Each of these has a role to play in fostering the first language development of potentially bilingual children, either by actively teaching the L1, or by supporting it. And each of the home, school, and community should perhaps be assessed and evaluated to ensure that maximum support is being made available for fostering first language development, if first language maintenance is a goal for individual minority language families. On the other hand, it is possible to imagine a situation in which, for reasons of trauma or political oppression, or even for more moderate reasons, families may choose to abandon the first language in order to gain psychological distance from the past, or in order to embrace the future. Therefore, far from wanting to question the wisdom of such parental choices, I feel that first language support should not be thrust on families, but rather, that it should be made available. Perhaps in such cases, support and understanding could be directed toward helping parents and their children successfully acquire a common language.

McKay and Weinstein-Shr (1993) remind us that, among their many competing survival agendas, immigrant adults have equally pressing needs to,

> [support] children in their social and moral development as human beings; [help] grandchildren know the story of their past; [create] circumstances in which their children can succeed without rejecting who they are and where they have come from; [and ensure] that their children will stay connected enough to take care of them when they are old. (p. 415)

They go on to stress that "the degree to which there is a shared language will determine the extent to which this is possible" (p. 415-416). Wiley (1993) warns that failure to ensure that generations share a language may result in a situation similar to that in the 1920s and 1930s in which "widespread loss of parental authority" led to "the rise of juvenile delinquency among European American immigrant youth" (p. 426). This research project, too, hints at the potential for social strife when first languages, or common languages, are not supported and maintained. Within each story we come up against at least one "what if" question: What if Helena had rebelled against her family, but had not applied herself to finishing her education? what if her questions had not been about menstruation, but about STDs? what if Brian had chosen a less constructive lifestyle? what if Richard had not returned to his linguistic and cultural homeland? what if Ariana had completely rejected the influence of her parents and siblings? what if Lara had not found strength and direction in her siblings?

Beyond this, I dare not go. This is not for reasons of epistemological or political allegiance; my reasons have more to do with restraint. I feel that I could say nothing more which the subjects of this research have not already said better, and, more prosaically, I am concerned that readers' saturation thresholds may have been reached. Instead of concluding, therefore, I would ask readers to live with these stories as I have, to borrow of this research anything of value that may influence pedagogy, politics or the practice of research, to "taketh the fruit, and lat the chaf be stille" (Chaucer, *The Canterbury Tales*, The Nun's Priest's Tale, line 623), according to individual talent and taste. I have done so, and have found my own practice to be profoundly affected. If nothing else, I have vicariously learned the personal value of preserving minority languages, and I have learned the power of story.

Implications

As to implications for further research, there are many. Given that first language loss is not spontaneous, but occurs during second language acquisition, more study of this simultaneous process seems warranted. Although there seems to have been a surge of interest in first language loss in the 6 years since the publication of Wong Fillmore's (1991) influential article (e.g., Aivazian, 1995-1996; Li, 1995-1996; Murray & Kouritzin, 1997; Parsons Yazzi, 1995-1996; Waas, 1993-1994), first language loss still appears to attract relatively little research attention. In 1982, Oxford wrote that "if nourished with a combination of creative intelligence, technical skill, team cooperation, time, and funds, language loss may be born as a coherent and very important research field in the not too distant future"[3] (p. 167). Yet, still at the margins of second language acquisition research, first language loss inquiry, even 17 years after this announcement, seems to remain a research field nestled in the stork's beak on the verge of being born.

This research project has also raised many issues which may be best expressed as questions. Why do so many subjects feel that they would regain L1 fluency in 6 months? Related to this, do languages get lost, or do they go to sleep? How are minority-language children viewed by educators? Do parents believe that maintaining the L1 will aid or impede academic performance or social development? Whose responsibility is L1 maintenance? Why do people stop speaking a language and start speaking a different one? How can we foster a multilingual mindset, one that is supportive of all minority languages, without limiting students' access to ESL? Each of these questions requires a multifaceted approach.

Reflections

It is difficult for me to talk of the tears and friendships I shared over the last year of my life without sounding "hokey," but I shall try to set it in context. I began this research project in the early stages of pregnancy, buoyed by thoughts of growing together, of expansion, and of giving birth in real and figurative terms. My earliest interviews filled me with optimism and with happiness, as I realized that, not only was I becoming a mother, but I was getting what I wanted in terms of data as well. Then, early in the second trimester, I found out that my baby had died; it was my fourth miscarriage. Hopes and plans that I had allowed myself to nurture were pried away as my wonderful natural pregnancy became a medical procedure. Sick and sick at heart, I was unable to do anything more than contact the people I was interviewing (and those I was planning to interview later because I had given all selected participants a future contact date that needed to be revised) and explain to them what had happened to me. I asked that they give me a little time, and then we would resume. I slowly went back to work, but at a much less frenetic pace.

But, it changed us. During the interviewing process, I became pregnant again, against medical advice. The people I was interviewing knew of my miscarriage history, and they asked me how I was, what I was feeling; they coddled me. No longer was I the interviewer questioning the participants about their language loss. No longer were they vulnerable, exposing their own pain, and me invulnerable. I no longer represented the university and institutional authority; I became only too human. Although once I had tried to make them feel comfortable and at ease, a guest in their homes who exuded confidence and dominated the atmosphere, I then became a little like a lost soul who could understand loss. Our relationships became gentler, kinder, and more caring, features that are lost in my constant clinical reference to "the subjects" throughout this paper. So, they helped me. They told me their stories, and they made me laugh and made me cry and, in so doing, they ensured that I would never knowingly misrepresent them, that I would always try to be responsible, that I would somehow earn their magnificent benedictions. For the generosity, the many kindnesses, the enthusiasm and care, the time, the reflection, and the affection, that have been bestowed upon me, I am forever grateful.

And so here I am on the threshold. This project has been about loss and endings but also about new beginnings. It is difficult, if not impossible, to fully express my gratitude for the confidences I have shared over the last 3 years, but it is important to try. I asked the subjects of this collective story if it had been a difficult decision for them to telephone, to volunteer, to be interviewed. They told me, almost to a wo/man, that they had read about this research project, and then had immediately, automatically telephoned. They had wanted to talk about their loss. They had questions. They wanted to know more about other people who had lost their first languages. In the end, several of the subjects told me that telling their stories had helped them, and that they felt connected to each other as a community, even though they did not meet one another. Many of them thanked me. Others, having read my research, or having listened to me speak about it, have given me encouragement by sharing with me some small parts of their linguistic and cultural lives, orally and in writing. Lara, having reflected on her participation for a year, has chosen to pick up the chalice where I have [temporarily] dropped it, and to challenge the limits of our "settlement" discourses by creating a guidebook for minority language parents. Many of them felt that speaking about their language loss had brought some small measure of comfort and healing—as it did for me.

I would like to give the last words to Richard who was able to redeem his loss; he experienced a linguistic rebirth. Because he finally dis/un-covered what it was he had lost, he was able to try to put it into words for all of the subjects of this polyphonic story the importance of one's language. He seems to suggest that our first languages are like parents, connecting us to our ancestry and our origins, shaping and molding the way we view the world and our positions in it:

> The soul or the spirit, the Cree spirit, is sustained by the earth which is sustained by the language of the earth. It speaks to you—the trees, the animals—the putting all those things together, makes a language, and that's where the language emits from....I don't think someone could have sat down in a cave and said "well I'm going to invent this language and this is how it's

*going to be written and this is what it will look like and this is what all these
other things will mean." There was no Adam or Eve to name all the animals;
the animals named themselves and we vocalized that spirit of that animal.
Everything I think in Cree comes from the earth; the earth was first, spirituality
was second, and Cree was third and I am the fourth. That's how I imagine it.*
(September 5th, 1995)

And, that's how I have grown to imagine it, too.

ENDNOTES

1. I do, however, acknowledge that I have remained in control, as I have chosen
   the subject matter, the subjects, and the methodology. I do not make any
   postmodern claims to having "decentered" myself in this research project;
   rather, I prefer to acknowledge the centrality of my role.
2. I do not believe that these cases are atypically negative. These are stories of
   people who would be considered successful in their working and social lives,
   and who, even after experiencing success, continue to feel regret, frustration,
   anger, or ambivalence about their first language loss. I feel that it is
   particularly interesting that such people as the subjects of this research have
   found language loss to be profoundly negative. I am uncertain whether their
   intellectual reflexivity has enabled them to think through their language loss
   experiences, or whether even people who have lost a language and did not
   achieve the outward markers of success would have similar (or even more
   intense) reactions.
3. Oxford was referring to both first and additional language loss.

APPENDIX A: LIFE HISTORY SELECTION CRITERIA

Establishing criteria for determining which five life stories to select proved difficult. Some broad parameters were established to guide the selection process. First, I decided to represent two Asian, two European, and one Indigenous language. Although this is not really representative of the current ESL population in Vancouver, it is balanced, and is also fairly representative of second language learners in 20th-century Canada. Second, I chose to include three female and two male voices because (a) females outnumbered males about 3 to 1 in volunteering for this study, (b) the women had seemed more comfortable with narration of their experiences, and (c) because I wanted to answer claims in feminist literature that more males than females are researched, resulting in gendered knowledge.

Third, a more controversial decision, I eliminated the "outliers," that is, people who were profoundly negatively affected by their language loss, or subjects who claimed to be completely untroubled by it. I did this because there were only three outliers (two profoundly affected, one unaffected), and I imagined a future in which subjects profoundly affected by first language loss recognized themselves and realized for the first time how much they lacked in comparison with others. Moreover, the one person who claimed to be completely unaffected by language loss was too strident in her claims and too bitter for her words to have the ring of truth, yet the two who were profoundly affected by language loss had not truly mastered any language (i.e., "semilingual") and therefore were not sufficiently articulate to frame coherent life stories. Fourth, and finally, I wanted to represent first (immigrant), second (parental immigrant) and third (grandparental immigrant) generations in the stories. I wanted to include the stories not only of immigrants, but also of subjects born into dynamic minority-language communities.

I then further narrowed the field by, (a) choosing two stories from two languages that had strong oral traditions and three from languages that didn't, (b) eliminating all stories from people who were fostered or adopted away from their first languages because of the other emotional issues impinging on language development, (c) including only subjects whose families supported bilingual development rather than monolingual development in English, (d) eliminating all stories from people in the public eye who could be readily identified, (e) ensuring that all stories represented different languages, (f) choosing stories that, taken together, touched on most of the themes that I planned to discuss in the thematic analysis, (g) trying to include stories from people of a variety of ages, and (h) including stories from people with varying levels of skill in both their first and second languages—from complete L1 loss to some understanding to completely relearning the L1 as an adult, and from extremely good oral English skills to quite poor oral English skills.

APPENDIX B: SUBJECT BIOGRAPHICAL INFORMATION

NAME	AGE AT TIME	FIRST LANGUAGE	SEX	GENERATION	OCCUPATION
Nadia	30	Ukrainian	F	grandparents immigrated	nurse
William	56	Welsh	M	adult immigrant	college professor (Biology)
Dhiet	18	Vietnamese	M	child immigrant	not legally employed
Greta	52	Dutch	F	child immigrant	writer and wife/mother
Ariana	33	Cantonese	F	grandparents immigrated	ESL teacher
Lara	45	Finnish	F	child immigrant (early)	computer systems analyst
Alexandra	53	German	F	parents immigrated	retired from IBM
Richard	46	Cree	M	indigenous	writer, actor
Kuong	18	Vietnamese	M	child immigrant (early)	not legally employed
Kurt	40	Polish	M	adult immigrant	business communications
Cameron	12	Polish	M	child immigrant (late)	elementary student
Julian	9	Polish	M	child immigrant (early)	elementary student
Brian	19	Korean	M	parents immigrated	university student (Physics)
Alex	40	Russian & Polish	M	child immigrant (early)	computer programmer
Naomi	51	Japanese	F	grandparents immigrated	wife and mother
Hana Kim	29	Korean	F	child immigrant (early)	news reporter/television
Minette	49	French	F	child immigrant (early)	news reporter/newspaper
Nellie	28	Cantonese	F	child immigrant (early)	university student (Education)
Michael	38	Portuguese	M	child immigrant (early)	graduate student/minister
Charles	21	Japanese	M	parents immigrated	college student (Kinetics)
Helena	25	Hungarian	F	parents immigrated	Marketing representative

216

REFERENCES

Aivazian, C. R. (1995-1996). A participatory study of the reflections and attitudes of Filipino high school additive and subtractive bilingual students toward the maintenance of Filipino (Doctoral dissertation, University of San Francisco, 1995). *Dissertation Abstracts International, 56,* 3027.

Amin, N. (1997). Race and the identity of the nonnative ESL teacher. *TESOL Quarterly, 31,* 580-583.

Ammon, U. (1994). On the German language in North Carolina. *Unterrichtspraxis/ Teaching German, 27,* (2) 34-42.

Anderson, R. W. (1982). Determining the linguistic attributes of language attrition. In R. D. Lambert & B. F. Freed (Eds.), *The loss of language skills* (pp. 83-118). Rowley, MA: Newbury House.

Anzaldúa, G. (1990). How to tame a wild tongue. In R. Ferguson, M. Gever, T. Trinh, & C. West (Eds.), *Out there: Marginalization and contemporary cultures* (pp. 203-211). Cambridge, Mass.: MIT Press.

Appel, R., & Muysken, P. (1987). *Language contact and bilingualism.* London: Edward Arnold.

Bannerji, H. (1990). The other family. In L. Hutcheon & M. Richmond (Eds.), *Other solitudes: Canadian multicultural fictions* (pp. 141-152). Toronto: Oxford University Press.

Ben-Rafael, E. (1994). *Language, identity, and social division.* New York: Oxford University Press.

Berotte Joseph, C. M. (1992/3). A survey of self-reports of language use, self-reports of English, Haitian, and French language proficiencies and self-reports of language attitudes among Haitians in New York (Doctoral dissertation, New York University, 1993). *Dissertation Abstracts International, 53,* 4183.

Bertaux, D. (Ed.). (1981a). *Biography and society: The life history approach in the social sciences.* Beverly Hills, CA: Sage.

Bertaux, D. (1981b). From the life history approach to the transformation of sociological praxis. In D. Bertaux (Ed.), *Biography and society: The life history approach in the social sciences* (pp. 29-46). Beverly Hills, CA: Sage.

Bertaux, D., & Bertaux-Wiame, I. (1981). Life stories in the bakers' trade. In D. Bertaux (Ed.), *Biography and society: The life history approach in the social sciences* (pp. 169-189). Beverly Hills: Sage.

Bertaux, D. & Kohli, M. (1984). The life story approach: A continental view. *Annual Review of Sociology, 10,* 215-237.

Bhabha, H., interviewed by P. Thompson. (1994). Between identities. In R. Benmayor & A. Skotnes (Eds.), *International yearbook of oral history and life stories: Vol. 3. Migration and identity* (pp. 183-200). New York: Oxford University Press.

Boyd, D. (1994, October 5). Time to chalk up the all-expenses-paid ESL education into history. *The Vancouver Sun,* p. B1.

Bretzer, J. (1992). Language, power, and identity in multiethnic Miami. In J. Crawford (Ed.), *Language loyalties: A source book on the Official English controversy,* (pp. 209-216). Chicago: University of Chicago Press.

Carey, S. T. (1991). The culture of literacy in majority and minority language schools. *The Canadian Modern Language Review, 47,* 950-976.

Chaucer, G. (1962). *The Canterbury tales.* In M. H. Abrams, E. T. Donaldson, H. Smith, R. M. Adams, S. H. Monk, L. Lipking, G. H. Ford, & D. Daiches (Eds.), *The Norton anthology of English literature* (3rd ed., pp. 85-212). New York: Norton.

Chong, D. (1995). *The concubine's children.* Toronto: Penguin Books Canada Ltd.

Clandinin, D. J., & Connelly, F. M. (1994). Personal experience methods. In Y.

Lincoln & N. K. Denzin (Eds.), *The handbook of qualitative research* (pp. 413-427). Thousand Oaks, CA: Sage.

Coleridge, S. T. (1962). *The rime of the ancient mariner*. In M. H. Abrams, E. T. Donaldson, H. Smith, R. M. Adams, S. H. Monk, L. Lipking, G. H. Ford, & D. Daiches (Eds.), *Norton anthology of English literature* (3rd ed., pp. 364-381). New York: Norton.

Collier, V. P. (1989). How long? A synthesis of research on academic achievement in a second language. *TESOL Quarterly, 23,* 509-531.

Coward, K. (1994, October 1). Who should pay for ESL - The taxpayers or those who need it? [letter to the editor]. *The Vancouver Sun,* p. A22.

Crawford, J. (1992a). *Hold your tongue: Bilingualism and the politics of "English Only."* New York: Addison-Wesley.

Crawford, J. (Ed.) (1992b). *Language loyalties: A sourcebook on the Official English controversy.* Chicago: University of Chicago Press.

Cruikshank, J., in collaboration with A. Sidney, K. Smith, & A. Ned. (1990). *Life lived like a story: Life stories of three Yukon native elders.* Vancouver: University of British Columbia Press.

Cummins, J. (1979). Linguistic interdependence and the educational development of bilingual children. *Review of Educational Research, 49,* 222-251.

Cummins, J. (1989). Language and literacy acquisition in bilingual contexts. *Journal of Multilingual and Multicultural Development, 10,* 17-32.

Dean, G. E. (1994, September 26). We wanted Canadian way of life [letter to the editor]. *The Vancouver Sun,* p. A9.

De Bots, K., & Clyne, M. (1989). Language reversion revisited. *Studies in Second Language Acquisition, 11,* 167-177.

De Bots, K., & Clyne, M. (1994). A 16-year longitudinal study of language attrition in Dutch immigrants in Australia. *Journal of Multilingual and Multicultural Development, 15,* 17-28.

De Bots, K., Gommans, P., & Rossing, C. (1991). L1 loss in an L2 environment: Dutch immigrants in France. In H. W. Seliger & R. M. Vago (Eds.), *First language attrition: Structural and theoretical perspectives* (pp. 87-98). Cambridge: Cambridge University Press.

De Bots, K., & Weltens, B. (1991). Recapitulation, regression, and language loss. In H. W. Seliger & R. M. Vago (Eds.), *First language attrition: Structural and theoretical perspectives* (pp. 31-52). Cambridge: Cambridge University Press.

Denzin, N. K. (1986). Interpreting the lives of ordinary people: Sartre, Heidegger and Faulkner. *Life Stories, 2,* 6-20.

Denzin, N. K. (1989). *Interpretive biography.* Qualitative research methods series 17. Newbury Park, CA: Sage.

de Vries, J. (1992). Language maintenance and shift: Problems of measurement. In W. Fase, K. Jaspaert, & S. Kroon (Eds.), *Maintenance and loss of minority languages* (pp. 211-222). Philadelphia: Benjamins.

Dolson, D. P. (1985). The effects of Spanish home language use on the scholastic performance of Hispanic pupils. *Journal of Multilingual and Multicultural Development, 6,* 135-156.

Dorian, N. C. (1982). Language loss and maintenance in language contact situations. In R. D. Lambert & B. F. Freed (Eds.), *The loss of language skills* (pp. 44-59). Rowley, MA: Newbury House.

Extra, G. (1989). Ethnic minority languages versus Frisian in Dutch primary schools: A comparative perspective. *Journal of Multilingual and Multicultural Development, 10,* 59-72.

Farrow, M. (1994, October 21). Immigration rules leave man feeling "angry and frustrated". *The Vancouver Sun,* p. B2.

Fase, W., Jaspaert, K., & Kroon, S. (1992). Introductory remarks. In W. Fase, K. Jaspaert, & S. Kroon (Eds.), *Maintenance and loss of minority languages* (pp. 2-13). Philadelphia: Benjamins.

Fielding, N. G., & Fielding, J. L. (1986). *Linking data*. Qualitative research methods series, no. 4. London: Sage.

Findley, T. (1986). *The telling of lies*. New York: Viking Press.

Fischer, L. R. (1983). Sociology and life history: Methodological incongruence? *International Journal of Oral History, 4*, 29-40.

Fitzgerald, F. S. (1945). *The Crack-up/F. Scott Fitzgerald, with other uncollected pieces, notebooks and unpublished letters; together with letters to Fitzgerald from Gertrude Stein, Edith Wharton, T. S. Eliot, Thomas Wolfe, and John Dos Passos; and essays and poems by Paul Rosenfeld, Glenway Wescott, John Does Passos, John Peale Bishop and Edmund Wilson; edited by Edmund Wilson*. New York: J. Laughlin.

Fitzgerald, F. S. (1953). *The Great Gatsby*. New York: Scribner's. (Original work published 1925)

Freed, B. F. (1983). Language loss: Current thoughts and future directions. In R. D. Lambert & B. F. Freed (Eds.), *The loss of language skills* (pp. 1-6). Rowley, MA: Newbury House.

Folmer, J. (1992). Dutch immigrants in New Zealand: A case study of language shift and language loss. *Australian Review of Applied Linguistics, 15*(2), 1-18.

Giles, H., Bourhis, R. Y., & Taylor, D. M. (1977). Towards a theory of language in ethnic group relations. In H. Giles (Ed.), *Language, ethnicity, and intergroup relations* (pp. 307-348). New York: Academic Press.

Goodson, I. G. (Ed.). (1992). *Studying teachers' lives*. New York: Routledge.

Grescoe, T. (1996, November 21-28). Stilled voices. *The Georgia Straight*, pp. 15, 17, 18, 19.

Hakuta, K., & D'Andrea, D. (1992). Some properties of bilingual maintenance and loss in Mexican background high school students. *Applied Linguistics, 13*, 72-99.

Harley, B., Hart, D., & Lapkin, S.. (1986). The effects of early bilingual schooling on first language skills. *Applied Psycholinguistics, 7*, 295-322.

Harres, A. (1989). "Being a good German": A case study analysis of language retention and loss among German migrants in North Queensland. *Journal of Multilingual and Multicultural Development, 10*, 383-400.

Heath, S. B. (1989). Language ideology. In E. Barnouw (Ed.), *International encyclopedia of communications, 2* (pp. 393-395). New York: Oxford University Press.

Hoffman, E. (1989). *Lost in translation: A life in a new language*. New York: Dutton.

Jamieson, P. (1980). The pattern of urban language loss. *Australian and New Zealand Journal of Sociology, 16*, 102-109.

Jaspaert, K., & Kroon, S. (1992). From the typewriter of A.L.: A case study in language loss. In W. Fase, K. Jaspaert, & S. Kroon (Eds.), *Maintenance and loss of minority languages* (pp. 137-147). Philadelphia: Benjamins.

Johnson, D. M. (1987). The organization of instruction in migrant education: Assistance for children and youth at risk. *TESOL Quarterly, 21*, 437-459.

Kaufman, D., & Aronoff, M. (1991). Morphological disintegration and reconstruction in first language attrition. In H. W. Seliger & R. M. Vago (Eds.), *First language attrition: Structural and theoretical perspectives* (pp. 175-189). Cambridge: Cambridge University Press.

Keillor, G. (1985). *Lake Wobegon Days*. New York: Viking Penguin.

Kenny, K. D. (1993). Language loss and hesitation frequency: The case of Ramallawi Arabic in Detroit (Doctoral dissertation, University of Michigan, 1993). *Dissertation Abstracts International, 54*, 915.

Kirby, S., & McKenna, K. (1989). *Experience, research, social change: Methods from the margins*. Toronto: Garamond Press.

Kohli, M. (1981). Biography: Account, text, method. In D. Bertaux (Ed.), *Biography and society: The life history approach in the social sciences* (pp. 61-75). Beverly Hills, CA: Sage.

Kouritzin, S. (1995). *Bringing life to research/bringing research to life: Life history and ESL.* Paper presented at the meeting of the Canadian Society for the Study of Education, Montreal, Quebec.

Kravin, H. (1992). Erosion of a language in bilingual development. *Journal of Multilingual and Multicultural Development, 13,* 307-325.

Lambert, R. D. (1982). Setting the agenda. In R. D. Lambert & B. F. Freed (Eds.), *The loss of language skills* (pp. 6-10). Rowley, MA: Newbury House.

Lambert, W. E. (1975). Culture and language as factors in learning and education. In A. Wolfgang (Ed.), *The education of immigrant students* (pp. 55-83). Toronto: Ontario Institute for Studies in Education.

Lambert, W. E. (1981). Bilingualism and language acquisition. In H. Winitz (Ed.), *Native language and foreign language acquisition* (pp. 9-22). New York: New York Academy of Science.

Landry, R. & Allard, R. (1991). Can schools promote additive bilingualism in minority group children? In L. M. Malave & G. Duquette (Eds.), *Language, culture and cognition* (pp. 198-231). Avon: Multilingual Matters.

Landry, R., & Allard, R. (1992). Subtractive bilingualism: The case of Franco-Americans in Maine's St. John Valley. *Journal of Multilingual and Multicultural Development, 13,* 515-544.

Lanoue, G. (1991). Language loss, language gain: Cultural camouflage and social change among the Sekani of northern British Columbia. *Language in Society, 20,* 87-115.

Larson-Freeman, D. & Long, M. (1991). *An introduction to second language acquisition research.* New York: Longman.

Li, J. J. (1995-1996). Heritage language retention in second-generation Chinese Americans (Doctoral dissertation, University of California, Los Angeles, 1995). *Dissertation Abstracts International, 56,* 3937.

MacKinnon, K. (1990). Language maintenance and viability in the contemporary Scottish Gaelic speech community: Some social and demographic factors. In D. Gorter, J. F. Hoekstra, L. G. Lammert, & J. Ytama (Eds.), *Fourth international conference on minority languages: Vol. II: Western and eastern European papers* (pp. 69-90). Avon: Multilingual Matters Ltd.

Maher, J. (1991). A crosslinguistic study of language contact and language attrition. In H. W. Seliger & R. M. Vago (Eds.), *First language attrition: Structural and theoretical perspectives* (pp. 67-86). Cambridge, MA: Cambridge University Press.

Major, R. C. (1992). Losing English as a first language. *Modern Language Journal, 76,* 190-208.

Markey, T. L. (1987). When minor is minor and major is major: Language expansion, contraction and death. *Journal of Multilingual and Multicultural Development, 8,* 3-22.

Marranca, B., Robinson, M., & Chaudhuri, U. (1991). Criticism, culture, and performance: An interview with Edward Said. In B. Marranca & G. Dasgupta (Eds.), *Interculturalism and performance: Writings from PAJ* (pp. 38-59). New York: PAJ Publications.

Martin-Jones, M., & Romaine S. (1986). Semilingualism: A half-baked theory of communicative competence. *Applied Linguistics, 7,* 26-38.

McGroarty, M. (1992). English instruction for linguistic minority groups: Different structures, different styles. In M. Celce-Murcia (Ed.), *Teaching English as a second or foreign language* (2nd ed., pp. 372-385). Boston: Heinle & Heinle.

McInnis, D. (1994, October 13). Advantages of living in Canada should justify ESL contribution [letter to the editor]. *The Vancouver Sun,* p. A20.

McKay, S. L., & Weinstein-Shr, G. (1993). English literacy in the U.S.: National policies, personal consequences. *TESOL Quarterly, 27,* 399-420.

Merino, B. J. (1983). Language loss in bilingual Chicano children. *Journal of*

Applied Developmental Psychology, 4, 277-294.

Middleton, S. (1993). *Educating feminists: Life histories and pedagogy.* New York: Teachers' College Press.

Morin, F. (1982). Anthropological praxis and life history. *International Journal of Oral History, 3,* 5-30.

Murray, G., & Kouritzin, S. (1997). Re-thinking second language instruction, technology and autonomy: A manifesto. *System, 25,* 185-196.

Nero, S. J. (1997). English is my native language...or so I believe. *TESOL Quarterly, 31,* 585-590.

Nunan, D. (1992). *Research methods in language teaching.* Cambridge, MA: Cambridge University Press.

Okamura-Bichard, F. (1985). Mother tongue maintenance and second language learning: A case of Japanese children. *Language Learning, 35,* 63-89.

Olshtain, E., & Barzilay, M. (1991). Lexical retrieval difficulties in adult language attrition. In H. W. Seliger & R. M. Vago (Eds.), *First language attrition: Structural and theoretical perspectives* (pp. 139-150). Cambridge, MA: Cambridge University Press.

Oxford, R. (1982). Research on language loss: A review with implications for foreign language teaching. *Modern Language Journal, 66,* 160-169.

Pan, B. A., & Berko-Gleason, J. (1986). The study of language loss: Models and hypotheses for an emerging discipline. *Applied Psycholinguistics, 7,* 193-206.

Parsons Yazzi, E. (1995/6). A study of reasons for Navajo language attrition as perceived by Navajo-speaking parents (Doctoral dissertation, Northern Arizona University, 1995). *Dissertation Abstracts International, 56,* 4644.

Peirce, B. N. (1995). Social identity, investment, and language learning. *TESOL Quarterly, 29,* 9-31

Pellerin, D. (1995, August 30). Mom told to speak English to daughter: Spanish-only habit ruled child abuse. *The Vancouver Sun,* p. A20

Phillipson, R. (1992). *Linguistic imperialism.* New York: Oxford University Press.'

Pütz, Martin. (1991). Language maintenance and language shift in the speech behaviour of German-Australian migrants in Canberra. *Journal of Multilingual and Multicultural Development, 12,* 477-492.

Pye, C. (1992). Language loss among the Chilcotin. *International Journal of the Sociology of Language, 93,* 75-86.

Rodriguez, R. (1981). *Hunger of memory: The education of Richard Rodriguez.* Boston: David R. Godine.

Schieffelin, B., & Ochs, E. (1986). Language socialization. *Annual Review of Anthropology, 15,* 163-191.

Schmidt, A. (1991). Language attrition in Boumaa Fijian and Dyirbal. In H. W. Seliger & R. M. Vago (Eds.), *First language attrition: Structural and theoretical perspectives* (pp. 113-124). Cambridge, MA: Cambridge University Press.

Segalowitz, N. (1991). Does advanced skill in a second language reduce automaticity in the first language? *Language Learning, 41,* 59-83.

Shaw, B. (1977). *Major Barbara.* New York: Penguin. (Original work published 1905)

Shields, C. (1993). *The stone diaries.* Toronto: Vintage Books.

Silverman, D. (1993). *Interpreting qualitative data: Methods for analysing talk, text and interaction.* London: Sage.

Skutnabb-Kangas, T. (1984). Why aren't all children in the Nordic countries bilingual? *Journal of Multilingual and Multicultural Development, 5,* 301-315.

Smolicz, J. J. (1992). Minority languages as core values of ethnic cultures: A study of maintenance and erosion of Polish, Welsh, and Chinese languages in Australia. In W. Fase, K. Jaspaert, & S. Kroon (Eds.), *Maintenance and loss of minority languages* (pp. 277-305). Philadelphia: Benjamins.

Sohm, K. (1994, October 13). Advantages of living in Canada should justify ESL contribution [letter to the editor]. *The Vancouver Sun,* p. A14.

Spolsky, B. (1989). Bilingualism. In F. J. Newmeyer (Ed.), *Linguistics: The Cambridge survey, IV. Language: The socio-cultural context* (pp. 100-118). Cambridge, MA: Cambridge University Press.

Stake, R. E. (1995). *The art of case study research*. Thousand Oaks, CA: Sage.

Stevens, G. A. (1982). Minority language loss in the United States (Doctoral dissertation, University of Wisconsin-Madison, 1982). (University Microfilms No. 8208331).

Taft, R., & Cahill, D. (1989). Mother tongue maintenance in Lebanese immigrant families in Australia. *Journal of Multilingual and Multicultural Development, 10,* 129-144.

Tang, C. (1997). On the power and status of nonnative ESL teachers. *TESOL Quarterly, 31,* 577-580.

Tierney, W. G. (1995). (Re)presentation and voice. *Qualitative Inquiry, 1,* 379-390.

Toohey, K. (1992). We teach English as a second language to bilingual students. In B. Burnaby & A. Cumming (Eds.), *Socio-political aspects of ESL* (pp. 87-96). Toronto: The Ontario Institute for Studies in Education.

Toohey, K. (1998). "Breaking them up, taking them away": ESL students in Grade 1. *TESOL Quarterly, 32,* 61-84.

Turian, D., & Altenberg, E. P. (1991). Compensatory strategies of child first language attrition. In H. W. Seliger & R. M. Vago (Eds.), *First language attrition: Structural and theoretical perspectives* (pp. 205-226). Cambridge, MA: Cambridge University Press.

Van Maanen, J. (1988). *Tales of the field: On writing ethnography*. Chicago: University of Chicago Press.

Van Manen, M. (1992). *Researching lived experience: Human science for an action sensitive pedagogy*. London, Canada: The Althouse Press.

Veltman, C. (1983). *Language shift in the United States*. New York: Mouton.

Verhoeven, L., & Boeschoten, H. E. (1986). First language acquisition in a second language submersion environment. *Applied Psycholinguistics, 7,* 241-256.

Waas, J. (1993/4). Language attrition among German speakers in Australia: A sociolinguistic inquiry (Doctoral dissertation, Macquarie University, Australia, 1993). *Dissertation Abstracts International, 55,* 702.

Weltens, B., & Cohen, A. (1989). Language attrition research: An introduction. *Studies in Second Language Acquisition, 11,* 127-133.

Widdowson, H. (1994). The ownership of English. *TESOL Quarterly, 28,* 377-387.

Wiley, T. G. (1993). Discussion of Klassen & Burnaby and McKay & Weinstein-Shr: Beyond assimilationist literacy policies and practices. *TESOL Quarterly, 27,* 421-430.

Wilton, J. (1994). Identity, racism, and multiculturalism: Chinese-Australian responses. In R. Benmayor & A. Skotnes (Eds.), *International yearbook of oral history and life stories: Vol. 3. Migration and identity* (pp. 183-200). New York: Oxford University Press.

Winfield, O. (1994, October 20). English onus is on immigrant [letter to the editor]. *The Vancouver Sun*, p. A12.

Wolcott, H. F. (1990). *Writing up qualitative research*. Newbury Park, CA: Sage.

Wong Fillmore, L. (1991). When learning a second language means losing the first. *Early Childhood Research Quarterly, 6,* 323-346.

Wong Fillmore, L. (1992). When learning a second language means losing the first. *Educator, 6,* 4-11.

Wong Fillmore, L. (1996). What happens when language are lost?: An essay on language assimilation and cultural identity. In D. Slobin, J. Gerhardt, A. Kyratzis, & J. Guo (Eds.), *Social interaction, social context, and language* (pp. 435-446). Mahwah, NJ: Lawrence Erlbaum Associates.

Woolard, K., & Schieffelin, B. (1994). Language ideology. *Annual Review of Anthropology, 23,* 55-82.

Wright, S. (1993/4). Bilingualism and educational achievement: A study of young bilinguals in Birmingham schools and Colleges (England) (Doctoral dissertation, Aston University, UK, 1993). *Dissertation Abstracts International, 55*, 12.

Yin, R. K. (1994). *Case study research: Design and methods* (2nd ed.). London: Sage.

AUTHOR INDEX

A

Aivazian, C. R., 211
Allard, R., 13, 18
Altenberg, D., 16, 18
Amin, N., 9
Ammon, U., 15
Anderson, R. W., 13
Anzaldúa, G., 7
Appel, R., 14
Aronoff, M., 16, 18

B

Bannerji, H., 4
Barzilay, M., 16, 18
Ben-Raphael, E., 17, 22-23, 150
Berko-Gleason, J., 14, 16, 102
Berotte Joseph, C. M., 15
Bertaux, D., 20
Bertaux-Wiame, I., 20
Bhabha, H., 73, 145
Boeschoten, H. E., 11
Bourhis, R. Y., 14
Boyd, D., 207
Bretzner, J., 151

C

Cahill, D., 13, 15
Carey, S., 13
Chaucer, G., 29, 99, 154, 211
Chaudhuri, U., 149, 177
Chong, D., 5
Clandinin, D. J., 20
Clyne, M., 14, 15, 18
Cohen, A., 16
Coleridge, S. T., 4
Collier, V., 16
Connelly, M., 20
Coward, K., 207
Crawford, J., 8, 150
Cruikshank, J., 19
Cummins, J., 17, 22-23, 84, 195

D

D'Andrea, D., 14, 15, 18, 175
De Bots, K., 12, 13, 14, 15, 18
de Vries, J., 12, 18
Dean, G. E., 207
Denzin, N. K., 20

Dolson, D. P., 17
Dorian, N. C., 13, 14

E

Extra, G., 14, 16, 175

F

Farrow, M., 207
Fase, W., 12
Fielding, J. L., xii
Fielding, N.G., xii
Findley, T., 4
Fischer, L. R., 176
Fitzgerald, F. S., 76, 130, 179
Folmer, J., 14, 175
Freed, B. F., 13

G

Galindo, R., 151
Giles, H., 14
Gommans, P., 12, 14
Goodson, I., 20
Grescoe, T., 72

H

Hakuta, K., 14, 15, 18, 175
Harley, B., 16
Harres, A., 14, 15, 175
Hart, D., 16
Heath, S. B., 8
Hoffman, E., 19, 208

J

Jamieson, P., 14, 15
Jaspaert, K., 12, 16, 18
Johnson, D. M., 17

K

Kaufman, D., 16, 18
Keillor, G., 3
Kenny, K.D., 16, 18
Kirby, S., 20
Kohli, M., 20
Kouritzin, S., 20, 21, 211
Kravin, H., 13, 16, 18
Kroon, S., 12, 16, 18

L

Lather, P., xii
Lambert, R. D., 13, 18, 22-23
Landry, R., 13, 18
Lanoue, G., 13, 54
Lapkin, S., 16
Larsen-Freeman, D., 20
Li, J. J., 211
Long, M., 20

M

MacKinnon, K., 18
Maher, J., 16
Major, R. C., 16, 18
Markey, T. L., 14
Marranca, B., 149, 177
Martin-Jones, M., 22-23
McGroarty, M., 17
McInnis, D., 207
McKay, S. L., 15, 210
McKenna, K., 20
Merino, B. J., 14, 15, 16, 18, 41
Middleton, S., 20
Morin, F., 20
Murray, G., 21, 211
Muysken, P., 14

N

Nero, S. J., 9
Nunan, D., 20

O

Ochs, E., 15
Okamura-Bichard, F., 15, 18
Olshtain, E., 16, 18
Oxford, R., 211, 214

P

Pan, B. A., 14, 16, 102
Parsons Yazzi, E., 211
Peirce, B. N., 8
Pellerin, D., 208
Phillipson, R., 7
Pütz, M., 14
Pye, C., 13, 60

R

Robinson, M., 149, 177
Rodriguez, R., 19
Romaine, S., 22-23

Rossing, C., 12, 14

S

Said, E., 149, 177, 179
Schieffelin, B., 8, 15
Schmidt, A., 13, 203
Segalowitz, N., 16, 18
Shaw, B., 10
Shields, C., 3, 5
Silverman, D., xii
Skutnabb-Kangas, T., 17
Smolicz, J. J., 13
Sohm, K., 207
Spolsky, B., 22-23
Stake, R. E., 20, 21
Stevens, G. A., 18

T

Taft, R., 13, 15
Tang, C., 9
Taylor, D. M., 14
Tierney, W. G., 42
Turian, D., 16, 18

V

Van Maanen, J., 21
Van Manen, M., 20
Veltman, C., 18
Verhoeven, L., 11

W

Waas, J., 211
Weinstein-Shr, G., 15, 210
Weltens, B., 13, 16
Widdowson, H., 9
Wiley, T. G., 210
Wilton, J., 17, 42
Winfield, O., 208
Wolcott, H. F., 209
Wong Fillmore, L., 9, 10, 11, 14, 15, 17, 187
Woolard, K., 8
Wright, S., 14

Y

Yin, R. K., 20

SUBJECT INDEX

A

Academic truth, definition, 3
Accessibility of research, 34
Adaptation, 150
Adoption, 157, *see also* Foster care
AIDS, 127
Alex, 160-161, 169, 172, 173, 180,
    204, 216
Alexandra, 158-159, 179, 185, 216
Anger, 39, 169, 174
Anonymity, 54, 215
Antilinguicism, xi
Ariana, 179, 198, 201
    interview context, 31-34
    introduction, 31-42
    life history context, 34-37
    narrative context, 37-42
Ariana's story, 43-49
Assimilation, 183, 188
Attitudes, public, 207

B

Balanced biculturalism, 183
Banning of first languages, 190
Belgium, 163
Benign neglect, 41, 102
Bilingual development, *see also*
    Language development
Bilingual education, 196
Borderlands, 149, 153
Brian, 180, 188, 203, 216
    interview context, 97-99
    introduction, 97-108
    life history context, 100-106
    narrative context, 106-108
Brian's story, 111-117, 178

C

Cameron, 160, 190, 216
Canadian Pacific Railway, 34
Canadianization, 40, 165, 179
Cannibalism, 156
Cantonese, 32, 43, 164, 171
Case study, ix, 12, 20, 209
Census, 84
Charles, 165-166, 180, 216
Cheating, 199
Child abuse, 157

Choice of words, subject, 39, 133,
    161, 183
Christine, 171
Codeswitching, 121, 144, 166
Common culture, ix
Communication, familial, *see*
    Family relationships
Concerns about stupidity, 177
Conclusion, 209-214
Conventional ideology, 209
Crime, 159, *see also* Drugs
Criterion variables, 18
Cultural defiance, 189
Cultural hegemony, 150
Cultural identity, ix, xi, 40, 44, 49,
    90, 96, 120, 130, 132, 139, 149,
    158, 177, 178-185
Cultural insensitivity, 43
Cultural isolation, 79
Cultural rejection, 48
Cultural standards, 128, 165, 172

D

Deception of parents, 173
Deliberate rejection, 170
Demotion, school, 195
Dhiet, 23, 156-157, 216
Discordance, x
Discrimination, 34, 80, 91, 157, 161,
    184
    covert, 190
    overt, 191
Dominant language, 203
Drugs, 127, 159, 174, 199
Dutch, 157

E

Economic advantage, 203
Embarrassment, 189
Emic perspective, ix
Emiko's story, 7-11
English ability, 92, 93, 156
English as a second language, x, 126
English dominance, 64
English language ability, parental,
    88, 111, 115, 120, 124, 143, 163,
    182
English language ability, subject, 83,
    105, 121, 135, 159, 196

writing, 45, 64, 108, 116, 140
English ownership, 7
Envy, 47, 49
Error correction, 197
ESL classes, 192
ESL students, 37, 102, 111
    treatment of, 32, 36, 45, 191
ESL teachers, 32, 82, 101, 116, 180,
    192
Exile, 149

F

Familial communication, 100, 127
Familial consequences, 61, 169, 176
Familial influence, 155
Familial relationships, 46, 93, 126-
    129, 138, 142, 164, 169-176
Fear, 159, 175
Fiction, ix
Finland, 78, 82, 87
First language ability, 83, 94, 104,
    111, 114, 116, 136, 141, 160, 161,
    162
First language consciousness, 206
First languages, banning, 190
First Nations, 47, 51, 154
    land claims, 53
Fluency, 183, 201
Foster care, 157, 158, see also
    Adoption
French, 163, 174, 183
French as a second language, 142
French horn, compared to
    interview, 27
Frustration, 184

G

German, 158
Gifts, 52
Good vs. evil, 61
Grandparents, 34, 43, 46, 111, 139,
    161, 169
Greta, 75, 158, 172, 174, 180, 181,
    187, 197, 216
Guilt, 49
Gustafson Lake, 52, 53

H

Halfie, use of term, 161
Hana Kim, 162-163, 170, 190, 216
Helena, 173, 188, 189, 196, 216
    interview context, 119-123
    introduction, 119-133

life history context, 123-129
    narrative context, 129-133
Helena's story, 135-145
Hong Kong, 164
Honorarium, 52
Hungarian mentality, 132
Hybrids, 150
Hyphenated Canadians, 179
Hyphens, 150

I

Iceberg metaphor, 84, 196
Identity, 35, 155, 177, 201
    cultural, ix, xi, 40, 44, 49, 90, 96,
    120, 130, 132, 139, 149, 158, 177,
    178-185
Identity crises, 179
Immersion, 63, 181, 184
Immigrant experience, ix
Immigration policy, 185
Imperfect learning, 14
Importance of names, 79, 138, 161,
    180
Indian Movement, 57
Instruction, need for, 131, 140, see
    also Helena's story
Internment camp, 75, 161
Interview, 175
    control, 54
    description, 27-28
Interview context, definition, x
Interview strategy, 123
Inversion of family relationships,
    171
Invitational texts, x

J

Japanese, 161, 166, 184
Julian, 160, 190, 195, 216

K

Kalavalas, 78, 81
Kindergarten, importance, 80
Korean, 111, 162
Kuong, 23, 159-160, 171, 191, 198,
    216
Kurt, 169, 188, 190, 195, 216

L

Lakeland, 79
    memories of, 88
Land claims, 53

Language,
definition, 18, 19, 71
personification, 71
Language-culture connection, 70,
154
Language attrition, 13
Language change, 13
Language death, 13
Language development, xi, 63, 83,
103, 112, 125, 135
Language erosion, 13
Language hybrid, 83
Language ideology, 17
Language instruction, 131, 140, *see
also* Helena's story
Language loss,
acceleration, 11
causes, 15, 19
consequences, 15-16, 211
definition, ix, 11, 203
first vs. second, 12
individual, 16
meaning, 63, 66, 76-77, 97, 117,
163, 201-206
realization, 69
synonyms, 12
Language maintenance, 17, 38, 58-
59, 210
Language obsolescence, 13
Language regression, 13
Language shift, 12, 14-15, 101, 192
Language soundtracks, 89
Languages, relearning, 57, 69-71,
141, 183
Lara, 172, 192, 196, 204, 213, 216
interview context, 75-77
introduction, 75-85
life history context, 77-81
narrative context, 81-85
Lara's story, 96
Life history, ix, 19-21, 59
telling, 5
writing, 5
Life history context, definition, x
Linguistic borderlands, 153
Linguistic capital, 8
Linguistic dispossession, 208
Linguistic identity, 46
Literacy policy, 78
Literature, use of fiction and poetry,
ix, 3
Lived experiences, ix, 20
Losing out, 38, 184
Loss of first language ease, 202
Love of English, 64, 68, 197
Lyricism, 76, 95, 155, 202

M

Macrostories, definition, 106
Majority-language culture, 16-18
Marketability, 203
Martial law, 160
Member checks, 32-34, 122
Michael, 165, 170, 174, 181, 191, 193,
197, 216
Microstories, definition, 106
Minette, 75, 164, 170, 174, 182, 183,
201, 204, 216
Minority-language community, 95
Minority-language families, xi
Monolingual development, *see*
Language development
Mortality, parental, 75, 169, 204
Motivation, 195
Multiculturalism, xi, 35, 38-39, 43,
44, 47, 189
policy, 184

N

Nadia, 154-155, 170, 174, 177, 178,
185, 187, 203, 216
Names, importance of, 79, 138, 161,
180
Naomi, 75, 161-162, 178, 184, 189,
191, 216
Narrative, 76, 99, 107, 129, 154, 209
Narrative context, definition, x
Need for instruction, 131, 140 *see*
Helena's story
Nellie, 164-165, 170, 172, 178, 184,
187, 189, 196, 216
Nonstandard speech, 40-41, 60, 108,
115, 122, 130, 136, 156, 193
Nordic sagas, *see* Kalavalas
Nostalgia, 156, 204

O

Objectivity, 33
Oral cultures, 59, 83
Oral history, 89
Outliers, 97, 157-158, 215
Ownership of English, 7
Ownership of languages, 183
Ownership of research, 33

P

Pan Indianism, 54, 64
Parental characteristics, 41-42, 45,
84-85, 87, 88, 98, 100, 115, 124,

125, 172
Parental influence, 137, 143
Parental language ability, 88, 111,
    115, 120, 124, 143, 163, 182
Parental mortality/decline, 75, 169,
    204
Parental reaction, 98
Peer pressure, 187
Performance, school, 81, 91, 103,
    113, 126, 137, 165, 195-199
Pilot study, 171
Polish, 160, 161
Politics of destruction, 67
Polyphony, x
Portuguese, 165
Predictor variables, 18
Public attitudes, 207
Public education, 185
Public school, 43

R

Racism, 37, 43-44, 105, 161, 166, 189
    self-directed, 37, 48, 158, 177-
    178, 188
Rage, 207
Refugee, 156, 160
Regret, 205
Relationships,
    family, 46, 93, 126-129, 138, 142,
    164, 169-176
    school, 80-81, 90-91, 112-113,
    187-193
Relearning languages, 57, 69-71,
    141, 183
Reparations, 87
Research process, 212, 215
Researcher experience, ix
Resentment, 80
Residential schools, 56, 61, 63, 64, 65
Richard, 174, 177, 181, 183, 201, 213,
    216
    interview context, 51-55
    introduction, 51-61
    life history context, 55-59
    narrative context, 59-61
Richard's story, 63-72
Royal Canadian Mounted Police, 52
Russian, 160

S

School performance, 81, 91, 103,
    113, 126, 137, 165, 195-199
School relationships, 80-81, 90-91,
    112-113, 187-193

Segregation, see Separate schools
Self-consciousness, 144
Self-esteem, xi, 199
Self-image, 177-185, 196
    cultural, 37
Semilingualism, 13, 22-23, 156
Separate schools, 185
Shame, 44, 67, 121, 138, 155, 162, 175
Siblings, 34, 55, 63, 78, 79, 135, 159,
    164, 195
Social isolation, 195
Stereotypes, 198, see also
    Discrimination
Storytelling, 60, 107
Stupidity, concerns about, 177
Subject characteristics, 21, 77, 216
Subject English language ability, 83,
    105, 121, 135, 159, 196
    writing, 45, 64, 108, 116, 140
Submersion, 63
Subtractive bilingualism, 13
Sundance ceremony, 52

T

Taiwanese, 166
Treaties, 58
Truth, ix

U

Ukrainian, 135, 154, 160, 170
United States, 124
University of British Columbia, 97

V

Vancouver Sun, 31
Van River, 55, 56, 63, 202
    school system, 56
Vietnam, 156, 159
Vignette, explanation, x

W

WASP, 40
Welsh, 155
William, 155-156, 193, 196, 197, 216
Word choice, 39, 133, 161, 183
World War II, 75, 82, 87, 89, 123, 161
    reparations, 82

Z

Zaibatsu, 8